Nuclear Weapons and Foreign Policy

Henry A. Kissinger has combined an academic career with active participation in the councils of government. He received his A.B., M.A., and Ph.D. degrees at Harvard University, where he has been professor of government, director of the National Security Studies program, and a member of the Center for International Affairs. He served as a consultant to the Department of State, the U.S. Arms Control and Disarmament Agency, the National Security Council, and other government bodies. In 1968, he was appointed assistant to President Nixon for National Security Affairs, and subsequently served as Secretary of State from 1973 to 1977. Since leaving office, Mr. Kissinger has published the first volume of his memoirs, *White House Years.*

In addition to *Nuclear Weapons and Foreign Policy,* a best-selling and prize-winning study that has greatly influenced American strategic thinking, Mr. Kissinger has also written *American Foreign Policy* (Third Edition); *The Troubled Partnership: A Reappraisal of the Atlantic Alliance; The Necessity for Choice: Prospects of American Foreign Policy;* and *A World Restored: Castlereagh, Metternich, and the Problems of Peace, 1812–1822.*

Nuclear Weapons and Foreign Policy

HENRY A. KISSINGER

Abridged Edition

W · W · NORTON & COMPANY

New York · London

The Council on Foreign Relations is a nonprofit institution devoted to the
study of political, economic, and strategic problems as related to American
foreign policy. It takes no stand, expressed or implied, on American policy.
The authors of books published under the auspices of the Council are responsible for their statements of fact and expressions of opinion. The Council
is responsible only for determining that they should be presented to the public.

This is an abridgement of a clothbound edition of
Nuclear Weapons and Foreign Policy, published
for the Council on Foreign Relations by Harper &
Row, Inc.

Books That Live
The Norton imprint on a book means that in the publisher's
estimation it is a book not for a single season but for the years.
W. W. Norton & Company, Inc.

W. W. Norton & Company, Inc., 500 Fifth Avenue, New York, N.Y. 10110
W. W. Norton & Company Ltd., 37 Great Russell Street, London WC1B 3NU

ISBN 0-393-00494-5

PRINTED IN THE UNITED STATES OF AMERICA

9 0

Preface to this Edition

TWELVE years ago, in the concluding chapter to this book, I wrote: "Whatever the problem — whether it concerns questions of military strategy, of coalition policy, or of relations with the Soviet bloc — the nuclear age demands above all a clarification of doctrine. At a time when technology has put in our grasp a command over nature never before imagined, the value of power depends above all on the purpose for which it is to be used."

Significant changes have taken place in the relations between nations since those words were written. Even though the world order is still dominated in a military sense by two superpowers, other countries have joined the nuclear club, the Soviet and Western alliance systems have lost cohesiveness, the United States and the Soviet Union have faced each other directly in confrontations over Berlin and Cuba and indirectly in flashpoint conflicts elsewhere in the world, and American forces have been committed on a large scale in an attenuated struggle in Viet Nam.

These events have altered the international climate. But they have intensified, rather than lessened, the need to seek a clarification of doctrine and a new international order.

HENRY A. KISSINGER

Washington
January 1969

Foreword to the Abridged Edition

When *Nuclear Weapons and Foreign Policy* was first published in June 1957, it had an immediate and profound impact on American thinking about the political world in which we live with such terrible insecurity. Generals and statesmen studied it, Congressmen read it to their colleagues on Capitol Hill, and enough ordinary citizens perused its long and sometimes difficult pages to keep it on the best-seller list for fourteen weeks. Although it is too early to judge the full extent of the book's influence on American policy, we can at least speculate on the reasons why *Nuclear Weapons and Foreign Policy* made such a deep impression both here and abroad.

First, it succeeded in articulating with great clarity the fears and reservations that many Americans had been feeling about certain of our postwar policies and failures—especially about our reliance on massive retaliation, the conflicts among our military services, and the inability to use our vast strength to achieve reasonable political objectives.

Second, the book was perhaps the first to examine the postwar world comprehensively, applying an understanding of nuclear technology and military strategy to political questions and showing the interrelationship between force and diplomacy. Readers found in Dr. Kissinger a first-rate intelligence which had succeeded in cutting through many of the false assumptions and contradictions in our policies to propound a fresh conception of the realities of the nuclear age.

Third, though free of wishful thinking, the book was yet hopeful in showing a reasoned way between the alternatives of thermonuclear devastation and the prospect of being nibbled to death by the Russians. It was that rare work which not only showed what was wrong but was fertile in ideas on how our policies might be set right.

And finally, the book carried added weight, perhaps, because it was the outgrowth of a study conducted by the Council on Foreign Relations, which called together a panel of exceptionally qualified individuals to explore all factors involved in the making and implementing of foreign policy in the nuclear age. Thus, although the book is the work of an individual, Dr. Kissinger had the benefit of the wisdom and experience of experts and men of affairs in all the relevant fields, such as government, diplomacy, science, engineering, the military services, and weapons production.*

For these reasons—and perhaps others—*Nuclear Weapons and Foreign Policy* fulfilled a great need in this country, a need that has not been lessened by the speed with which the missile age has since come upon us. The present edition is an effort to bring to a larger audience all the essentials of the original book, omitting only some of the documentation and amplification. Only two of the original twelve chapters have been dropped entirely—one a detailed examination of NATO in the light of concepts developed in an earlier chapter, and an expository chapter on the technical characteristics of nuclear weapons. Except for the advanced student or the critic, the abridged edition will,

* Members of the Study Group were: Gordon Dean, Chairman, Frank Altschul, Hamilton Fish Armstrong, Hanson W. Baldwin, Lloyd V. Berkner, Robert R. Bowie, McGeorge Bundy, William A. M. Burden, John C. Campbell, Thomas K. Finletter, George S. Franklin, Jr., Lieutenant General James M. Gavin, Roswell L. Gilpatric, N. E. Halaby, Caryl P. Haskins, James T. Hill, Jr., Joseph E. Johnson, Mervin J. Kelly, Major General Richard C. Lindsay, Major General James McCormack, Jr., Frank C. Nash, Paul H. Nitze, Charles P. Noyes, Frank C. Pace, Jr., James A. Perkins, Don K. Price, I. I. Rabi, David Rockefeller, Oscar M. Ruebhausen, General Walter Bedell Smith, Henry DeWolf Smyth, Shields Warren, Carroll L. Wilson, Arnold O. Wolfers.

I believe, be as serviceable as the original. It was prepared by Philip W. Quigg, Assistant Editor of *Foreign Affairs*.

Dr. Kissinger has produced what in my opinion is the most profound and constructive study that has yet been made of one of the toughest problems facing our country. There is a way out of our dilemma if we keep our heads, and Dr. Kissinger's book is an appeal to the head and to the way to keep it.

GORDON DEAN

CONTENTS

Nuclear Weapons and Foreign Policy

CHAPTER ONE

The Challenge
of the Nuclear Age

I

In Greek mythology the gods sometimes punished man by fulfilling his wishes too completely. It has remained for the nuclear age to experience the full irony of this penalty. Throughout history humanity has suffered from a shortage of power and has concentrated immense effort on developing new sources and special applications of it. It would have seemed unbelievable even fifty years ago that there could ever be an excess of power, that everything would depend on the ability to use it subtly and with discrimination.

Yet this is precisely the challenge of the nuclear age. Ever since the end of the Second World War brought us not the peace we sought so earnestly but an uneasy armistice, we have responded by what can best be described as a flight into technology: by devising ever more fearful weapons. The more powerful the weapons, however, the greater becomes the reluctance to use them. At a period of unparalleled military strength President Dwight D. Eisenhower summed up the dilemma posed by the new weapons technology in the phrase "there is no alternative to peace."

It is only natural, of course, that an age which has known two world wars followed by a cold war should have as its central problem the attainment of peace. It is paradoxical, however, that so much hope should concentrate on man's most destructive capabilities. We are told that the growth of thermonuclear stockpiles has created a stalemate which makes war, if not too risky, at least unprofitable. The

power of the new weapons is said to have brought about a
tacit nonaggression treaty: a recognition that war is no
longer a conceivable instrument of policy and that for this
reason international disputes can be settled only by means
of diplomacy. And it has been maintained that the peaceful uses of nuclear energy have made irrelevant many of
the traditional motives for wars of aggression, because each
major power can bring about a tremendous increase in its
productive capacity without annexing either foreign territory or foreign labor.

These assertions fit in well with a national psychology
which considers peace as the "normal" pattern of relations
among states and which has few doubts that reasonable
men can settle all differences by honest compromise. So
much depends, however, on the correctness of such propositions that they must be subjected to close scrutiny.

This is particularly urgent in a revolutionary period like
the present, when change is more desired than harmony.
Contemporary international relations would, therefore, be
difficult at best but they take on a special urgency because
never have so many different revolutions occurred simultaneously. On the political plane, the postwar period has seen
the emergence into nationhood of a large number of peoples hitherto under colonial rule. To integrate so many new
states into the international community would not be a simple matter at any time; it has become increasingly formidable because many of the newly independent states continue
to inject into their policies the revolutionary fervor that
gained them independence. On the ideological plane, the
contemporary ferment is fed by the rapidity with which
ideas can be communicated and by the inherent impossibility of fulfilling the expectations aroused by revolutionary
slogans. On the economic and social plane, millions are re-
belling against standards of living as well as against social
and racial barriers which had remained unchanged for centuries. Moreover, all these revolutions have been taking
place at a moment when international relationships have
become truly global for the first time; there are no longer
any isolated areas. Any diplomatic or military move imme-

diately involves world-wide consequences. And these problems, serious enough in themselves, are manipulated by the Sino-Soviet bloc, which is determined to prevent the establishment of an equilibrium and which is organized to exploit all hopes and dissatisfactions for its own ends.

Statesmanship has never faced a more fearful challenge. Diplomacy is asked to overcome schisms unparalleled in scope and to do so at a moment when the willingness to utilize the traditional pressures available to it—even during periods of harmony—is constantly diminishing. To be sure, the contemporary revolution cannot be managed by force alone; it requires a consistent and bold program to identify ourselves with the aspirations of humanity. But when there is no penalty for irresponsibility, the pent-up frustrations of centuries may seek an outlet in the international field instead of in internal development. To the extent that recourse to force has become impossible, the restraints of the international order may disappear as well.

Moreover, whatever the possibilities of identifying ourselves with the aspirations of the rest of humanity, we are confronted by two revolutionary powers, the U.S.S.R. and Communist China, which pride themselves on their superior understanding of "objective" forces and to which policies unrelated to a plausible possibility of employing force seem either hypocrisy or stupidity. Because harmony between different social systems is explicitly rejected by Soviet doctrine, the renunciation of force will create a vacuum into which the Soviet leadership can move with impunity. Because the Soviet rulers pride themselves on their ability to "see through" our protestations of peaceful intentions, our only possibility for affecting their actions resides in the possession of superior force. For the Soviet leadership has made every effort to retain its militancy. It has been careful to insist that no technological discovery, however powerful, can abolish the laws of history and that real peace is attainable only *after* the triumph of communism. "We will bury you," Nikita S. Khrushchev has said, and the democracies would have been spared much misery had they not so often insisted that dictators do not mean what they say.

"Political power," Mao Tse-tung has said, "grows out of the barrel of a gun . . . Yes . . . we are advocates of the omnipotence of the revolutionary war, which . . . is good and is Marxist."[1]

The dilemma of the nuclear period can, therefore, be defined as follows: the enormity of modern weapons makes the thought of war repugnant, but the refusal to run any risks would amount to giving the Soviet rulers a blank check. At a time when we have never been stronger, we have had to learn that power which is not clearly related to the objectives for which it is to be employed may merely paralyze the will. No more urgent task confronts American policy than to bring our power into balance with the issues for which we are most likely to have to contend. All the difficult choices which confront us—the nature of our weapons systems, the risks diplomacy can run—presuppose an ability on our part to assess the meaning of the new technology.

This task is complicated by the very novelty of the challenge. Until power is used, it is—as Colonel George A. Lincoln, of the United States Military Academy, has wisely said—what people think it is. But except for the two explosions of now obsolete weapons over Hiroshima and Nagasaki, no nuclear weapons have ever been set off in wartime; there exists, therefore, no body of experience on which to draw. To a considerable extent the impact of the new weapons on strategy, on policy, indeed on survival, depends on our interpretation of their significance.

I I

It is the task of strategic doctrine to translate power into policy. Whether the goals of a state are offensive or defensive, whether it seeks to achieve or to prevent a transformation, its strategic doctrine must define what objectives are worth contending for and determine the degree of force appropriate for achieving them. As a *status quo* power, the

[1] Mao Tse-tung, *Selected Works* (New York: International Publishers, 1954), v. 2, p. 272.

basic strategic problem for the United States is to be clear about what strategic transformations we are prepared to resist. The crucial test of our strategic doctrine is, therefore, what it defines as a threat.

In determining what transformations to resist, our strategic doctrine has been inhibited, however, by the seeming lessons of our history. We have confused the security conferred by two great oceans with the normal pattern of international relations; we have overlooked that concepts of aggression developed in a period of relative safety may become dangerously inadequate in the face of a new type of challenge. A power favored by geography or by a great material superiority, as we have been through most of our history, can afford to let a threat take unambiguous shape before it engages in war. And because many other states had to be attacked long before the threat to our security became apparent, we could always be certain that some powers would bear the brunt of the first battles and hold a line while we mobilized our resources. Thus we came to develop a doctrine of aggression so purist and abstract that it absolved our statesmen from the necessity of making decisions in ambiguous situations and from concerning themselves with the minutiae of day-to-day diplomacy.

But the destructiveness and speed of modern weapons have ended our historic invulnerability, and the polarization of power in the world has reduced our traditional margin of safety. The intermediary states having lost either the power or the will to resist aggression by themselves, we can no longer count on other powers to hold a line while we are assessing events or organizing our defenses. Resistance to aggression henceforth is no longer a problem of our coming into a battle long in progress in order to tilt the scales, as was the case with our entry into World War I and World War II. It depends not only on our strength, but also on our ability to recognize aggression. In the nuclear age, by the time a threat has become unambiguous it may be too late to resist it.

Moreover, nuclear technology makes it possible, for the first time in history, to shift the balance of power solely through developments *within* the territory of another sovereign state. No conceivable acquisition of territory—not even the occupation of Western Europe—could have affected the strategic balance as profoundly as did the Soviet success in ending our atomic monopoly. Had a power in the past sought to achieve a comparable strategic transformation through territorial expansion, war would have been the inevitable consequence. But because the growth of nuclear technology took place within sovereign territory, it produced an armaments race instead of war.

Finally, as the power of weapons has increased the forms of attack have multiplied. The age of the hydrogen bomb is also the age of internal subversion, of intervention by "volunteers," of domination through political and psychological warfare.

In such circumstances, our notion of aggression as an unambiguous act and our concept of war as inevitably an all-out struggle have made it difficult to come to grips with our perils. Because the consequences of our weapons technology are so fearsome, we have not found it easy to define a *casus belli* which would leave no doubt concerning our moral justification for using force. We have been clear that we would resist aggression, the goal of which we have identified with world domination, and our military policy has prescribed all-out war for meeting this contingency. But, faced with the implications of our power, we have had to learn that world domination need not be aimed at directly by means of a final showdown. Even Hitler's attack on the international order took the form of such issues as his claims to Danzig and the Polish Corridor, which at the time seemed to the United States not to warrant embarking on war. In the face of the methodical, almost imperceptible advances of the Kremlin, subtly adjusted so that no one of its individual steps seems "worth" an all-out war, it has become even more apparent that the willingness to resist aggression depends importantly on the price that must be paid. We may wait a long time for that "pure" case of aggression in which our military doctrine, the provocation, and our principles are all in harmony.

We have, therefore, been vulnerable to Soviet maneuvers in two ways. Because we have considered the advantage of peace so self-evident, we have been tempted to treat each act of Soviet intransigence as if it were caused by a misunderstanding of our intentions or else by the malevolence of an individual. There is a measure of pathos in our continued efforts to discover "reasonable" motives for the Soviet leaders to cease being Bolsheviks: the opportunities to develop the resources of their own country, the unlimited possibilities of nuclear energy, or the advantages of expanding international trade. The Kremlin has been able to exploit this attitude by periodically launching policies of "peaceful coexistence," which have inevitably raised the debate whether a "fundamental" shift has occurred in Soviet purposes, thus lulling us before the next onslaught. On the other hand, because our strategic doctrine recognized few intermediate points between total war and total peace, we have found it difficult, during periods of Soviet belligerency, to bring the risks of resistance into relationship with the issues which have actually been at stake.

Much has been made of the "nuclear stalemate" which is supposed to have come about with the development by the Soviet Union of thermonuclear weapons and the ability to deliver them. But so far as the effect on our national policy is concerned, the stalemate is nothing new. In fact, it has been with us ever since the explosions over Hiroshima and Nagasaki. To be sure, in the first postwar years it was not a physical stalemate. For nearly a decade the United States was virtually immune to Soviet retaliation. It was a stalemate, none the less, in the sense that we never succeeded in translating our military superiority into a political advantage. This was due to many factors: a theory of war based on the necessity of total victory, the memory of the wartime alliance with the Soviet Union, humanitarian impulses, lack of clarity about the process in which we found ourselves involved. Whatever the reason, our atomic monopoly had at best a deterrent effect. While it may have prevented an even greater expansion of the Soviet sphere, it did not enable us to achieve a strategic transformation in our favor. Indeed, even its importance as a deterrent is questionable. Assuming that there had never been an atomic bomb, would we really have acquiesced in a Soviet occupation of all of Europe? And would the Kremlin have risked a general war so soon after having suffered large-scale devastation by the Germans and having lost, by the most conservative estimate, ten million dead? Not even a dictatorship can do everything simultaneously.

Apart from the questionable assumption that an all-out war was prevented by our atomic monopoly, the decade witnessed the consolidation of Soviet control over the satellite orbit in Eastern Europe, the triumph of communism in China, and, most fundamental of all, the growth of the Soviet atomic stockpile. Those who think that the problems of the nuclear period are primarily technical would therefore do well to study American reactions after Nagasaki and Hiroshima. No foreseeable technological breakthrough is likely to be more fundamental than our discovery of the atomic bomb. Yet possession of it did not enable us to prevent a hostile power from expanding its orbit and developing a capability to inflict a mortal blow on the United States.

How did this come about? Primarily because we added the atomic bomb to our arsenal without integrating its implications into our thinking. Because we saw it merely as another tool in a concept of warfare which knew no goal save total victory and no mode of war except all-out war.

The notion that war and peace, military and political goals, were separate and opposite had become so commonplace in our strategic doctrine by the end of World War II that the most powerful nation in the world found itself hamstrung by its inability to adjust its political aims to the risks of the nuclear period. In every concrete instance, even in the matter of the regulation of the atom, which affected our very survival, we found ourselves stalemated by our preconceptions. Our policy became entirely defensive. We possessed a doctrine to repel overt aggression, but we could not translate it into a strategy for achieving positive goals. Even in the one instance where we resisted aggression by military power, we did not use the weapons around which our whole military planning had been built. The gap between military and national policy was complete. Our power was not commensurate with the objectives of our national policy, and our military doctrine could not find any intermediate application for the new weapons. The growth of the Soviet atomic stockpile has merely brought the physical equation into line with the psychological one; it has increased our reluctance to engage in war even more. It has not, however, changed the fundamental question of how our political and military doctrines can be harmonized, how our power can give impetus to our policy rather than paralyze it.

III

Perhaps this quandary is inherent in the new weapons themselves, rather than in the strategic doctrine. In the face of the horrors of nuclear war, perhaps force has ceased to be an instrument of policy save for the most naked issue of national survival. Here it may be useful to touch on some of the fundamental characteristics of the new technology.

Nuclear weapons, only a short decade ago a difficult and delicate engineering feat, have now become plentiful. They can be produced in all sizes, from weapons of a fraction of the explosive power of the bombs used over Hiroshima and Nagasaki, to thermonuclear devices (popularly called H-bombs) which represent the same increase of explosive power over the Hiroshima bomb as the original atomic bomb did over the largest "blockbusters" of World War II: a thousandfold increase. The Hiroshima and Nagasaki bombs had an explosive equivalent of 20 thousand tons TNT (20 kilotons). Today "tactical" nuclear weapons as small as 100 tons of TNT equivalent have been developed. Thermonuclear devices exist which have an explosive equivalent of 20 million tons of TNT (20 megatons), and there is no upper limit: thermonuclear and nuclear weapons can be made of any desired explosive power.

Moreover, there is no "secret" about the manufacture of

nuclear weapons or even of thermonuclear devices. Given a certain level of technology, any industrialized state will be able to produce them. With the spread of the peaceful uses of atomic energy, it can be expected that many secondary powers will enter the nuclear race by either making their own weapons or purchasing them from the constantly growing list of countries which will possess a nuclear armaments industry. For better or for worse, strategy must henceforth be charted against the ominous assumption that any war is likely to be a nuclear war.

And the new technology *is* awesome. The lethal radius of the weapons dropped over Hiroshima and Nagasaki—the area within which destruction was total and the proportion of fatalities was in excess of 75 per cent—was 1½ miles. Their blast and heat effects destroyed or set fire to buildings within a radius of another 4.4 square miles in Hiroshima and 1.8 square miles in Nagasaki. The explosions of the first atomic bombs killed between 70 thousand and 80 thousand in Hiroshima and 35 thousand in Nagasaki; the direct injuries were between 100 thousand and 180 thousand in Hiroshima and between 50 thousand and 100 thousand in Nagasaki. The collateral effects of radiation may not become fully apparent for several decades.

For all their horror the atom bombs dropped on the two Japanese cities were puny compared to present weapons. The damage they caused was restricted to a relatively small area, and even the effects of radiation were generally confined to the area covered by heat and blast damage. The thermonuclear weapons, on the other hand, do not possess this relative measure of discrimination. A 20 megaton weapon has a lethal radius of 8 miles; its area of total destruction is 48 square miles. Within that area at least 75 per cent of the population would be killed and all the remainder severely injured.

Nor are the damage and casualties exhausted by the direct effects. If it touches the ground, the fireball of a megaton weapon sucks up particles of earth and buildings and deposits them downwind as radioactive material. Depending on meteorological conditions, the radioactive fall-out may cover an area of 10,000 square miles or a territory larger than the state of New Jersey. A successful attack on fifty of the most important metropolitan areas of the United States would thus bring under fire 40 per cent of our population, 50 per cent of our key facilities and 60 per cent of our industry.

At this scale of catastrophe it is clear that the nature of war has altered. Our traditional insistence on reserving our military effort for an unambiguous threat and then going all out to defeat the enemy may lead to paralysis when total war augurs social disintegration even for the victor. During the period of our atomic monopoly, it was possible to rely on our nuclear stockpile to deter all forms of aggression because we could inflict punishment without fear of retaliation. But in the face of the new-found Soviet capability to inflict devastating damage on the United States, our reluctance to engage in an all-out war is certain to increase. To be sure, we shall continue to insist that we reject the notion of "peace at any price." The price of peace, however, cannot be determined in the abstract. The further development of Soviet rockets and missiles is certain to widen the line between what is considered "vital" and what is "peripheral" if we must weigh each objective against the destruction of New York or Detroit, of Los Angeles or Chicago.

It can be argued that the fear of all-out war is bound to be mutual, that the Soviet leaders will, therefore, share our reluctance to engage in any adventures which may involve this risk. But though each side may be equally deterred from engaging in all-out war, it makes all the difference which side can extricate itself from its dilemma *only* by initiating such a struggle. If the Soviet bloc can present its challenges in less than all-out form, it may gain a crucial advantage. Every move on its part will then pose the appalling dilemma of whether we are willing to commit suicide to prevent encroachments, no one of which seems to threaten our existence directly but which may be a step on the road to our ultimate destruction.

The growing Soviet nuclear stockpile, coupled with the

diversification of nuclear technology, places precisely this possibility in the hands of the Soviet leadership. It can engage in military actions ranging from the employment of conventional forces to the use of "tactical" nuclear weapons of a size which will raise serious doubt as to whether they "warrant" the resort to all-out war. Every Soviet move of this nature will provide us with an incentive to defer a showdown to a more propitious moment or to a clearer provocation. An all-or-nothing military policy will, therefore, play into the hands of the Soviet strategy of ambiguity which seeks to upset the strategic balance by small degrees and which combines political, psychological, and military pressures to induce the greatest degree of uncertainty and hesitation in the minds of the opponent.

The attempt to develop a doctrine for a more flexible application of our power is made more difficult by the pace at which new weapons are being developed. Were technology stable, an equilibrium might come about between the power of the new weapons and the fear of their consequences. But far from being stable, technology is advancing at a constantly accelerating rate. Almost up to the outbreak of World War II, a weapons system would be good for a generation at least. Today a weapons system begins to be obsolescent when it has barely gone into production. The B-17 Flying Fortress of World War II remained in operational use for a decade; the B-36 intercontinental bomber was obsolescent within less than seven years; and the B-52 heavy jet bomber, the most recent addition to our strategic striking force, will probably be outdated within five years. As weapons must be replaced at ever shorter intervals, their complexity increases. The F-51, a late World War II fighter plane, required 154,000 engineering man-hours to build and cost $21,000; the F-100, its 1957 equivalent, requires 404,000 engineering man-hours and costs $486,000 to perform a similar strategic mission.

The technological race also multiplies the choices which must be made by the military services. Today there are scores of different weapons systems, each with differing characteristics and implying differing strategies. By the

1960's choices will have to be made among hundreds of types. Moreover, each choice permits a wide variety of combinations, so that the number of conceivable weapons systems reaches fantastic figures.

Another aspect of the technological race is an unparalleled specialization of functions. Traditionally, weapons which were useful for offense were broadly useful for defense as well. Now this no longer holds true to the same extent. A superior tank could dominate the battlefield, but a superior bomber does not necessarily dominate the skies. For bombers do not fight each other. Their performances can be compared only in terms of their ability to reach their target, and this depends on superiority vis-à-vis the opposing defensive system. The test of a modern weapon is not so much whether it is better than its equivalent on the other side, but whether it can perform its strategic mission. The victim of an H-bomb will find small consolation in the knowledge that the delivery system which dropped it was inferior to that of his own country. If two hostile bomber fleets pass each other in the sky, the superior performance of one will be meaningless if both are able to reach their targets.

This is not to argue that we can afford to fall behind in the technological race. It is simply to emphasize the complexity of the current strategic problem. The technological race is not between weapons which have the same mission; rather it is between offensive and defensive capabilities. And because the offensive and defensive weapons systems have different characteristics, one of the most important problems for strategy is to decide on the relative emphasis to be given to each and on the "mix" which will provide the greatest security and flexibility.

In these circumstances it is not surprising that there exists more concern with technology than with doctrine. The penalty for miscalculation in the technical field is obvious and demonstrable. The penalty for falling behind in the field of strategic doctrine, though catastrophic, is not immediately discernible. Mastering the technical problems is so difficult that it leaves little time for considering the strategic implications of the new technology. It gives rise to the notion that strategy is identical with the technical analysis of weapons systems, obscuring the fact that both the development and the use of weapons systems are impossible without strategic doctrine.

Maximum development of power is not enough, for with modern technology such a course must paralyze the will. We must have the ability to meet the whole spectrum of possible challenges and not only the most absolute one. To be sure, the first charge on our resources must be the capability for waging all-out war, because without it we would be at the mercy of the Soviet rulers. But while our strategic striking power represents the condition which makes possible all other measures, it cannot be the exclusive preoccupation of our military planning. Given the power of modern weapons, it should be the task of our strategic doctrine to create alternatives less cataclysmic than a thermonuclear holocaust. In 1936, the French General Staff possessed no doctrine for any conflict except all-out war and it believed in no strategy save the defensive. It failed to provide for any contingency except a direct attack on the Franco-German border. Nor did it anticipate that the strategic balance might be upset by small stages, each of which, in itself, did not seem "worth" all-out war. As a result, when Hitler remilitarized the Rhineland, French leadership was paralyzed. It recoiled before the consequences of full mobilization, but its strategic doctrine provided for no other military measures. Faced with the prospect of all-out war and obsessed by the memory of 1914, France could not decide whether to rely on Germany's professions of peaceful intent or on its own military strength. In order to justify its vacillations, the French General Staff ascribed to Germany a military capability it did not possess. By adjusting its estimates of the enemy strength to its strategic doctrine, instead of the reverse, the French General Staff vindicated its theory of all-out war, the very war which the country dreaded and which France was unable to wage except with allies that proved reluctant or ill-prepared. Finally France recoiled, seeking refuge in yet another guarantee of its frontiers, which substituted a legal for a physical safeguard and contributed to France's sense of impotence, even while its Army was still thought to be the world's finest. Only four years later, when France faced the unambiguous aggression for which French strategic doctrine had provided, the attack even then was not directed at the Maginot line on which France had expended so many resources. The penalty for doctrinal rigidity was military catastrophe.

The basic challenge to United States strategy is to formulate a military policy which will avoid this very dilemma. We cannot base all our plans on the assumption that war, if it comes, will be inevitably all-out. We must strive for a strategic doctrine which gives our diplomacy the greatest freedom of action and which addresses itself to the question of whether the nuclear age presents only risks or whether it does not also offer opportunities.

This is a complex task, different from any before in our history; for there is little experience to guide us. The theory we develop will determine our response to the challenges which will inevitably confront us. The Soviet capability to inflict a catastrophic blow on the United States is increasing year by year, and just beyond the horizon lies the prospect of a world in which not only two superpowers will possess nuclear weapons, but also many weaker and perhaps more irresponsible nations, with less to lose. Henceforth, our problem will be one long familiar to less favored nations: how to relate the desirable to the possible and above all how to live with possible catastrophe.

CHAPTER TWO

The Dilemma
of American Security

I

One of the most difficult challenges a nation confronts is to interpret correctly the lessons of its past. For the lessons of history, as of all experience, are contingent: they teach the consequences of certain actions, but they leave to each generation the task of determining which situations are comparable. So long as development is gradual, no particular problem arises. New problems will be sufficiently similar to past experience so that even inaccurate analogies will have a certain validity. It is different, however, when events occur which transcend all past experience. Then the very success of the past may inhibit an understanding of the present. An era of unparalleled success may make it difficult to come to grips with a period of possible disaster. The fact that every problem has found a final solution in the past may stand in the way of the realization that henceforth only partial remedies are possible.

This has been the problem which has haunted American military thinking since World War II. Its dilemma can be defined as the conflict between the quest for absolute answers and the risks of the nuclear age, between the realization that we have become infinitely vulnerable and our rebellion against it.

Because we have won two world wars by outproducing our opponent, we have tended to equate military superiority with superiority in resources and technology. Yet history demonstrates that superiority in strategic doctrine has been

the source of victory at least as often as superiority in resources. In 1940 superior doctrine enabled the Germans to
defeat an allied army superior in numbers, at least equal
in equipment, but wedded to an outmoded concept of warfare. Superior mobility and superior use of artillery, a better relationship between fire and movement, provided the
basis of Napoleon's victories. Similar examples were the
victories of the Roman legions over the Macedonian pha-
lanx, of the English archers against the medieval knights.
All these were victories not of resources but of strategic doctrine: the ability to break the framework which had come
to be taken for granted and to make the victory all the more
complete by confronting the antagonist with contingencies
which he had never even considered.

Thus the key to a proper doctrine is the correct understanding of the elements of one's superiority and the ability to apply them more rapidly than the opponent, whether
through the choice of an advantageous battlefield or
through the superior utilization of available weapons systems.

Our effort to assess the meaning of the new technology
has been difficult, however, because our experience makes
us more comfortable with technology than with doctrine
and because such strategic doctrine as we *had* developed
has been made irrelevant by the power and speed of the
new weapons. The traditional expression of our strategic
doctrine was the allocation of roles and missions among
the military services—until the end of World War II, the
Army and the Navy. Each of these services had the mission of defeating its enemy counterpart: the Army had primary responsibility for the land battle, and the Navy for
control of the seas. Although these missions were based, in
effect, on means of locomotion, with everything moving on
land assigned to the Army and everything moving by water
assigned to the Navy, they represented meaningful and distinguishable strategic tasks. The Army was powerless on the
sea beyond the range of its coastal artillery, and the Navy
was unable to project itself far inland. The Air Force was
not yet independent, and the range of its planes was suffi-

ciently short to permit the division of functions between the Navy and Army air arms to follow roughly that between the senior services. Each service was, therefore, able to control all the weapons it considered essential for achieving its mission. It could, in effect, develop its own strategy without too much concern with that of the sister service or without too much dependence on the interpretation of a sister service as to what constituted an essential target.

But the long-range airplane, the ballistic missile, and the incomparable destructiveness of weapons have almost obliterated the traditional boundaries among the services. Today no service can achieve its primary mission without either trespassing on the role of the other services or calling on them for assistance. And co-operation among the services is difficult unless there is agreement, at least, as to what constitutes an essential target. Is the sea controlled by bombing shipyards from carriers or by destroying the enemy's industrial potential? Is a land battle possible without having won air supremacy and is it necessary after the air battle has been won?

So long as there is no agreed strategic doctrine, each service will give its own reply. And the reply will be an effort to treat new weapons by analogy to familiar functions: Are missiles analogous to artillery because they are fired like shells or to aerial warfare because they fly through the air?—this is a bone of contention between the Army and the Air Force. Is the carrier a naval weapon or do the resources devoted to it detract from our long-range striking force?—this is the source of wrangling between the Navy and the Air Force. Is a 1,500-mile ballistic missile a tactical or strategic weapon? In the absence of a doctrinal answer, each service is pushing its own research in the hope that the service which develops a weapons system first will also control its use in combat.

So long as each service has the primary mission of defeating its enemy counterpart, and so long as there does not exist an agreed strategic doctrine, no service can afford to relinquish control over a weapon which it considers essential for the performance of its mission. For the Navy's conception of what is essential to win control of the seas may conflict with the Air Force's notion of its requirements for winning the air battle. And in view of the necessity for quick reaction imposed by the increasing speed and power of modern weapons, each service feels compelled to hoard as many weapons as possible. Thus the Army, the Air Force, and the Navy are each developing a 1,500-mile missile; the Navy is developing a long-range seaplane, which our mechanistic approach to doctrine treats as a naval weapon because it takes off from water; and the Strategic Air Command is reported to have established a kind of ground force of its own to protect its air bases.

The division of functions which worked relatively smoothly for a century and a half has become a source of bitter rivalry in the nuclear age. Each new weapon has led to a bitter wrangle as to which service should control it. It was thus with the A-bomb; it is now the case with missiles. And in each instance the doctrinal issue was evaded by permitting each service to develop its own weapon, even if it duplicated the efforts of a sister service.

Such a solution is costly. It also defers coming to grips with the doctrinal problem until some crisis brooks no further confusion or until some other pressures bring the interservice dispute into the open. Thus the chief impetus to our strategic thought has come from international crises, particularly from the Korean War, and even more importantly from the periodic economy drives of the Administration and of the Congress.

In a period of national emergency when budgets were generous, each service has protected itself by procuring the entire gamut of possible weapons, a course which, whatever the budgetary level, will soon be foreclosed by the extraordinary variety of possible choices. During periods of budgetary squeeze, each service must make a choice among the weapons systems available to it, because it cannot afford them all, and it can make this choice only in terms of a doctrine. When funds are scarce, each service faces the problem not only of establishing priorities among the weapons available to it but of justifying its role vis-à-vis the other services. When the services become competitors for available appropriations, an incentive is provided for developing a doctrine about the purpose of war and about the contribution which each service can make to our security.

While budgetary pressures have spurred consideration of strategic doctrine, their influence has not been entirely wholesome. They have fostered a tendency to create doctrines as tools in the interservice battle for appropriations; the incentive they have provided is for a theoretical elaboration of a service view and not of an over-all doctrine.

Aware that the budgetary rewards are in the field of strategic striking power, the Army and Navy have been tempted to emphasize that part of their mission which approximates long-range warfare. In budgetary hearings, at least, the Navy has stressed the offensive power of its carriers over its less dramatic antisubmarine role, and since 1955 the Army has emphasized its medium-range missiles as much as the subtler applications of its power. This has set up another vicious circle. The more the other services have extended the range and power of their weapons, the more closely they have approached what the Air Force considers its primary mission, thus opening the way to endless jurisdictional disputes. In the process, the basic strategic problem of the nuclear age has rarely been faced up to explicitly: whether it is possible to find intermediate applications for our military strength; whether our strategic thinking can develop concepts of war which bring power into balance with the willingness to use it.

Against the background of interservice rivalry the attempts to reconcile clashing views have resulted in instruments more akin to an agreement among sovereign states than to a workable doctrine. They have had the same vagueness, leaving each service free to interpret them largely according to its own preconceptions. The present assignment of roles and missions among the services dates from 1948, when Secretary James Forrestal took the Joint Chiefs of Staff to Key West in order to formulate common doctrine. What emerged as the Key West agreement was little more than a reformulation of traditional roles. The primary mission of the Air Force was restated to be control of the air, that of the Navy control of the seas, and that of the Army to defeat the enemy ground forces. This formula missed the essential point of interservice rivalry, perhaps deliberately. The disputes have arisen not because the services have sought to take over each other's primary mission —although this too has happened occasionally—but because in pursuit of their *own* missions they have been impelled by the conflicting pressures of technology and of budget-making into developing overlapping weapons systems. The real difficulty has been that the power, speed, and range of modern weapons have obliterated the traditional distinctions between ground, sea, and air warfare. It is no longer possible to define a distinguishable strategic mission on the criterion of different means of locomotion.

As a result the Key West agreement could receive concrete meaning only in terms of the dispute that had produced the interservice wrangling in the first place: the disagreement over which service should control the nuclear weapons. This was an important issue, because possession of nuclear weapons was the prerequisite to any claim to be able to contribute to the strategy of an all-out war and was, therefore, the best support for budgetary requests. The upshot was a compromise which demonstrated that the neat distinctions set forth in the general principles of the Key West agreement were inapplicable in practice: the Air Force was recognized as possessing the sole right to maintain a strategic air arm, but the Navy was granted the use of the A-bomb against specifically naval targets. It was also permitted to proceed with the construction of its giant aircraft carrier, designed to handle planes capable of carrying the A-bomb. No effort was made to define what constituted a "naval" target or to distinguish the use of atomic bombs against port facilities from strategic bombing. And, like many diplomatic instruments, the Key West agreement contained an unwritten understanding—the concept of balanced forces, in which significantly the balance was achieved not by doctrine but by the budget: each service was promised approximately the same yearly appropriation. In short, the

Key West agreement had not been the expression of a strategic doctrine but a way to postpone difficult choices.

Within eighteen months even the vague division of functions established by the Key West agreement had disappeared in the explosion produced by the "revolt of the admirals" against Secretary Louis A. Johnson's edict canceling the construction of the giant carrier. And within another year, the Korean War revealed that our almost exclusive concern with all-out war and with the most destructive type of strategy had obscured the most likely security problem: the attempt by the Soviet leaders to upset the strategic balance, not at one blow, but piecemeal.

I I

It has often been remarked that nothing stultifies military thought so much as a victorious war, for innovation then must run the gamut of inertia legitimized by success. It was no different with United States military thought after World War II. The war had not only been won, but its course had run true to our notion of what a war should be. The aggression had been unambiguous and had been directed against United States territory. We had brought to bear our superior resources and inflicted a terrible retribution. The enemy had been utterly defeated by a strategy of attrition unencumbered by political considerations. No wonder that we tended to elevate a particular set of circumstances into general maxims and to turn the strategy applied in defeating Germany and Japan into universal military doctrine. "In case of another major war," testified Lieutenant General Raymond S. McLain, in defense of the Army appropriation for 1948, "the pattern would probably take the following form: First the blitz, using all modern means. If this should succeed, the war would be over. . . . If the blitz, however, is stopped the second phase would be a softening-up phase in which bases, industries, and ports would be bombarded. The final phase would be a struggle between complete teams, air, sea, and ground, in which the accompanying attrition would finally point to the victor."[1]

Thus, whatever the technological transformations of the postwar period, we sought to fit them into a concept of war which we had perhaps learned too well. ". . . any aggressor nation seeking domination of the earth," said General Dwight D. Eisenhower in 1947, "must defeat the United States and must defeat us before we can achieve our maximum strength. Therefore, if global war comes to us again, the first blow will be struck not at Warsaw but at Washington; not at London but at Los Angeles; not even at Pearl Harbor but at Pittsburgh."[2]

The notion that a new war would inevitably start with a surprise attack on the United States has been basic to our thinking; reinforced by the memory of Pearl Harbor, it has provided the background for our preponderant concern with the problem of all-out war. Thus a vicious circle has been set up. The more total the sanctions of our weapons technology have become, the more absolute we have imagined the provocation that would alone justify unleashing it. The more we have become convinced that a war would start with an attack on the continental United States, the more fearsome the strategy we have devised to resist it. In the process, we have not realized how abstract and one-sided the notion of a surprise attack has been, particularly at a time when the Soviet Union possessed neither a nuclear arsenal nor a long-range air force. We have failed to see how vulnerable it has left us to the preferred form of Soviet aggression: a strategy which seeks its objectives by small increments of power, by avoiding "all-out" provocation, and by inducing lesser powers to do its fighting. By concentrating on measures to defeat a Soviet attempt to neutralize us physically, we have given the Soviet leadership an opportunity to strive to neutralize us psychologically by

[1] U. S. House, *Military Establishment Appropriation Bill for 1948*, Hearings before the Subcommittee of the Committee on Appropriations, 80th Cong., 1st Sess. (Washington: GPO, 1947), pp. 1,241.

[2] Same, p. 77.

so graduating their actions that the provocation would never seem "worth" an all-out war, the only form of war our doctrine took into account.

If our military doctrine in the immediate postwar period had difficulty in coming to grips with our most likely dangers, it had few doubts about the strategy for conducting any war that might break out. A war would be global and it would be won by our superior industrial potential. Since war would start with a surprise attack, our best defense lay in "our ability to strike back quickly with a counteroffensive, to neutralize the hostile attack at its source . . . by striking at the vitals of the aggressor."[3] The doctrine of massive retaliation was far from new at the time Secretary John Foster Dulles proclaimed it.

There was, to be sure, an awareness that our monopoly would be fleeting. But there was also an air of unreality about these prophecies. In 1945 it was said that the Soviet Union would break our atomic monopoly within five years, and the prediction remained the same with each passing year. A leading military analyst estimated in 1947 that the Soviet Union would produce one atomic bomb some time between 1950 and 1957, that it would then take it another twenty years to build up a significant stockpile, and that in any case the U.S.S.R. was not likely to develop a delivery system for a long time. These views reflected the realities of the national psychology, if not necessarily the intelligence reports.

Our complacency with respect to Soviet progress in the nuclear field, coupled with the notion that war was likely to start with a surprise attack on us, lent a quality of unreality to all thinking about military problems in the immediate postwar period. It gave rise to this syllogism, psychologically if not actually: (1) War must start with a surprise attack; (2) the Soviet Union will not possess an

[3] General Carl Spaatz before the Subcommittee of the Committee on Appropriations, *Military Establishment Appropriation Bill for 1947*, U. S. House, 79th Cong., 2nd Sess. (Washington: GPO, 1946), p. 402.

atomic capability for a long time; (3) therefore, there will not be a war.

As a result, our thinking about nuclear weapons oscillated between exaggerating their horror (which was to some extent reassuring) and underrating their strategic significance. The latter was particularly noticeable among the traditional services, which were afraid that their roles would be impaired by the new technology. In 1947 both the Army and the Navy made known this assessment of the strategic implications of the new weapons. Neither service considered that nuclear weapons would affect its role fundamentally. The Navy, in particular, deprecated the implications of the new technology. A 1,000-mile missile, it argued, was almost impossible. Such a weapon did not simply represent an extension of the German experience with rockets in World War II, but required an altogether new order of physics. In short, for the next ten to fifteen years any new war would not only be fought with a World War II strategy, but with World War II weapons, with the atomic bomb merely added to increase the power of our strategic arsenal.

The advent of the long-range bomber, the B-36, upset the finely wrought concept of the "balanced forces" which permitted each service to do what it had always done, only with more powerful weapons. For if deterrence was to be achieved by retaliatory power and if retaliatory power was identical with offensive air power, the only justification for the other services was their utility in providing or holding air bases. But if it was possible to launch long-range attacks from the United States, the doctrine of balanced forces might represent a diversion of resources.

Had defense appropriations been larger, this argument might not have been pressed to its logical conclusion. But with a new Secretary of Defense, Louis Johnson, convinced that one of Stalin's aims was to induce the United States to spend itself into bankruptcy, the allocation of missions and with it the availability of scarce defense dollars became a matter of overriding concern. When the Defense Department stopped the construction of the Navy's 65,000-ton aircraft carrier *United States* and ordered the procurement of additional B-36 bombers, the first important postwar debate on strategic doctrine was inevitable. No longer restrained by an uneasy partnership with the Air Force in the possession of long-range air power, the Navy now gave full expression to the disagreement among the services over the nature of strategy, the definition of essential targets, and the best means for attacking them.

The debate over the B-36 would have taken on added significance had it not been bound up so intimately with the battle for appropriations. As matters stood, the Navy's case, which attacked the efficacy of strategic bombing, gave the impression of having been constructed out of pique at the decision to end its equivalent of long-range aviation, the giant carrier *United States*. And the Navy's case was further weakened by the fact that the Chief of Naval Operations had not dissented from any of the formulations of strategic doctrine during the postwar period. Nevertheless, the Navy case, ably marshaled by Admiral Arthur W. Radford, for the first time raised issues which have become the core of present disputes about military policy. It attacked the notion of a quick war to be won by air power alone. It emphasized the importance of working out the relationship between military and political objectives. And it rejected the doctrine that a massive retaliatory attack represents our primary deterrent. "One member of the defense team in one branch of the Government asserts," said Admiral Radford, "that the best guaranty for America's security lies first in preventing war by the threat of atomic annihilation, and second in prosecuting such a war of annihilation if we have to fight. . . . This theory of warfare is not generally concurred in, I believe, by military men. Aside from any moral or political considerations . . . many reject the theory on the grounds that it will fail to bring victory. . . . [Moreover,] future war will extend far beyond the province of the military. In planning to wage a war . . . we must look to the peace to follow. . . . A war of annihilation might possibly bring a Pyrrhic military victory, but it would be politically and economically senseless.

. . . The results of two world wars have demonstrated the fact that victory in war is not an end in itself."[4]

In the process, the Navy brought into the open the inadequacies of our method of arriving at strategic decisions. According to this procedure, three service chiefs, whose primary task is the maintenance of the morale and efficiency of their respective services, are also required to make over-all strategic judgments which may well run counter to their basic task. As long as the views of the three services on the most effective strategy are in accord, this presents few problems. If they are at variance—as they have been since 1949—only two solutions are possible. In periods of budgetary plenty, as between 1951 and 1954, each service will build up the weapons systems it considers appropriate for its mission without a too careful concern with doctrinal harmony or overlapping functions. In periods of relative budgetary scarcity it will lead to bitter rivalry over the assignment of missions. And since the presentation of a budget is facilitated by maintaining the *appearance* of interservice harmony, there usually occurs just enough compromise to prevent a resolution of the doctrinal conflict. The necessity of fighting doctrinal battles at intervals set by the budgetary process, with appropriations as the prize, almost insures the perpetuation of the doctrinal disagreements behind the scenes.

To be sure, the "revolt of the admirals" demonstrated that the Navy's disagreement was not so much with doctrine as with the technical implementation of a strategy which could not envisage any form of conflict short of all-out war. The Navy had posed the question of the relationship between political and military objectives, but not because it doubted that every war would be a war of unconditional surrender. Rather, it insisted that unconditional surrender should be achieved by a strategy which did not inflict so much devastation that the victor would be forced to rehabil-

---

[4] U. S. House, *The National Defense Program—Unification and Strategy*, Hearings before the Committee on Armed Services, 81st Cong., 1st Sess. (Washington: GPO, 1949), pp. 50–1.

itate occupied enemy territory. It raised for the first time the issue whether our strategy should be nuclear or conventional and it opposed what it considered the overemphasis on strategic air power. But it did so primarily because carrier planes were said to be able to perform the same missions more effectively and more economically. The B-36 was termed a billion-dollar blunder, but only because Navy fighters and therefore presumably the Soviet defense could outmaneuver it.

The B-36 controversy thus only hinted at the outline of the American strategic dilemma. Our military policy was directed to only two contingencies: a direct attack on the United States and a direct attack on Western Europe. It offered no solutions either to Soviet moves in other areas or to the gradual overturning of the balance of power through subversion, guerrilla activity, or indeed the ending of our atomic monopoly. In fact, it denied that these were the concern of our military policy. In its insistence on a "pure" cause of war, it had developed a *casus belli,* surprise attack on the territorial United States, which did not happen to fit any of the issues actually in dispute, such as the division of Germany, the East European satellites, or international control of the atom. This was the real gap between our military policy and our diplomacy, and compared to it the dispute between the Air Force and the Navy over allocation of missions paled in significance.

III

This was the strategy of a satisfied power, content with its place in the world, eager to enjoy its benefits undisturbed. Its defensiveness was a symptom of our desire to project the pattern of our domestic affairs abroad, to construct an international order animated entirely by the consciousness of the evident advantages of harmony. But the more we protested our horror of war, the more we removed the Soviet leaders' inhibitions against expanding their influence.

Our reaction to the ending of our atomic monopoly was,

therefore, as ambivalent as our doctrine of power. On the one hand, we postulated a nuclear stalemate which was still far from real and used it as one more justification for our existing inhibitions against using force. On the other hand, we hastened to create an even more powerful weapon, the thermonuclear bomb, which in turn caused us to defer the consideration of the strategic transformation wrought by the disappearance of our atomic monopoly.

The literalness of our notion of power made it impossible to conceive of an effective relationship between force and diplomacy. A war which started as a surprise attack on us had of necessity to be conducted in a fit of righteous indignation, and the proper strategy for waging it was one of maximum destructiveness. By the same token, now that the risks of war had grown so fearsome, the task of diplomacy was to attempt to settle disputes by the process of negotiation, and this, in turn, was conceived as a legal process in which force played a small role, if any. The objective of war was conceived to be victory, that of diplomacy, peace. Neither could reinforce the other, and each began where the other left off. We proved unable to use our atomic monopoly to exert pressure or to exploit our unilateral disarmament as a symbol of our peaceful intentions. Since our atomic monopoly was considered to be in the realm of strategy and our unilateral disarmament in the realm of domestic policy, these were treated as unsuitable for being injected into the process of negotiation. This attitude was well expressed when General Marshall said that he would be reluctant to risk American lives for purely political objectives.

This approach to the problem of power and its uses came to full expression in our key postwar policy. The policy of containment was based on the assumption that military strategy and diplomacy represented successive phases of national policy: it was the task of military policy to build strength and thereby to contain Soviet aggression. After containment had been achieved, diplomacy would take over. ". . . what we must do," testified Secretary Acheson at the MacArthur hearings, "is to create situations of strength; we must build strength; and if we create that strength, then I think that the whole situation in the world begins to change . . . with that change there comes a difference in the negotiating positions of the various parties, and out of that I should hope that there would be a willingness on the side of the Kremlin to recognize the facts . . . and to begin to solve at least some of the difficulties between east and west."[5]

But international relations do not permit such absolute divisions. Secretary Acheson's definition of containment implied that strength was self-evident, that power would supply its own rationale. It did not deal with the question of how the position of strength was to be demonstrated in the absence of a direct attack on us or on our allies. It did not supply a doctrine for translating our power into policy except as a response to Soviet initiative. Nor did it make clear what would happen if the Soviet leaders refused to negotiate after we had achieved a "position of strength" and instead concentrated their efforts on eroding it or turning its flank. In short, our posture was bellicose enough to lend color to Soviet peace offensives but not sufficiently so to induce Soviet hesitations.

So it came about that the only time we resisted aggression by force we did so in an area which our doctrine had hardly taken into account and by means of a strategy it had explicitly rejected less than a year before. The problem of limited war was forced on American strategic thought despite itself.

IV

When reality clashes with our expectations of it, frustration is the inevitable consequence. Korea caught us completely unprepared, not only militarily but above all in doctrine. Secretary Acheson's speech of January 12, 1950,

[5] U. S. Senate, *Military Situation in the Far East,* Hearings before the Committee on Armed Services and the Committee on Foreign Relations, 82nd Cong., 1st Sess. (Washington: GPO, 1951), p. 2,083.

which excluded Korea from our defensive perimeter, was no more than an application of fundamental United States strategy, no different in content and almost identical in language with a statement made by General Douglas MacArthur nine months previously.[6] In an all-out war with the U.S.S.R., Korea was indeed outside our defensive perimeter, and its fate would depend on the outcome of a struggle fought in other theaters. As a result the Korean War fitted no category of our strategic thought. It was not initiated by a surprise attack against the United States, nor directed against Europe, nor did it involve the U.S.S.R. It was a war to which an all-out strategy seemed peculiarly unsuited. It has been remarked more than once that, had the Korean War not actually taken place, we would never have believed that it could have.

It was a courageous decision to resist an aggression so totally at variance with all previous planning. The penalty we paid for the one-sidedness of our doctrine, however, was the necessity for improvising a new strategy under the pressure of events. Throughout the Korean War we were inhibited by the consciousness that this was not the war for which we had prepared. The result was an endless conflict between the commanders, who, being responsible for fighting the war, sought to apply literally the doctrine that victory means crushing the enemy, and the responsible officials in Washington, who, in the light of their preconceptions and the global nature of their responsibilities, could only consider the Korean War a strategic diversion or a deliberate feint on the part of the adversary.

It would be a mistake, however, to consider the controversies produced by the Korean War as a dispute about the efficacy of an all-out strategy. On the contrary, both advo-

[6] In March 1949 General MacArthur told a reporter: "Now the Pacific has become an Anglo-Saxon lake and our line of defense runs through the chain of islands fringing the coast of Asia. It starts from the Philippines and continues through the Ryukyu archipelago which includes its broad main bastion, Okinawa. Then it bends back through Japan and the Aleutian Island chain to Alaska." New York *Times,* March 2, 1949.

cates and opponents of a greater effort in Korea agreed that war, by its nature, was an all-out struggle that could be won only by crushing the enemy totally. Where they differed was not in their notion of the nature of war but in their interpretation of the significance of the Korean War. MacArthur advocated a showdown in the Far East and specifically with China. His critics believed we must conserve our strength for a possibly imminent all-out test with the U.S.S.R. and specifically over Europe. The dispute over the Korean War was, therefore, less a conflict over the nature of strategy than a disagreement over the *area* in which it could best be applied.

MacArthur was only expressing accepted doctrine when he asserted that "the general definition which for many decades has been accepted was that war was the ultimate process of politics; that when all other political means failed, you then go to force; and when you do that, the balance of control . . . the main interest involved . . . is the control of the military. . . . I do unquestionably state that when men become locked in battle, that there should be no artifice under the name of politics, which should . . . decrease their chances for winning. . . ."[7] Precisely because they accepted this notion of war, MacArthur's opponents sought to keep the Korean War to the smallest proportions and to reserve our strength for the "real" test which by definition had to involve the Soviet Union: ". . . enlargement of the war in Korea to include Red China, would probably delight the Kremlin more than anything else we could do," argued General Bradley. "It would necessarily tie down . . . our sea power and our air power . . . in an area that is not the critical strategic prize. Red China is not the powerful nation seeking to dominate the world. Frankly, in the opinion of the Joint Chiefs of Staff, this strategy would involve us in the wrong war, at the wrong place, at the wrong time, and with the wrong enemy."[8]

The difficulty was, of course, that it was precisely the

[7] U. S. Senate, *Military Situation in the Far East,* cited, p. 45.
[8] Same, pp. 731–2.

global nature of our defense plans which left us unprepared for the challenges of the Korean War. The assumption behind our military planning had been that our wars would be fought against a principal enemy and a major challenge, but that our forces-in-being need only be powerful enough to gain us the time to mobilize our industrial potential. This doctrine presupposed two related contingencies: that other powers would bear the initial brunt of aggression and that the threat would be unambiguous.

But in the aftermath of World War II this doctrine was no longer adequate to the situation, because the smaller states had lost either the strength or the will to resist by themselves. Since their ability to resist aggression had now come to depend on our willingness to commit our forces at the very beginning of any war, and since their decision to resist at all depended more and more on their confidence in our ability to act at once, our forces-in-being would have to be strong enough to absorb the first blows and to strike back effectively without delay. When war came, it did not involve a principal enemy, nor did it appear as an all-out challenge. In Korea the opponent was first a satellite of the third order and then Communist China. The attack was directed not against us or our installations but against a remote area from which we had withdrawn our troops scarcely a year before. In such a situation, it is little wonder that our preoccupation with an all-out strategy caused us to consider the Korean War as an aberration and a strategic diversion.

Given the threat which we knew the Soviet Union must soon pose when it had developed its nuclear capability further, it is possible to doubt our assumption that time was on our side, or at least to raise the question whether the U.S.S.R. did not have more to lose from an all-out war than we did. Be that as it may, our announced reluctance to engage in all-out war gave the Soviet bloc a psychological advantage. We tended to be more aware of our risks than of our opportunities; in fact, in our eyes even opportunities became risks. Despite our strategic superiority, we thought we could not afford to win in Korea because we assumed Russia could not afford to lose.

The Korean War was a peripheral war, therefore, not only because of its geographic location but because of our difficulty in coming to grips with it. We kept it limited, not because we believed in limited war but because we were reluctant to engage in all-out war over the issues which were at stake in Korea. Whatever aspects of the Korean War we considered—geographic location, strategy for conducting it, or our preparedness—we resolved them into arguments for keeping it to the smallest possible proportions.

By denying the existence of any middle ground between stalemate and total victory, both MacArthur and his opponents inhibited a consideration of strategic transformations which would be compatible with a policy of limited objectives. It was perhaps true that the U.S.S.R. would not permit a thorough-going defeat of China in an all-out war leading to the overthrow of the Communist regime. But it did not follow that the U.S.S.R. would risk everything in order to forestall *any* transformations in our favor, all the more so as our nuclear superiority was still very pronounced. Had we pushed back the Chinese armies even to the narrow neck of the Korean peninsula, we would have administered a setback to Communist power in its first trial at arms with the free world. This might have caused China to question the value of its Soviet alliance while the U.S.S.R. would have been confronted with the dilemma of whether it was "worth" an all-out war to prevent a limited defeat of its ally. A limited war is inconsistent with an attempt to impose unconditional surrender. But the impossibility of imposing unconditional surrender should not be confused with the inevitability of a return to the *status quo ante.*

Our strategic doctrine made it very difficult, however, to think of the possibility of intermediary transformations. Its defensive assumptions led us to analyze Soviet reactions as if every move were equally open to the Kremlin. And the divorce between force and diplomacy tended to paralyze both. The objective of our campaign was varyingly stated as repelling aggression, resisting aggression, punishing aggression, or as the security of our forces.[9] Each of these objectives was defined in military terms and each assumed that diplomacy would take over only *after* a position of strength had been established.

The Korean War thus represented an application of the doctrine of containment. In fact, it was explicitly justified in those terms. But it suffered from the same drawbacks. Throughout the Korean War we made our objectives dependent on the military situation: they fluctuated with the fortunes of battle between repelling aggression, unification, the security of our forces, and a guaranteed armistice.

The fluctuation of our objectives demonstrated that it is impossible to conduct limited wars on the basis of purely military considerations. After Inchon, at a moment of maximum strength, we proved unable to create a political framework for settling the Korean War, and we thereby provided the enemy with an incentive, if any was needed, to seek to restore the military balance as a prerequisite to any negotiation. It is not clear that a generous and comprehensive offer, for example, to stop at the narrow neck of the peninsula and to demilitarize the rest of North Korea under United Nations supervision, would have been accepted; for purposes of this argument, it is sufficient to note that it was never made. The attempt by both sides to achieve a position of strength *prior* to negotiation resulted in a vicious circle of gradually expanding commitments which was brought to a halt only because an equilibrium was finally established between the physical inability of Communist China to invest more resources in the conflict and our psychological unwillingness to do so.

The same attitude toward power which kept our diplomacy from setting limits to our military aims after we had the upper hand also prevented us from drawing strength from our military posture after we had opened negotiations for an armistice. Our decision to stop military operations, except those of a purely defensive nature, at the *very be-*

[9] Same, p. 478 (General Marshall); p. 937 (General Bradley); pp. 1,225 and 1,191 (General J. Lawton Collins); p. 1,717 (Secretary Acheson); p. 570 (General Marshall).

ginning of the armistice negotiations reflected our conviction that the process of negotiation operated on its own inherent logic independently of the military pressures brought to bear. But by stopping military operations we removed the only Chinese incentive for a settlement; we produced the frustration of two years of inconclusive negotiations. In short, our insistence on divorcing force from diplomacy caused our power to lack purpose and our negotiations to lack force.

V

The same literal approach to power which affected our views about the strategy for fighting the Korean War also shaped our coalition policy. Our alliances were based on the same assumption as our strategic doctrine: that aggression is deterred by assembling the maximum force. As a result, we tended to place our hope of deterrence in a system of general collective security which gave rise to the notion that, unless all allies resisted aggression jointly, no resistance was possible at all. "The basis upon which we are building our security, in addition to the strength of our own Armed Forces, is collective security," said Secretary Acheson. ". . . [our allies] are the most fundamental forces in the security of the United States. Therefore, it is of transcendent importance that in our policies *in all parts of the world, where danger of war may be created, we work absolutely hand in hand with our allies.*"[10]

By such a course the inhibitions produced by our military policy were compounded by the vulnerabilities of our allies. A system of general collective security is effective only against a threat so overpowering that it obliterates all disputes about the nature of the threat or about the strategy for dealing with it. And it presupposes a military policy which offers each major ally a measure of protection against what it considers its greatest peril.

Neither condition held true in the Korean conflict. The

[10] Same, p. 1,764. [Emphasis added.]

attack was directed at a point at which the interests of our European allies were involved indirectly at best; yet our coalition policy treated the Korean War as if it were of world-wide concern. Our allies, conscious of the ability of the Red Army to overrun them, therefore magnified our own tendency to consider the Korean War only in terms of risks. No conceivable gains in Korea seemed "worth" the danger to their national existence which was implicit in the risk, however slight, that the Korean War might spread to Europe.

Thus our effort to assemble the maximum number of allies was the obverse of our all-out strategy and it involved the same problems: the greater the force, the greater the reluctance to employ it. Both our military and our coalition policy tended to make it difficult to undertake decisive action against peripheral threats: the former by posing risks disproportionate to the objectives in dispute, the latter by causing us to limit our actions to what could gain allied support. "This is the first time," said General Bradley, "we have had a United Nations field command . . . [we should] do anything we can to keep from breaking up a United Nations [field] command and discouraging them from taking United Nations action in the future."[11] For this reason, we rejected any expansion of the Korean War. Even "hot pursuit" of enemy planes beyond the Yalu seemed too risky in the face of the opposition of six of our allies.

To be sure, in the early stages of the Korean War the hesitations of our allies were not apparent; indeed the eagerness with which they offered military assistance seemed to prove the contrary. But the willingness of our allies to participate in the Korean War reflected their uncertainty as to whether we had actually outgrown our traditional isolationism and whether we could, in fact, be relied on to help them defend their homelands. Their interest in Korea was, therefore, largely symbolic: to commit us to the principle of collective security. Beyond this their willingness to run risks was limited by the consciousness of their weak-

[11] Same, p. 1,077.

ness. Since our commitment to the principle of collective security was established with our entry into the Korean War, the pressure of our allies from then on was in favor of a strategy of minimum risk. This is not to say that our allies were "wrong," only that they tended to look at the Korean War from the perspective of their vulnerabilities rather than from that of strategic opportunities.

The choice in Korea was not necessarily between collective action or isolation in a global war, as was so often maintained during the MacArthur hearings. In the first place, our allies could not in their own interest have stayed aloof from an all-out global war between the United States and Soviet Russia. But a more likely result of an expanded war in Korea was that the conflict would have spread in the Pacific without becoming all-out. In this event allied support would have been unnecessary, and Europe would have been protected by her neutrality instead of by our alliance. This is not to imply that it would have been wise to expand the war in Korea. It is simply to indicate that, by leaving no room between total war and stalemate and between complete allied support and neutrality, we posed alternatives for ourselves which did not, in fact, exhaust our options.

VI

Our reactions to the frustrations of the Korean War have illustrated how strongly strategic and political concepts linger on even after they have outlived their usefulness. Instead of reassessing our strategic doctrine we have been inclined to ascribe our difficulties to a departure from our traditional policy. Limited war has tended to be identified with a strategically unproductive holding operation. We have refused to admit that our strategic doctrine had created a gap between our power and our policy. Rather, our experience in Korea has reinforced our determination to reserve our all-out power for use in contingencies in which it could be utilized without restraint.

From our reaffirmation of strategic orthodoxy we have

drawn the conclusion that the United States should not exhaust itself in a war of attrition over peripheral areas nor keep in being forces so large as to drain our economy without adding to our effective strength on A-day (the hypothetical date of the outbreak of the nuclear war). Since the Sino-Soviet bloc possesses interior lines of communication and is therefore able to choose the point of attack, we should, according to the predominant view, not let ourselves be lured into areas where we would be operating at a strategic disadvantage. Instead we should inhibit aggression at its source by the threat of general war.

Thus the most recent public consideration of strategic concepts, the hearings on air power conducted by Senator Stuart Symington's Senate subcommittee, turned into restatements of familiar doctrine. All the services, except the Army, were in accord that the next war would start with a surprise attack; all agreed that it would be won by maximum offensive power.[12] It was little wonder, therefore, that deterrence was again identified with strategic striking power, as if the Korean War had never taken place. ". . . the key to the enemy decision [to attack]," said the Strategic Air Command briefing, "is our relative strength in 1958–65. We use the word 'relative' because our strength as compared to his determines what he has to pay in excess costs as to whatever action he undertakes. . . ."[13]

The notion that the decision between peace or war depends on the ability to inflict a greater level of damage than the enemy, demonstrates the traditionalism of our military thinking. In fact, the notion of "relative damage" may have become meaningless in an all-out war in which both sides have an abundance of nuclear weapons. For even the side which has mounted the stronger offensive may have to absorb a level of damage which drains its national

12 U. S. Senate, *Study of Airpower*, Hearings before the Subcommittee on the Air Force of the Committee on Armed Services, 84th Cong., 2nd Sess. (Washington: GPO, 1956), p. 50 (General Spaatz); p. 184 (Major General Curtis E. LeMay); p. 1,055 (Rear Admiral C. D. Griffin); p. 1,845 (General Nathan F. Twining).

13 Same, p. 185.

substance. With modern weapons, even an inferior retaliatory capacity may deter, not because it can inflict disproportionate damage but because it can inflict unacceptable losses. This, if anything, should have been the lesson of the Korean War, which we refused to press despite Soviet strategic inferiority.

Thus the clash of strategic doctrines which marked the pre-Korea period has continued. The three services, each in pursuit of its primary mission as laid down in the Key West agreement, have developed partially overlapping, partially inconsistent, strategies. The Air Force speaks of winning the air battle, the Navy of keeping the sea lanes open, and the Army of conducting brush-fire wars. And because their force levels are set on the basis of their primary missions, all the interservice pressures operate to perpetuate a division of functions which the power of modern weapons has rendered almost meaningless.

The Symington hearings revealed an attempt by each service to hoard weapons of maximum range and destructiveness, because, in the absence of an agreed over-all doctrine, no service can rely on a sister service's interpretation of what constitutes an essential target. The only way a service can be certain that its targets will in fact be attacked is to seek to obtain every weapon which can be used against them. ". . . if I was assured," said General Twining, "when we wanted to attack Russia on a strategic mission, that the naval carriers were assigned to General LeMay . . . fine. But that is not the case, and I don't know where those carriers are going to be. . . . So the Strategic Air Force has to be just as big, just as strong, and just as ready, regardless of this Navy contribution on these targets. . . ."[14] ". . . the primary function of the Army is the destruction of the enemy army," said General Maxwell D. Taylor, in justifying the Army's development of a 1,500-mile missile. "The primary function of the Air Force is to destroy enemy air power and for the Navy to destroy enemy naval power. . . . if you accept the fact that the

[14] Same, p. 1,840; see also p. 178 (General LeMay).

Army exists to destroy hostile armies, then any missile which will destroy hostile ground forces should be available to the Army."[15] "To control the sea," said Rear Admiral Arleigh A. Burke, "the Navy must be capable of destroying the source of weapons which threaten ships and operations at sea—submarine bases, airbases, missile bases and any other bases from which control of the sea can be challenged."[16] Secretary Charles E. Wilson summed up for all three branches: "Each of the armed services has its own particular military philosophy . . . [about] how wars should be fought."[17]

Given the range, speed, and power of modern weapons, the attempt to develop a weapons system capable of destroying every target that can affect a service's primary mission must lead to an attempt by each service to develop a strategic striking force. It prevents an adequate consideration of intermediate applications of power whose importance is now all the greater because of the changing nature of deterrence. The notion that deterrence can be achieved by only *one* of the two superpowers is no longer applicable, if it ever was. So long as the United States enjoyed an absolute atomic monopoly, even a small number of nuclear weapons exercised a powerful deterrent effect. Then we could protect many areas by the threat of massive retaliation. But as the Soviet nuclear stockpile has grown, the American strategic problem has been transformed. No matter how vast our remaining margin in the number and refinement of weapons, henceforth not only *they* but *we* must fear them. In this situation deterrence can no longer be measured by absolute numbers of bombs or planes. To seek safety in numerical superiority or even in superior destructiveness may come close to a Maginot-line mentality—to seek in numbers a substitute for conception. Moreover, in many fields where our present weapons system is already adequate to its mission, new technological advances will add much less to our effective strength than to that of the

15 Same, p. 1,285, p. 1,287.
16 Same, p. 1,343.
17 Same, p. 1,618.

Soviet bloc. This seems to be true for the Intercontinental Ballistic Missile and the atomic submarine. And when weapons can be made of any desired degree of destructiveness a point will be reached at which additional increments of destructive power yield diminishing returns. What is the sense in developing a weapon that can destroy a city twice over?

To be sure, the key to survival is the possession of an adequate retaliatory force. Without a powerful retaliatory force, either of planes or of missiles, no other measures are possible. But all-out surprise attack does not exhaust the range of our perils; although the greatest threat, it may, in fact, be the least likely danger. Mastery of the challenges of the nuclear age will depend on our ability to combine physical and psychological factors, to develop weapons systems which do not paralyze our will, and to devise strategies which permit us to shift the risks of counteraction to the other side. The pernicious aspect of the absence of doctrinal agreement among the services is that it tempts each of them to aim for absolute solutions in purely military terms. And it therefore inhibits the attempt to bridge the gap which has opened between power and the objectives for which power can be used.

Our difficulty in finding a strategic doctrine adequate to the dangers we face has been compounded by the apparent ambiguity of Soviet behavior since World War II. We cannot achieve an intelligent doctrine until we understand the nature of the threat, and this in turn requires a clear reading of the revolutionary challenge of the Soviet Union and Communist China.

CHAPTER THREE

The Strategy of Ambiguity—Sino-Soviet Strategic Thought

I

What is a revolutionary? Were the answer to this question self-evident, only the most moribund societies would ever collapse and few, if any, international orders would be overthrown. For it would then be possible to stifle at its inception the party or the state seeking to subvert the existing system or to remedy, in time, the situation that brought about its emergence. Instead, history reveals a strange phenomenon. Time and again states appear which boldly proclaim that their purpose is to destroy the existing structure and to recast it completely. And time and again, the powers that are the declared victims stand by indifferent or inactive while the balance of power is overturned. Indeed, they tend to explain away the efforts of the revolutionary power to upset the equilibrium as the expression of limited aims or specific grievances, until they discover—sometimes too late and always at excessive cost—that the revolutionary power was perfectly sincere all along, that its call for a new order expressed its real aspirations. So it was when the French Revolution burst on an unbelieving Europe and when Hitler challenged the system of Versailles. So it has been with the relations of the rest of the world toward the Soviet bloc.

How was it possible that from positions of extreme weakness these states could emerge as the most powerful in Europe and that the most recent of these challengers, the U.S.S.R., can bid for the domination of the world less than a generation after a group of die-hards were trying to hold Moscow against enemies converging from all sides?

Part of the answer is to be found in the tendency of the powers which represent the *status quo* to confront the revolutionary power with methods they learned in a more secure environment, in the difficulty they find in adjusting to the changed nature of international relations in a revolutionary international order. An international order in which the basic arrangements are accepted by all the major powers may be called "legitimate." A system which contains a power or a group of powers which rejects either the arrangements of the settlement or the domestic structure of the other states is "revolutionary." A legitimate order does not make conflicts impossible; it limits their scope. Wars may arise, but they will be fought *in the name* of the existing system, and the peace will be justified as a better expression of agreed arrangements. In a revolutionary order, on the other hand, disputes have to do, not with adjustments within a given framework, but with the framework itself.

Negotiations within a legitimate order have three functions: to formulate agreements or disagreements in a manner that does not open unbridgeable schisms; to perpetuate the international system by providing a forum for making concessions; to persuade by stating a plausible reason for settlement. But in a revolutionary period most of these functions have changed their purpose. The emphasis of traditional diplomacy on "good faith" and "willingness to come to an agreement" is a positive handicap when it comes to dealing with a power dedicated to overthrowing the international system. For it is precisely "good faith" and "willingness to come to an agreement" which are lacking in the conduct of a revolutionary power. Diplomats can still meet but they cannot persuade each other. Instead, diplomatic conferences become elaborate stage plays which seek to influence and win over public opinion in other nations; their purpose is less the settlement of disputes than the definition of issues for which to contend. They are less a forum for negotiation than a platform for propaganda.

While this changed function of diplomacy may be clear enough in retrospect, an understanding of it in the face of a revolutionary challenge is inhibited by the very factors which make for the spontaneity, indeed the existence, of a legitimate order. To be sure, no international order is ever stable *solely* because it is considered legitimate by its component states. The fact that each power within an international system is sovereign and that its intentions are, therefore, subject to change imposes a measure of precaution on all policy. No statesman can make the survival of his country entirely dependent on the assumed good will of another sovereign state, because one of his most effective guarantees for this will remaining good is not to tempt it by too great a disproportion of power. For this reason there always exists in international relations the temptation to strive for absolute security, to press the search for safety to the point of eliminating all possible sources of danger. But since absolute security for one power is unattainable except by the annihilation or neutralization of all the others, it can be achieved only by a cycle of violence culminating in the destruction of the multi-state system and its replacement by single-power domination. The quest for absolute security inevitably produces a revolutionary situation.

A legitimate order is distinguished by its willingness not to press the quest for security to its limits. Instead, safety is sought in a combination of physical safeguards and mutual trust. It is legitimate, not because each power is perfectly satisfied but because no power is so dissatisfied that it will seek its remedy in overthrowing the existing system. The confidence required for the operation of a legitimate order does not presuppose the absence of *all* tensions, but the conviction on the part of all major powers that the disputed issues do not threaten their national survival.

The powers that represent the *status quo* are, therefore, at a profound psychological disadvantage vis-à-vis a revolutionary power. They have everything to gain from believing in its good faith, for the tranquillity they seek is unattainable without it. All their instincts will cause them to seek to integrate the revolutionary power into the legitimate framework with which they are familiar and which to them seems "natural." They will ascribe existing tensions to misunderstanding, to be removed by patience and good will: ". . . we are dealing with people who are rather unpredictable," President Eisenhower has said of the Soviet leaders, "and at times they are just practically inexplicable, so far as we are concerned. So you go along announcing your views about peace in the world, what you are striving to do . . . and then for the rest of it, you meet them from time to time, or your diplomatic representatives do, in order to see whether it is possible to ameliorate the situation. . . ."[1]

A revolutionary power confronts the legitimate order with a fearful challenge. A long period of peace leads to the temptation to trust appearances and to seek to escape the element of conjecture in policy by interpreting the motives of other powers in the most favorable and familiar manner. Napoleon's conquests were made possible because the "legitimate" rulers surrendered after a lost battle according to the canons of eighteenth-century warfare; the familiar assumptions prevented them from conceiving the enormity of Napoleon's goals. Hitler could use the doctrines of his opponents in annexing Austria, because they wanted to believe that his aims were limited by the "legitimate" claim of national self-determination. And the Soviet rulers have expanded their power into the center of Europe and along the fringes of Asia by coupling each act of expansion with protestations of peace, democracy, and freedom.

The revolutionary power, therefore, gains a subtle advantage. If it displays any degree of psychological skill, it can present every move as the expression of limited aims or as caused by a legitimate grievance. The *status quo* powers, on the other hand, cannot be sure that the balance of power is in fact threatened or that their opponent is not sincere until he has demonstrated it, and by the time he

[1] New York *Times*, January 24, 1957. (Press Conference of January 23, 1957.)

has done so it is usually too late. However the physical balance may be weighted at first against the revolutionary power, this handicap is more than made up by the psychological advantage conferred by the absence of self-restraint.

In the past, conflicts between a legitimate and a revolutionary order have often had a tragic quality, for each side was unconscious of the role it was playing. To be sure, one side was attacking the *status quo* while the other defended it. But each contender spoke in the name of an absolute truth and each was wont to ascribe its victory to the superior validity of its maxims or its greater resolution. The particular dynamism of the Soviet system derives from its combination of revolutionary righteousness and psychological adeptness. Its leaders have studied not only the elements of their own doctrine—which is true of all revolutionary movements—but have consciously sought to press the psychological vulnerabilities of their opponents into their service. The liberal theory of the West preaches tolerance. Therefore the Communists in democratic states seek to present their organization merely as one of the contending parties and claim for it the equality of democratic opportunity which it will be their first act to deny their opponents should they come to power by parliamentary means. The empiricism of the free world teaches that resistance by force is justified only against overt aggression. Therefore the Soviet leaders graduate their moves so that the equilibrium is overturned by almost imperceptible degrees which magnify the inward doubts of the non-Soviet world. The West is reluctant to exert its power, and the uncommitted peoples exalt peace into an absolute principle. Thus Soviet policy alternates peace offensives with threats of the dire consequences if their demands are disregarded: while Bulganin and Khrushchev, during their visit to India, were loudly protesting their love of peace, a hydrogen bomb was set off in the Soviet Union. The timing could hardly have been accidental. The free world believes that peace is a condition of static equilibrium and that economic advance is a more rational objective than foreign adventures. Therefore the Communists appear periodically in the guise of the domestic reformer eager to spread the fruits of material advancement.

For each change of pace and tactic, the U.S.S.R. has found defenders among its victims, who justified its course not on the ground of Communist doctrine, but because it fitted in with the preconceptions of a legitimate order. The great advance of communism over the past generation has many causes, but chief among them is a spiritual crisis among its opponents. "We say to the powers," wrote Lenin long ago, "'. . . you . . . do not know what you want and . . . you are suffering from what is called a weak will which is due to your failure to understand economics and politics which we have appraised more profoundly than you.'"[2]

Whatever the validity of Lenin's statement, there is something remarkable about the reluctance of the defenders of the "legitimate" order to believe the publicly announced aims of the Communist leaders. Neither Lenin's published works nor Stalin's utterances nor Khrushchev's declarations have availed against the conviction of the non-Soviet world that peace is the natural relation among states and that a problem deferred is a problem solved. During World War II there was a general conviction among Western policy makers that after the war the U.S.S.R. would prefer to concentrate on the development of its own resources rather than engage in foreign adventures. And after the death of Stalin there took place a new outburst of speculation that a "basic" change had occurred in Soviet thinking. "The Soviet leaders," said Secretary Dulles in 1956, "are scrapping thirty years of policy based on violence and intolerance."[3]

The situation is doubly paradoxical because of the exasperation with which the Soviet leaders regularly have repudiated the notion that a change of tactics on their part

---

[2] V. I. Lenin, *Selected Works* (New York: International Publishers, 1943), v. 9, pp. 311–2, as quoted by Nathan Leites in *A Study of Bolshevism* (Glencoe, Ill.: The Free Press, 1953), p. 383.
[3] U. S. Department of State *Press Release No. 92*, February 25, 1956.

implies an abandonment of their basic doctrines. ". . . if anyone thinks," Khrushchev said at the height of the "peace offensive," "that we shall forget about Marx, Engels, and Lenin, he is mistaken. This will happen when shrimps learn to whistle."[4] "The theory of Marx, Engels, Lenin and Stalin is a 'universally applicable theory,'" Mao has written. "We should not regard their theory as a dogma, but as a guide to action. We should not merely learn Marxist-Leninist words and phrases, but study Marxism-Leninism as the science of revolution."[5] It is the insistence by the intended victims that the Bolsheviks do not "mean" what they have so often proclaimed which has given an air of unreality to the relations between the Soviet bloc and the rest of the world.

Throughout the decades when Mao and other Chinese Communist leaders were proclaiming their devotion to Marxist-Leninist doctrine, many analysts in the West were arguing that Chinese communism was inherently different from Soviet communism. And today, in many areas of Asia at least, there is a general belief in the peaceful character of the Chinese regime based on no more solid evidence than the natural desire of the peoples concerned and on the Chinese rulers' skill in using the term "peace" with all the ambiguity which attaches to it in Communist doctrine. Yet Mao has reiterated the world-revolutionary quality of Chinese communism in the most contemptuous terms: "We have a claim on the output of the arsenals of London as well as Hangyeng, and what is more, it is to be delivered to us by the enemy's own transport corps. This is the sober truth, not a joke."[6]

II

What, then, are the principles which constitute the "science of revolution"? In both Soviet and Chinese Commu-

[4] Denis Healey, "When Shrimps Learn to Whistle," *International Affairs*, v. 32 (January 1956), p. 2.

[5] Mao Tse-tung, *Selected Works* (New York: International Publishers, 1955), v. 2, p. 259.

[6] Same, v. 1, p. 253.

nist thought they derive from Marxism, as reinterpreted by Lenin. To be sure, many tenets of classical Marxism and even of Leninism have since been discarded or modified. But it is one thing to adapt doctrine to the tactical requirements of the moment; it is quite another to give up the belief which to Communists distinguishes theirs from all other movements: the confidence that Leninist theory will enable them to understand and to manage an inexorable historical development. For this reason a study of Marxist-Leninist theory is not considered an abstract philosophical exercise in Soviet countries but the prerequisite to effective action. It explains also the insistence by Marxist leaders that victory is achieved only by superior *theoretical* insight. In every Soviet school, whether technical or professional, a study of Marxist-Leninist theory takes up a large part of the curriculum: ". . . all those members of the Communist Party," wrote Mao, "who are fairly qualified to study must study the theory of Marx, Engels, Lenin and Stalin. . . . It is impossible for a party to lead a great revolutionary movement to victory if it has no knowledge of revolutionary theory. . . ."[7]

As a result, while Communist tactics are highly flexible, every effort is made to integrate them into a doctrine presented as unchanging and inflexible. Part of the reason for the misunderstanding by the non-Soviet world of Soviet motivations is that more attention is paid to Soviet announcements, meant for public consumption and couched in the simple slogans of propaganda, than to Soviet doctrinal discussions. Yet the latter are much more significant. Since the Soviet "legitimacy" is based on the claim to superior theoretical insight, every tactical move is justified as the expression of "pure" theory and every effort is made to maintain doctrinal militancy, whatever the tactical requirements of the moment. From Lenin, to Stalin, to Mao, and to the current Soviet leadership, the insistence on superior historical understanding, on endless and inevitable conflict

[7] Same, v. 2, p. 258.

with non-Soviet states, on ultimate victory, has been un-varying. This chapter deals with these underlying beliefs, compared to which Soviet tactics are like the visible tip of the iceberg in relation to the submerged mass. It pays particular attention to Lenin and Mao, for while they may become superseded on this point or that, they have established the basic orientation and the pattern of thinking of their society, including the attitudes of the current Soviet leadership which, as will be seen, have not been basically changed even by the enormity of the new technology.

Marxist-Leninist theory asserts that political events are only manifestations of an underlying reality which is defined by economic and social factors. Leninism is said to enable its disciples to distinguish appearance from reality and to avoid being deceived by what are only symptoms, often misleading, of deep-seated economic and social factors. The "true" reality resides not in what statesmen say, but in the productive process they represent. This process in all societies, except a communist one, is characterized by a class struggle between the exploiting classes and the proletariat. To be sure, in the industrially advanced countries the struggle may sometimes be obscured by the ability to exploit colonies and "semi-colonial countries." But the respite is only temporary. For imperialism transfers the class struggle to the international scene. The very effort to escape the contradictions of the capitalist economy at home sharpens international tensions and leads inevitably to an unending cycle of conflicts and wars among the imperialist powers. Thus all of political life is only a reflection of a struggle produced by economic and social changes. Statesmen are powerless to alter this fact; they can only guide it or utilize it for the ends of the dominant class.

The existence of a communist state results, according to Leninist theory, in intensifying the contradictions of capitalism. For a "socialist" state is not only a symbol of the possibility of revolutionary upheaval, its very existence limits the markets available to capitalism. Thus the larger the Soviet bloc, the smaller the stage on which the tensions of capitalism can work themselves out and the greater the resulting conflicts within the capitalist camp. Another consequence is that, whether they are aware of it or not, capitalist states must seek to destroy the socialist state if they are not to be destroyed by it. Thus the basic relationship between the two camps is one of inevitable conflict, and whether it is hot or cold at any given moment is largely a question of tactics.

Nor will statesmen be able to escape the operation of these economic laws by an act of will, for their role is determined by the economic structure of the society they represent. Conciliatory American statements will, therefore, appear to Soviet leaders either as hypocrisy or stupidity, ignorance or propaganda. Even when they accept the "subjective" sincerity of American statesmen, the Soviet leaders still believe them powerless to deal with the "objective" factors of American society which will make continuing conflict inevitable. Soviet statesmen consider diplomatic conferences a means to confirm an "objective" situation, and nothing is more futile than to seek to sway them by invocations of abstract justice or shared purposes.

As a result, relations between the Communist and the non-Communist world always have some of the attributes of war whatever form the contest may take at any given moment. It is not that the Soviet leadership glorifies war for its own sake; it is rather that it believes that the struggle is imposed on it by the task history has set it. Lenin wrote:

War is a great disaster. But a social-democrat [i.e., Communist] cannot analyze war apart from its historic importance. For him there can be no such thing as absolute disaster, or absolute welfare and absolute truth. He must analyze . . . the importance of war from the point of view of the interests of his class—the proletariat. . . . He must evaluate war not by the number of its casualties, but by its political consequences. Above the interests of the individuals perishing and suffering from war must stand the interests of the class. And if the war serves the interests of the proletariat . . . [it] is progress irrespective of the victims and the suffering it entails.[8]

"War," wrote Mao, "this monster of mutual slaughter among mankind, will be finally eliminated through the progress of human society. . . . But there is only one way of eliminating it, namely, to oppose war by means of war, to oppose counter-revolutionary war by means of revolutionary war. . . ."[9]

The image of a constant conflict between the Communist and the non-Communist world has given a completely different meaning to the Soviet notion of war and peace. To the non-Soviet world, peace appears as an end in itself and its manifestation is the *absence* of struggle. To the Soviet leaders, by contrast, peace is a *form* of struggle. To the nations which are heir to the liberal tradition of the West, man is an end in himself. In the Soviet concept, man is the product of a social experience, a datum to be manipulated for his own good.

There is a certain irony in the Communist image of the cunning capitalists devising or manipulating philosophies, religions, and systems of government in terms of their suitability for oppressing the proletariat. Had the capitalist powers been as aware of their interests, as coolly calculating, as cold-bloodedly manipulating as communism asserts, the Soviet state could never have come into being or flourished. It was because the non-Communist powers refused to believe in irreconcilable antagonisms that the U.S.S.R. has emerged in the center of Europe and China has achieved a dominant position in Asia. Had the non-Soviet world used its beliefs merely as a tool in the class struggle, the colonial peoples would still be subjugated. It was because the non-Communist powers *do* believe in their own principles that their resistance to independence movements has been so indecisive. Thus the Soviet leaders in some respects have constantly overestimated their opponents,

[8] V. I. Lenin, *Sochineniia* (3rd ed.; Moscow: 1935), v. 6, p. 457, as quoted by T. A. Taracouzio, *War and Peace in Soviet Diplomacy* (New York: Macmillan, 1933), p. 53.
[9] Mao Tse-tung, cited, v. 1, p. 179.

looking for devious manipulation in the most superficial gesture.

However incorrect the Communist assessment, it has given an increasing urgency to international relationships. Knowing its own motivations toward the non-Communist world, the Soviet leadership cannot credit any assertion of peaceful intention by its declared enemy. Against an opponent possessing the attributes ascribed to him by Soviet doctrine, relations have had to assume the form not only of a struggle but of a contest without quarter. "Until the final issue [between capitalism and communism] is decided," said Lenin, "the state of awful war will continue. . . . Sentimentality is no less a crime than cowardice in war."[10] "We . . . have no use for stupid scruples about benevolence, righteousness and morality in war," wrote Mao. "In order to win victory we must try our best to seal the eyes and ears of the enemy, making him blind and deaf. . . ."[11]

One way of achieving this aim has been through an unintended method, through making the most of the ambiguity inherent in Communist terminology. Because disciplined Communists see everything in relation to the class struggle, the concepts of war and peace, seemingly so unambiguous, have been turned into tools of Soviet political warfare. If wars are caused by the class struggle, and if the class struggle reveals the determining role of an exploiting class, all wars by non-Communist powers are unjust by definition. By contrast, all wars of the Soviet Union are just, since a government which has abolished the class struggle cannot fight any other kind. That peace can be achieved by war, that a war by a classless society is a form of peace—these are paradoxes dear to the heart of dialectically-trained Leninists. "Wars in history," wrote Mao following Stalin, "can be divided into two kinds: just and unjust. All progressive wars are just and all wars impeding progress are unjust. We Communists are opposed to all un-

[10] Lenin, *Selected Works*, cited, v. 9, pp. 242 and 267, as quoted by Leites, cited, p. 347.
[11] Mao Tse-tung, cited, v. 2, p. 217.

just wars that impede progress, but we are not opposed to progressive, just wars. . . . We [Communists] . . . aim at peace not only in one country but throughout the world, and we not only aim at temporary peace but at permanent peace. In order to achieve this objective we must wage a life-and-death war, must be prepared to sacrifice anything. . . ."[12]

Thus peace offensives have alternated in Soviet strategy with threats of war, depending on the Soviet assessment of the tactical requirements of the moment. Since, according to Soviet theory, permanent peace can be achieved only by abolishing the class struggle, and since the class struggle can be ended only by a Communist victory, any Soviet move, no matter how belligerent, advances the cause of peace, while any non-Communist policy, no matter how conciliatory, serves the ends of war. While Soviet tanks were shooting down civilians in Hungary in the fall of 1956, it was the United Nations which, in Soviet propaganda, threatened peace by debating Soviet intervention. And in 1939, it was the League of Nations which threatened peace by condemning the Soviet attack on Finland. Hence too the constant effort to expand the Soviet sphere and to fill every vacuum; any territory in the possession of a non-Communist state is considered, by virtue of its different social structure, a danger to the peace of the Soviet bloc. Therefore, finally, the skillful use of peace offensives and disarmament talks always aimed precisely at the psychological weak point of the non-Soviet world: that it considers peace as an end in itself, an attitude which Lenin once described as the "pitiful pacifism of the bourgeoisie." "The replacement of the slogan 'armament of the proletariat' by that of 'disarmament,'" proclaimed a thesis at the Sixth World Congress of the Comintern, "[can] serve . . . only as a revolutionary slogan. . . . The peace policy of a proletarian state in no way signifies that the Soviets have come to terms with capitalism. . . . It is merely another—in this situation a more advantageous—form of the struggle against capitalism. . . ."[13]

12 Same, v. 2, p. 199.
13 Taracouzio, cited, pp. 274–5.

What is striking, therefore, about relations between the Soviet and the non-Soviet world is not the flexibility of Soviet tactics, but that essentially the same pattern of Soviet behavior should time and again raise discussion about its "sincerity" or its "novelty." The Soviet leaders have advanced variations of the same disarmament proposals since the mid-1920's. Their recurrent peace offensives have consistently followed the line that the export of revolution was impossible. And their periods of belligerency have had the same justification, that a capitalist encirclement was threatening the Soviet bloc. Yet each new Soviet move has been taken at face value and has produced infinite arguments over whether the Soviet government was preparing for a "showdown" or ushering in a period of peace.

Nothing could be more irrelevant. For the one contingency which Soviet theory explicitly rules out is a static condition. Neither an all-out showdown nor a permanent peace is part of Soviet theory except as the former may be forced on them by an all-out attack like Hitler's or the latter may come about through achieving Communist hegemony over the entire world. Rather, the Soviet concept is one of seeking to manage the inevitable flow of history, to bring about the attrition of the enemy by gradual increments, and not to stake everything on a single throw of the dice.

Moreover, military actions are but one form of conflict and appropriate only to a specific relation of forces. The struggle is unchanging but its forms vary: "We Marxists," wrote Lenin, "have always been proud of the fact that by a strict calculation of the mass of forces and mutual class relations we have determined the expediency of this or that form of struggle. . . . At different moments of economic evolution, and depending on varying political, national, cultural, and other social conditions, different forms of struggle assume prominence, become the chief form of struggle, whereupon in their turn the secondary and supplementary forms of struggle also change their aspect."[14]

14 Lenin, *Sochineniia*, cited, v. 22, p. 265 and v. 10, pp. 80–1,

From the Soviet point of view, relations between the Soviet and non-Soviet world, therefore, reflect an equilibrium of forces in flux, in which the task of the Communist leadership is to tilt the scale by constant if imperceptible pressure in the direction predetermined by the forces of history. Neither personal feelings nor considerations of abstract principle can enter into this contest. The Soviet leadership can only be profoundly suspicious of overtures that ask it to demonstrate its "good faith" by a specific concession as a prelude to a permanent settlement. If the forces have been calculated correctly, a settlement will always be possible, according to Soviet theory, and if they have been misjudged, good faith cannot act as a substitute. Soviet negotiators typically adopt a posture of intransigence in order to squeeze the last possible gain from the existing relation of forces; and their professions of good will are always abstract, involving no practical consequences.

To the Soviet way of thinking, a settlement is not something to be achieved by the process of negotiation; rather an "objective" situation is ratified by the settlement. There is no value in making concessions. Either they are unnecessary on the basis of the relationship of forces and therefore a needless surrender; or else they reflect the relationship of forces and are, therefore, not concessions, strictly speaking. Not to take advantage of a strategic opportunity is to demonstrate not moderation but weakness.

As a result, the Soviet leaders never give up the chance to fill a vacuum, real or imagined, for the sake of winning the good will of the non-Communist world. The immense reservoir of sympathy built up during World War II was sacrificed without hesitation to obtain a bastion in Eastern Europe. The Geneva summit conference was used to perpetuate the Soviet position in East Germany and did not stand in the way of the Soviet arms deal with Egypt. Neither the "spirit of Geneva" nor the chidings of the uncommitted proved an obstacle to the ruthless use of Soviet force

as quoted by Raymond L. Garthoff in *Soviet Military Doctrine* (Glencoe, Ill.: The Free Press, 1953), p. 19.

in putting down the revolt in Hungary. In every policy choice the Soviet leaders identify security with a physical relationship of forces: they cannot have any confidence in the continued good will of powers whom Soviet doctrine defines as permanently hostile.

The nature of the Soviet challenge is, therefore, inherently ambiguous. It uses the "legitimate" language of its opponents in a fashion which distorts its meaning and increases the hesitations of the other side. The belief in an inevitable historical progress leads the Soviet leaders to maintain a constant pressure just short of the challenge which they believe would produce a final showdown. To be sure, the Soviet leadership may miscalculate and thus bring on a holocaust despite its most rational calculations. But meanwhile, all dividing lines between war and peace, aggression and the *status quo* are gradually eroded and in a manner which never presents a clear-cut issue to the West.

The combination of caution, persistence, and ambiguity is well illustrated by the Soviet sale of arms to Egypt. It was launched at the height of the "Geneva spirit," which was interpreted by the Soviet leaders not as a sign of relaxation of tensions but as a measure of the free world's yearning for release from tensions, and, therefore, as opening a new strategic opportunity. It was negotiated by Czechoslovakia in order to keep the Soviet line of retreat open in case the Western powers should react strongly. When the Soviet leaders saw that they could penetrate the Middle East without increasing the risk of counterpressures and, much less, of war, they gradually increased their commitment by increments so small that none of them seemed to justify serious alarm, until suddenly during the Suez crisis the U.S.S.R. emerged as a major Middle Eastern power, a contingency which would have been considered inconceivable a mere two years before.

The Soviet strategy of ambiguity can ultimately be countered only by a policy of precaution, by attempting to nip Soviet moves in the bud before Soviet prestige becomes so deeply engaged that any countermeasures increase the risk of war. Yet a policy of precaution is the most difficult

of all for *status quo* powers to implement. All their preconceptions tempt them to wait until the Soviet threat has become unambiguous and the danger has grown overt, by
which time it may well be too late. The Soviet leadership,
therefore, presents to the West a challenge which may be
moral even more than physical. Many of the Soviet gains
have been due in large part to a greater moral toughness,
to a greater readiness to run risks, both physical and moral,
than their opponents. And despite the moral bankruptcy of
Soviet theory, which with every passing year is demonstrated anew, the Soviet power center has made gains
which were not justified by the relation of forces but were
largely due to the inward uncertainty of their declared
victims.

III

The revolutionary dynamism of the U.S.S.R. and Communist China affects profoundly both the conduct of diplomacy and the conduct of war; indeed, it tends to blur the
distinction between them. To Leninist doctrine, negotiation
is one tool among many others in the conduct of the international class struggle, to be judged by its utility in advancing Soviet objectives but without any inherent moral value
in itself. To us, negotiation tends to be an end in itself. To
the Communists, a conference is a means to gain time or
to define the political framework of the next test of strength
or to ratify an "objective" situation. To us, the willingness
to enter a conference is in itself a symptom of reduced tension because we believe that reasonable men sitting around
a table can settle disputes in a spirit of compromise. To
the Soviet leaders, a settlement reflects a temporary relationship of forces, inherently unstable and to be maintained
only until the power balance shifts. To us, a treaty has a
legal and not only a utilitarian significance, a moral and not
only a practical force. In the Soviet view, a concession
is merely a phase in a continuing struggle: "Marxism-
Leninism," wrote Mao, "does not allow concessions to be regarded as something purely negative. . . . Our concession,

withdrawal, turning to the defensive or suspending action, *whether in dealing with allies or enemies,* should always be regarded as part of the entire revolutionary policy, as an indispensable link in the general revolutionary line. . . ."[15] To us, on the other hand, compromise is the very essence of the process of negotiation, and we are, therefore, prepared to meet the other side at least part way as a token of good faith.

Our belief that an antagonist can be vanquished by the reasonableness of argument, our trust in the efficacy of the process of negotiation, reflects the dominant role played in our diplomacy by the legal profession and its conception of diplomacy as a legal process. But the legal method cannot be applied in a revolutionary situation, for it presupposes a framework of agreed rules within which negotiating skill is exercised. Adjustments are achieved because agreement is itself a desirable goal, because there exists a tacit agreement to come to an agreement. It is not the process of negotiation as such which accounts for the settlement of legal disputes but a social environment which permits that process to operate.

The legalistic approach is, therefore, peculiarly unsuited for dealing with a revolutionary power. Law is a legitimization of the *status quo* and the change it permits presupposes the assent of two parties. A revolutionary power, on the contrary, is revolutionary precisely because it rejects the *status quo.* It accepts a "legal" framework only as a device for subverting the existing order. Diplomacy is based on the assumption of some degree of confidence in the "good faith" of the other side. But Soviet doctrine prides itself on its ability to cut through spurious protestations of good faith to the "objective" class relations which alone furnish a real guarantee of security. "With a diplomat," wrote Stalin, "words *must* diverge from acts. . . . Words are one thing and acts something different. . . . A sincere diplomat would equal dry water, wooden iron."[16]

[15] Mao Tse-tung, cited, v. 2, pp. 263–4. [Emphasis added.]
[16] Joseph Stalin, *Sochineniya* (Moscow: Gosudarstvennoe Izdatelstov Politicheskoi Literaturi, 1946), v. 2, pp. 276–7, as quoted by Leites, cited, p. 325.

For these reasons it is futile to seek to deal with a revolutionary power by "ordinary" diplomatic methods. In a legitimate order, demands once made are negotiable; they are put forward with the intention of being compromised. In a revolutionary order, they are programmatic; they represent a claim for allegiance. In a legitimate order, it is good negotiating tactics to formulate maximum demands because this facilitates compromise without loss of essential objectives. In a revolutionary order, where compromise is unlikely, it is good negotiating tactics to formulate minimum demands in order to gain the advantage of advocating moderation. In a legitimate order, proposals are addressed to the opposite number at the conference table. They must, therefore, be drafted with great attention to their substantive content and with sufficient ambiguity so that they do not appear as invitations to surrender. But in a revolutionary order, the protagonists at the conference table address not so much one another as the world at large. Proposals here must be framed with a maximum of clarity and even simplicity, for their major utility is their symbolic content. In short, in a legitimate order, a conference represents a struggle to find formulas to achieve agreement, in a revolutionary order, it is a struggle to capture the symbols which move humanity.

The major weakness of United States diplomacy has been the insufficient attention given to the symbolic aspect of foreign policy. Our positions have usually been worked out with great attention to their legal content, with special emphasis on the step-by-step approach of traditional diplomacy. But while we have been addressing the Soviet leaders, they have been speaking to the people of the world. With a few exceptions we have not succeeded in dramatizing our position, in reducing a complex negotiation to its symbolic terms. In major areas of the world the Soviets have captured the "peace offensive" by dint of the endless repetition of slogans that seemed preposterous when first advanced but which have come to be common currency through usage. The power which has added 120 million people to its orbit by force has become the champion of anticolonialism. The state which has utilized tens of millions of slave laborers as an integral part of its economic system appears as the champion of human dignity in many parts of the world. Neither regarding German unity, nor Korea, nor the satellite orbit have we succeeded in mobilizing world opinion. But Formosa has become a symbol of American intransigence, and our overseas air bases a token of American aggressiveness. We have replied to each new Soviet thrust with righteous protestations of our purity of motive. But the world is not moved by legalistic phrases, at least in a revolutionary period. This is not to say that negotiations should be conceived as mere propaganda; only that, by failing to cope adequately with their psychological aspect, we have given the Soviet leaders too many opportunities to use them against us.

As a result the international debate is carried on almost entirely in the categories and at the pace established by the Soviets. The world's attention is directed toward the horror of nuclear weapons but not toward the danger of Soviet aggression which would unleash them. The Soviet leaders negotiate when a relaxation of tension serves their purpose and they break off negotiations when it is to their advantage, without being forced to shoulder the onus for the failure.

The negotiations beginning with the summit conference at Geneva can serve to illustrate these points. We were right to agree to the summit conference and to the subsequent meeting of the foreign ministers, although it would have been wiser to combine the two and to relate a relaxation of tension to concrete political conditions. But it was not necessary to permit the Soviet leaders to build up a distinction between the President and the rest of the United States Government, so that any subsequent increase in tensions could be ascribed by them to the President allegedly having succumbed to the pressure of his advisers or of the "objective" factors of the American economy. Moreover, to the extent that the Soviet leaders believed the sincerity of our profession of peaceful intentions they realized that they might make gains perhaps not otherwise open to them on the basis of the existing relation of forces. As a result, on the way back from Geneva Khrushchev and Bulganin pledged themselves to maintain their East German satellite and thereby to perpetuate the division of Germany. And shortly thereafter the world learned of the Soviet-Egyptian arms deal which marked the active entry of Soviet policy into the Middle East.

Having established its acceptance of two *de facto* governments in Germany, Soviet diplomacy could permit the foreign ministers' conference on German unity to fail completely. Indeed the very abruptness of its failure demonstrated our impotence to affect events and laid the basis for Moscow to negotiate directly with West Germany, perhaps eventually to the exclusion of the Western powers. And in the Middle East the Kremlin used its new-found enthusiasm for Arab nationalism as a means to advance ambitions which had eluded Imperial Russia. In short, what many in the non-Soviet world considered the beginning of a relaxation of tensions was used by the Kremlin as a means to attempt to overturn the world balance of power.

Thus the canons of traditional diplomacy become a subtle device of Soviet pressure. They enable the Soviet spokesmen to define the moral framework of most disputes and to shift the debate to issues of maximum embarrassment to us. It is a cardinal principle of traditional diplomacy that negotiations should concentrate on the most soluble problems, lest the holding of a conference foredoomed to failure exacerbate existing tensions. The application of this principle to a revolutionary situation enables the Kremlin to demoralize the international order still further. Since we consider negotiation as inherently valuable while the Soviet leaders refuse to negotiate except when it serves their purpose, a fundamental inequality exists in the negotiating position of the two parties. The emphasis on "soluble" problems ensures that diplomatic conferences become means for Moscow to liquidate unprofitable disputes and to shift all points of tension to the non-Soviet side of the line. The invasion of Egypt was treated more urgently in the United Nations than the suppression of the Hungarian uprising because the latter seemed less soluble, and the issue of Formosa has been kept more prominently before world opinion than has the unification of Korea or of Germany. Diplomacy in this manner becomes an instrument of political warfare, which merges insensibly into military measures if the situation warrants it.

IV

The notion that international relations reflect the class struggle also underlies the Soviet theory of war. War is not a last resort to be invoked if all else fails. Rather it is one form of a continuing struggle; its use is mandatory if the relation of forces warrants it, and resort to it should be avoided if the power constellation is unfavorable. Soviet military doctrine, therefore, rejects the notion that there is such a thing as "purely" military considerations. "War," wrote Lenin, "is part of the whole. The whole is politics. . . . Appearances are not reality. Wars are most political when they seem most military."[17]

These comments were written by Lenin as marginalia to Clausewitz, the non-Soviet thinker who has had perhaps the profoundest impact on Soviet military thought. War, to Clausewitz, was not an isolated act but part of a continuing political process in which will, popular attitudes, and the nature of objectives play a cardinal role. "War," he wrote, "can never be separated from political intercourse and if . . . this is done in any way, all the threads of the different relations are, to a certain extent, broken, and we have before us a senseless thing without an object."[18] These lines were underscored by Lenin in a volume which he inscribed: "This volume is composed of nothing but fine points."[19]

The essence of Clausewitz's teaching is his insistence that

[17] For a complete list of Lenin's marginalia and the appropriate text, see Bertholdt C. Friedl, "Cahier de Lénine No. 18674 des Archives de l'Institut Lénine à Moscou," *Les Fondements Théoriques de la Guerre et de la Paix en URSS* (Paris: Editions Médicis, 1945), pp. 47–90.

[18] Carl von Clausewitz, *On War* (London: Kegan Paul, Trench, Trubner, 1940), v. 3, p. 122.

[19] Friedl, cited, p. 72.

the relationship between states is a dynamic process in which war constitutes only one aspect, and even a period of peace can become an instrument for imposing a nation's will. ". . . with the conclusion of peace, a number of sparks are always extinguished which would have smouldered on quietly, and the excitement of the passions abates, because all those whose minds are disposed to peace, of which in all nations and under all circumstances there is always a great number, turn themselves away completely from the road to resistance."[20] That the skillful use of peace offensives by Soviet policy has not been accidental is demonstrated by Lenin's marginalia "exactly" along this passage. And this is confirmed by another aphorism of Clausewitz on which Lenin remarked and which has been paraphrased in Soviet thought on several occasions: "The conqueror," he said, "is always a lover of peace. . . . He would like to enter our territory unopposed."[21]

The passage which most appealed to Lenin and which Stalin in 1946 emphasized as a cardinal tenet of Marxist thought concerned the relationship of war to politics. War, argued Clausewitz, can never be an act of pure violence because it grows out of the existing relations of states, their level of civilization, the nature of their alliances, and the objectives in dispute. War would reach its ultimate form only if it became an end in itself, a condition which is realized only among savages and probably not even among them. For war to rage with absolute violence and without interruption until the enemy is completely defenseless is to reduce an idea to absurdity.

The intimate relation in Clausewitz's thought between policy and war was characterized by Stalin in 1946 as "having confirmed a familiar Marxist thesis." It has been paraphrased by a leading Soviet military authority: "If war is a continuation of politics, only by other means, so also peace is a continuation of struggle, only by other means."[22]

[20] Clausewitz, cited, v. 1, p. 28.
[21] Friedl, cited, p. 58.
[22] Boris M. Shaposhnikov, *Mozg Armii* (Moscow-Leningrad: Gosizdat, 1929), v. 3, p. 239, as quoted by Garthoff, cited, p. 11.

And it has been quoted with approval by Mao. It accounts for the Soviet preference for indirect attack—the conflict in which physical and psychological factors are combined in the proportion best calculated to produce the maximum confusion and hesitation on the part of the enemy. Buttressed by Marxist theory, this concept has been applied to Soviet military doctrine with its emphasis on morale, deception, and a "main thrust" at the enemy's weakest link —all attributes which seek to place psychology and policy at the service of a strategy based on never-ending struggle. Therefore too the most substantial Communist contribution to the theory of war has been in the area of limited war— the conflict in which power and policy are most intimately related, in which everything depends on gearing the psychological to the physical components of policy. Both Soviet and Chinese Communist theory emphasize the integral relationship between peace and war as alternating or combined methods for conducting a conflict.

Significantly, the best theoretical statement of Communist military thought is found not in Soviet, but in Chinese writings. This is no accident. The expansion of the U.S.S.R. has been due largely to a skillful use of political warfare and to the vast opportunities created by the collapse of German power in Central Europe. Chinese communism owes its entire success, indeed its survival, to its ability to derive political benefits from military operations.

Written in the 1930's at the beginning of the war against Japan, Mao's essays on "Protracted War" and on "Strategic Problems of China's Revolutionary War" are remarkable for their sense of proportion and their skill in adapting the Leninist orthodoxy to Chinese conditions. Mao summed up the correct military line in three propositions which he considered the prerequisite for victory: "[1] to fight resolutely a decisive engagement in every campaign or battle when victory is certain; [2] to avoid a decisive engagement in every campaign or battle when victory is uncertain; and [3] to avoid absolutely a strategic decisive engagement which stakes the destiny of the nation."

The basic military strategy of Chinese communism was

defined as "protracted limited war." The relationship of forces being unfavorable for waging an all-out war, the kind of war in which absolute power reigns supreme, the Communist goal has to be a series of transformations, none of them decisive in themselves, the cumulative effect of which, however, should be to change the balance of power.

Mao's theory of war, therefore, rejects the notion of a quick, decisive war conducted on the basis of purely military considerations, which underlies so much of American strategic thought. It abounds with exhortations that the psychological equation of war is as important as the physical one; indeed, that it is not strength which decides war, but the ability to use it subtly and to the enemy's maximum disadvantage. Mao never tires of counseling a strategy of maximum ambiguity, in which the enemy's impatience for victory is used to frustrate him. He expresses this principle in sixteen words: "Enemy advances, we retreat; enemy halts, we harass; enemy tires, we attack; enemy retreats, we pursue."[23]

His concern with winning a war through the psychological exhaustion of his opponent led Mao, like Stalin, to pay particular attention to the strategic counteroffensive. If part of the confusion of war is caused by the inadequacy of intelligence about the enemy's intentions, one way of reducing this uncertainty is to induce the enemy to advance in a predetermined direction. As the opponent advances into hostile territory he may make mistakes through overconfidence or he may become discouraged about his inability to fight a decisive engagement against an elusive hostile force. Moreover, it will then be easier to deny the enemy the information he requires to act purposefully. Sometime in the course of the enemy advance a point is usually reached at which, according to Mao, Communist psychological superiority outbalances the physical superiority of the opponent. This will particularly be true if it is possible to attack columns on the move. For then the absolute superiority of the enemy can be transformed into

[23] Mao Tse-tung, cited, v. 1, p. 212.

a relative inferiority on the battlefield. The art of warfare is to isolate enemy units, however great their combined superiority, and to defeat them in detail: "We defeat the many with the few . . . [by defeating] the few with the many—this we say to the separate units of the enemy forces that we meet on the battlefield. This is no longer a secret, and the enemy in general is by now well acquainted with our habit. But he can neither deprive us of our victories nor avoid his losses, because he does not know when and where we shall strike. That we keep secret. The Red Army's operations are as a rule surprise attacks."[24]

For this reason Mao inveighs against "desperadoism" and "adventurism"—the tendency to cling to territory at all cost or the quest for a quick victory. The strength of Communist strategy, according to Mao, is precisely its willingness to accept withdrawals as long as they are related to an over-all strategic plan. The Communist superiority resides in the fact that in a protracted war the internal contradictions of the capitalist enemy are certain to mature: "The . . . objective of retreat is to induce the enemy to commit mistakes and to detect them. . . . we can skilfully induce the enemy to commit mistakes, by staging a 'feint,' as Sun Tzu called it (i.e., 'make a noise in the east but strike in the west' . . .)."[25] ". . . in order to draw the enemy into a fight unfavourable to him but favourable to us, we should often engage him when he is on the move and should look for such conditions favourable to ourselves as the advantageousness of the terrain, the vulnerability of the enemy, the presence of inhabitants who can blockade information, and fatigue and inadvertence on the part of the enemy. This means that we should allow the enemy to advance and should not grudge the temporary loss of part of our territory. . . . We have always advocated the policy of 'luring the enemy to penetrate deep'. . . ."[26]

If necessary, Chinese Communist theory maintains, even negotiations can be utilized to magnify the psychological

[24] Same, v. 1, p. 242.
[25] Same, v. 1, pp. 217–8.
[26] Same, v. 2, pp. 223–4.

pressure on the opponent or to deprive him of the fruits of his victory. Like a judo artist, Mao therefore proposes to paralyze the enemy when seeming to be most pliable and to use the opponent's strength to defeat him by attacking him when most off balance. The desire of the opponent for a rapid victory is considered a sign of weakness to be exploited by skillful Communist strategy and to be used to frustrate the enemy when success seems nearest. It will be noted that the strategy advanced by Mao in the 1930's was followed almost precisely during the Korean War.

Thus limited war is not considered by Soviet doctrine as a strategic aberration but as a strategic opportunity. It is the form of conflict best suited to take advantage of the preconceptions and inhibitions of *status quo* powers. It permits the posing of risks in such a manner that they will always seem out of proportion to the objectives in dispute. And this strategy is given an additional impetus by the horrors of modern weapons. For against a power which is committed to an all-out strategy either by its strategic doctrine or by its weapons systems, the Communists' favored strategy of ambiguity can be carried out with considerable chances of success. Mao's strategy of protracted war can be effective, after all, only against an opponent unprepared either physically or psychologically for limited war; an opponent to whom a war without total victory seems somehow beyond reason.

A war waged against Communist powers, therefore, presupposes an ability to relate the physical to the psychological balance of international relations, to find a mode of action in which power and the willingness to use it are most nearly in harmony. Mao understood that in the subtle adjustments of the psychological balance the side least eager for peace has a negotiating advantage because it can outwait, if not outfight, its opponent. Thus in any conflict with Communist powers it is important, above all, to be clear at the outset about the precise objectives of the war. *And no conditions should be sought for which one is not willing to fight indefinitely and no advance made except to a point at which one is willing to wait indefinitely. The side which is willing to outwait its opponent—which is less eager for a settlement—can tip the psychological balance, whatever the outcome of the physical battle.* The great advantage of communism has been that its doctrine of protracted conflict has made it less uncomfortable with a contest seemingly without issue than we have been with our belief in the possibility of achieving total victory. In any concept of limited war, it is imperative to find a mode of operation and to create a psychological framework in which our impetuosity does not transform time into an enemy ally. Henceforth patience and subtlety must be as important components of our strategy as power.

V

But is not a change of course possible? May not the Soviet leaders be sincere in their protestations of peaceful intentions? Have not the death of Stalin and his subsequent downgrading radically altered the situation? It is difficult to know what sincerity means where self-interest is identical with the avoidance of all-out war. So long as the "relation of forces" is not clearly in the Soviet favor, Leninist theory counsels keeping the provocation below the level which might produce a final showdown. Peaceful coexistence would thereby become the most efficient offensive tactic, the best means to subvert the existing order.

What is permanent in Soviet theory is the insistence upon the continuing struggle, not the form it takes at any given moment. Conflict between opposing social systems is inevitable, but its nature must be adapted to changing conditions. "Communists," said Stalin to H. G. Wells in 1934, "do not in the least idealize methods of violence. . . . They would be very pleased to drop violent methods if the ruling class agreed to give way to the working class."[27]

Nor is the slogan of peaceful coexistence the invention

[27] Joseph Stalin, "Marxism vs. Liberalism: An Interview between Joseph Stalin and H. G. Wells," 1934, as quoted by Garthoff, cited, p. 11 (f.n.).

of the group which succeeded Stalin. Since 1918 it has reappeared in Soviet policy at periodic intervals. In the 1920's it was ushered in by Lenin's statement: ". . . we shall make every possible concession within the limits of retaining power. . . ."[28] And it was justified in 1926 by Stalin in the only terms which make sense in Marxist doctrine: that peaceful coexistence was produced by a temporary equilibrium of forces and was justified only by tactical considerations: "A certain degree of *provisional* equilibrium has been established between our country of socialist construction and the countries of the capitalist world. This equilibrium characterizes the present stage of the 'peaceful co-existence.' . . ."[29]

In the 1930's peaceful coexistence had a similar tactical significance. Notably, it followed upon an unsuccessful overture to Nazi Germany. This overture was made, not because the Soviet leaders preferred Fascist Germany to the Western powers; it was simply that they saw no essential difference between the social structure of Nazi Germany and the Western democracies. The best way to protect the Soviet Union was to set the capitalist powers against each other, to deflect German energies, if at all possible, toward the West. ". . . we are far from being admirers of the Fascist régime in Germany," said Stalin soon after Hitler came to power. "The importance, however, lies not in Fascism, if for no other reason than the simple fact that Fascism in Italy, for instance, did not prevent us from establishing most cordial relations with that country. . . . We are oriented as we were before, and as we are now . . . only toward the U.S.S.R. And if the interests of the Soviet Union demand that we approach one country or another . . . we shall do so without hesitation."[30]

Only when the overture to Germany had failed, and it

28 Lenin, *Selected Works*, cited, v. 9, p. 242, as quoted by Leites, cited, p. 491.
29 Joseph Stalin, *XIV S'ezd Vsesoiuznoi Kommunisticheskoi Partii* (*b*) 18–31 Dekabria 1925, Stenograficheskii Otchet, p. 8, as quoted by Taracouzio, cited, p. 138. [Emphasis added.]
30 Stalin, *XVII S'ezd Vsesoiuznoi Kommunisticheskoi Partii*, cited, p. 14, as quoted by Taracouzio, cited, pp. 181–2.

seemed as if the Soviet Union might become the first victim of the often predicted capitalist "contradictions," did the U.S.S.R. emerge as the champion of collective security. Then the League of Nations, only recently derided as an instrument of capitalist hypocrisy, became the focal point of Soviet diplomacy. As always during such periods, the international aspect of communism was played down. And once more eager advocates in the West accepted the Soviet statements at face value and contrasted the consistent anti-Fascism of the U.S.S.R. with the vacillations of the Western powers. Had they read Stalin's statement in 1933, they would have been less shocked about the Nazi-Soviet pact, the treaty which made inevitable the war so long predicted by Soviet theory.

There was nothing inconsistent about the Nazi-Soviet pact nor anything immoral in it from the Soviet point of view. It was the logical application of a policy announced by Stalin a decade previously: ". . . a great deal . . . depends on whether we shall succeed in deferring the inevitable war with the capitalist world . . . until the time . . . when the capitalists start fighting with each other. . . ."[31] Less than six months before his death, Stalin ushered in the most recent period of peaceful coexistence precisely with the argument that a period of *détente* would sharpen the conflicts among the capitalist powers whose difficulties had increased with the growth of the Communist bloc.

Any policy which is based on the assumption of a change in Soviet purposes bears the burden of proving that the change now is "real," that the Soviet leadership is now interested in a basic and lasting accommodation. This would be tantamount to asserting that the Soviet leaders have ceased being Bolsheviks. A genuine settlement between different social systems can come about in Marxist eyes only with the end of the class struggle. In any other situation the Communists assign themselves the task of exacerbating all tensions. Moreover, while it is easy to see how the Soviet

[31] Stalin, *Sochineniya,* cited, v. 10, pp. 288–9, as quoted by Leites, cited, p. 501.

leaders might refrain from a certain course of action because the relation of forces seemed to them unfavorable, it is difficult to find a reason for their giving up a theory which thus far has served them so well. Now that Mao rules 600 million people and China has emerged as the strongest state of Asia, why should he abandon a doctrine which seemed valid when he was reduced to 20,000 adherents in the mountains of Yenan? Why should the Soviet leaders give up a system of analysis which has been taught in all their schools for over a generation and in whose dogmas their thought has been steeped for many decades? Why should they do so, when they see how their state has transformed itself within twenty-five years from an international outcast to a position where it is feared or respected throughout virtually the entire world?

Nor is there any evidence that they have any intention of modifying the basic Soviet doctrine. *Pravda,* at the close of 1956, was again insisting that the downgrading of Stalin referred only to the cult of his personality and that it did not affect the ideological posture of communism. And Khrushchev maintained at the same time that, when it came to fighting imperialism, all Communists were Stalinists.

Even the speech with which Khrushchev opened the Twentieth Congress of the Communist Party in February 1956, hailed in the West as opening an era of peaceful coexistence, was, in fact, a restatement of familiar Leninist doctrine. Its significance did not rest in its invocations of peace, but in the fact that after almost forty years of Communist rule the non-Soviet world had still not learned the peculiar Communist use of such terms as "peace" and "democracy." Neither the doctrine of revolutionary struggle nor of the increasing contradictions within the capitalist economy was given up by Khrushchev. On the contrary, they were reaffirmed and bolstered with quotations from Lenin.[32] To be sure, Khrushchev did not draw any explicit

<hr />

[32] Nikita S. Khrushchev, "Report to the Party Congress," *Current Digest of the Soviet Press,* v. 8 (March 7, 1956), pp. 4, 5, 10 and 11.

conclusions regarding the inevitability of war; indeed, he gave an ambiguous definition of "peaceful coexistence" hardly different in substance and almost identical in words with the "peaceful coexistence" theme of the 1920's and 1930's. But before a group trained in Marxist dialectics it was not necessary to draw such obvious lessons. All of them knew, even if Western readers did not, what would happen if both the domestic and international contradictions of capitalism matured at the same time. Thus the most remarkable aspect of Khrushchev's speech was not its content, but that after thirty years such shopworn phraseology could still lull the non-Soviet world and be seriously debated as ushering in a new era of Soviet behavior.

Khrushchev's speech began in correct Soviet style with a description of the economic and social conditions which underlay international relationships. He contrasted the constantly improving position of the Soviet economy with a capitalist economy "developing in the direction of still greater enrichment of the monopolies, more intensive exploitation and . . . lowering of . . . living standards . . . sharpening of the competitive struggle among capitalist states, maturing of new economic crises and upheavals." He warned his listeners not to be confused by the seeming prosperity of the capitalist economy. Quoting Lenin, he emphasized that the decay of capitalism does not preclude its rapid growth: ". . . only a temporary coincidence of circumstances favorable to capitalism prevented existing crises phenomena from developing into a deep economic crisis. . . . The capitalists and the learned defenders of their interests are circulating a 'theory' . . . [of] salvation from economic crises. The representatives of Marxist-Leninist science have [often] pointed out that this is a hollow illusion. The arms drive does not cure the disease, but drives it deeper. . . . present-day technology does not remove the contradiction, only emphasizes it. . . . Crises are inherent in the very nature of capitalism; they are inevitable."[33]

[33] Same, pp. 4–5.

The consciousness of impending catastrophe has impelled the capitalist powers, according to Khrushchev, to resort to the inevitable expedient of forming aggressive military pacts to restore their position by military means. But the Soviet leaders were not fooled, argued Khrushchev, by the hypocrisy of calling the alliances defensive. "We know from history that, when planning a redivision of the world, the imperialist powers have always lined up military blocs. Today, the 'anti-Communism' slogan is again being used . . . to cover up one power's claims for world domination."[34]

According to Khrushchev, however, there existed a basic difference between the position of the U.S.S.R. before World War II and at present: the growth of the Socialist bloc "dedicated to peace and progress." And the newly emergent peoples in Asia and Africa constituted another counterweight to imperialist war aims: "The whole course of international relations in recent years shows that great popular forces have risen to fight for the preservation of peace. The ruling imperialist circles cannot ignore this. Their more farsighted representatives are beginning to admit that the 'positions of strength' policy . . . has failed. . . . These public figures still do not venture to state that capitalism will find its grave in another world war . . . but they are already obliged to admit openly that the socialist camp is invincible."[35]

In short, since long-term trends were favorable, a period of peaceful coexistence was tactically advisable. But, as in all past periods of peaceful coexistence, Khrushchev was at pains to point out that this change of tactics did not imply a modification of revolutionary goals: "Our enemies like to depict us Leninists as advocates of violence always and everywhere. True, we recognize the need for the revolutionary transformation of capitalist society into socialist society. It is this that distinguishes the revolutionary Marxists from the reformists, the opportunists. There is no doubt that in a number of capitalist countries violent overthrow

[34] Same, p. 6.
[35] Same, p. 7.

of the dictatorship of the bourgeoisie . . . [is] inevitable. But the forms of social revolution vary. . . . moreover, achieving these forms need not be associated with civil war under all circumstances. . . . The greater or lesser intensity which the struggle may assume, the use or non-use of violence in the transition to socialism depend on the resistance of the exploiters. . . . Of course, in those countries where capitalism is still strong, where it possesses a tremendous military and police machine serious resistance by reactionary forces is inevitable."[36]

Thus the capitalist powers were given the option—as indeed they had under Stalin—of surrendering peacefully. Khrushchev's speech was given particular poignancy by later events. For the only examples of the "peaceful" triumph of communism he could think of were Czechoslovakia and Hungary.

The emerging middle class in Russia may, of course, in time ameliorate the rigors of Soviet doctrine. It has happened before in history that a revolutionary movement has lost its messianic *élan*. But it has usually occurred only when such a movement came to be opposed with equal fervor or when it reached the limit of its military strength. The Turks did not stop voluntarily at the gates of Vienna or the Arabs in southern France. Rather, a line was established because they had been defeated in battle, and the decay did not set in until the West for several centuries exercised unremitting pressure to push them back.

But the important question is: To what extent can we afford to gear our policy to assumptions regarding the possible transformation of Soviet society? The test of policy is its ability to provide for the worst contingency; it can always escape its dilemmas by relying on history or the good will of the opposing states. A wise policy will keep under its own control all factors essential to survival. It will not count too much on changes in domestic structures of other states, particularly of avowedly revolutionary powers like the U.S.S.R. or Communist China, where both the histori-

[36] Same, pp. 11–2.

cal record and the often-repeated proclamations should inspire caution.

Moreover, there may be some prices we are unable to pay even for a domestic Soviet transformation. Perhaps a long period of peace would alter the Soviet regime. But we cannot give up the Middle East to purchase it. Perhaps a policy of inactivity on our part would magnify all the internal tensions of the Soviet system. But it may also give the Soviet leaders the breathing spell needed to overcome them and to gather forces for a renewed onslaught. There is, in short, no means of escaping the inextricable element of international relations: in a system of sovereign states, policy always has somewhat of a "precautionary" aspect. It must guard not only against current intentions of another power, but against the possibility that these intentions may change. It is risky to trust that history will accomplish what the structure of international relations imposes as the duty of statesmanship.

To be sure, the United States should utilize all opportunities to bring about a more moderate course within the Soviet bloc. But, while we should always leave open avenues for a basic change in Soviet leadership, we should have few illusions about the degree to which these can be promoted by a conciliatory American policy. For when we have been most conciliatory, as after the Geneva summit conference, the Soviet leaders have been most insistent about feeling threatened. They are probably sincere in these assertions but, whether or not they feel threatened, the point to bear in mind is that nothing can reassure them. Because their doctrine *requires* them to fear us, they strive for absolute security: the neutralization of the United States and the elimination of all our influence from Europe and Asia. And because absolute security for the U.S.S.R. means absolute insecurity for us, the only safe United States policy is one which is built on the assumption of a continued revolutionary struggle, even though the methods may vary with the requirements of the changing situation.

Nevertheless the likelihood of a continuing revolutionary conflict should not be confused with the imminence of an all-out showdown. An all-out attack is the least likely form of Soviet strategy, either politically or militarily. Yet this is the kind of conflict for which our military and strategic doctrine best prepare us. From this the Soviet leaders derive two basic advantages. In the political field, we tend to look for the "pure" case of aggression which their doctrine teaches the Soviet leaders to avoid by all means. And in the military field it causes us to look for absolute solutions in a contest which Moscow will seek to transform into a subtle blend of political, economic, psychological, and, incidentally, military warfare.

We have thus been inhibited by two contradictory motivations. We have refused to take at face value the often repeated Soviet assertions that they mean to smash the existing framework and we have sought to interpret every Soviet maneuver in terms which we have come to consider as "legitimate." On the other hand, we have conducted our relations with the Soviet bloc, whether military or diplomatic, as if it were possible to conceive of a terminal date to the conflict. Many of our pronouncements have implied that an over-all diplomatic settlement is at least conceivable, and much of our military thought centers around the possibility of victory in an all-out war which would put an end to international tensions once and for all.

Both contingencies are explicitly rejected by Communist doctrine. As long as the class struggle continues—until, that is, the Communist system has triumphed all over the world —conflict between the Soviet and non-Soviet world is considered to be inevitable, although its forms may vary with the tactical requirements of the situation. Nor would Soviet doctrine counsel risking everything in an all-out showdown unless the disproportion of power in their favor became overwhelmingly clear. Thus both the free world's quest for legitimacy and its search for absolute answers increase its vulnerability to the Soviet strategy of ambiguity: the former by taking at face value every tactical move by the Soviets; the latter by producing an excessive concern with the least likely danger.

Effective action against the Soviet threat, therefore, must

presuppose that the contest with the Soviet bloc is likely to be protracted, a fact from which we cannot escape, because the Soviet leaders insist on it. Both in our diplomacy and in our military policy we must be able to gear firmness to patience and not be misled by Soviet maneuvers or by our preference for absolute solutions. The United States must study the psychology of its opponents as carefully as they have studied ours. We must learn that there are no purely political solutions any more than purely military solutions and that, in the relation among states, will may play as great a role as power. We must know that revolutionary powers have never been brought to a halt until their opponents stopped pretending that the revolutionaries were really misunderstood legitimists.

Everything depends, therefore, on our ability to graduate our actions, both in our diplomacy and in our military policy. To the extent that we succeed in seeing policy as a unity in which political, psychological, economic, and military pressures merge, we may actually be able to use Soviet theory to our advantage. The Soviet and Chinese regimes are not likely to risk everything to prevent changes adverse to them so long as their national survival is not directly affected. They are even less likely to stake everything to achieve a positive gain. To be sure, the Soviet leaders have sought skillfully to paralyze opposition by creating the impression that a withdrawal from any territory once occupied by Soviet troops or in which Soviet influence has been growing, as in Egypt, is inconceivable, and that any attempt to bring it about may lead to all-out war. But both history and Soviet theory would seem to indicate that this is a form of atomic blackmail. Mao has repeatedly labeled the refusal to yield, when confronted with superior force, as "desperadoism." One need only study the abject effort of the Politburo to achieve an accommodation with the Nazis in the weeks before the German invasion of Russia to realize that, when confronted with an unfavorable relation of forces, the Communist regimes would not hesitate to apply Lenin's dictum: one step backward, two steps forward. We too often forget that, when faced with determined United States opposition, the Kremlin in 1946 withdrew its troops from Iran.

Most of the discussion in this chapter has been in terms of a Soviet doctrine developed before the first explosion of the atomic bomb. Has nuclear power brought about a change in Soviet theory?

CHAPTER FOUR

The Soviet Union
and the Atom

I

For all its confidence in its skill in manipulating social forces, for all its pride in its ability to predict the course of history, the end of World War II confronted the Soviet leadership with a fearful challenge. At the precise moment when Soviet armies stood in the center of a war-wrecked Europe, and Lenin's prophecies of the doom of capitalism seemed on the verge of being fulfilled, a new weapon appeared far transcending in power anything previously known. Was the dialectic of history so fragile that it could be upset by a new technological discovery? Was this to be the result of twenty years of brutal repression and deprivation and of four years of cataclysmic war that at its end the capitalist enemy should emerge with a weapon which could imperil the Soviet state as never before?

It must have been disheartening for the men in the Kremlin to enter a postwar world where the ascendancy of the U.S.S.R. as a world power, seemingly confirmed by the outcome of the conflict, was again put into question. The purely ideological problems were no less formidable. If capitalism could extricate itself from its difficulties by a new technological discovery, the structure of the economy was not as crucial as Soviet doctrine postulated; it was less fundamental in fact than the state of technology. If the predictive power of Leninism failed at so vital a point, the whole dogma based on superior prescience was put into question.

But the Soviet leadership reacted with the iron discipline it had learned during its history of militancy. It refused to recognize an inconsistency between Leninist theory and reality, for to do so would have been to give up its reason for existence. Rather it took the position that the new developments confirmed accepted doctrine and that the decay of capitalism, far from being arrested by the more powerful weapons at its disposal, would be accelerated by it.

Nor was this display of discipline merely an exercise in abstract theory. On the contrary, the Soviet leaders put their doctrinal training to good use in the eminently practical task of surviving as a revolutionary power. They had learned all their lives that appearances were deceiving and that a political situation reflected a combination of political, economic, psychological, and military factors. They had been taught that the emphasis on any one of these factors to the exclusion of the others was self-defeating. They were convinced that superiority in one category of power could be compensated by a manipulation of the others. Thus while Soviet leadership could not do anything immediate about our possession of the atomic bomb, it might undermine the will to use it by a world-wide campaign against the horrors of nuclear warfare. And domestically Soviet leadership was even more sure of itself. Since the Kremlin controlled all the media of communication, it could establish the framework of thinking about nuclear matters within the Soviet Union both by withholding information and by interpreting it to fit the tactical requirements of the Soviet line.

The result was a tour de force, masterful in its comprehension of psychological factors, brutal in its consistency, and ruthless in its sense of direction. With a cold-blooded effrontery, as if no other version of reality than its own were even conceivable, through all the media and organizations at its disposal, through diplomacy and propaganda, the Kremlin advanced three related themes. One was that the decisiveness of nuclear weapons was overrated; this was designed to demonstrate that the U.S.S.R. remained predominant in the essential categories of power. A second maintained that, although not decisive, nuclear weapons were inherently in a special category of horror from other weapons and should, therefore, be banned. By means of diplomatic notes, peace congresses, resolutions, and propaganda, this campaign sought not only to paralyze our will to use our most potent weapon but to create a climate of opinion that would make use of the atomic bomb as politically disadvantageous as possible. A third and subordinate theme was that the only legitimate use of the atom was its peaceful application, in which field the U.S.S.R. was prepared to take the lead. This position reinforced the previous one; it gave impetus to Soviet peace offensives and strengthened its appeal to the uncommitted powers.

All three themes recur in Soviet doctrine since 1945, with changes of emphasis but little alteration in content. It is possible to distinguish two phases, however, in Soviet efforts to come to grips with the atom: the period of our atomic monopoly, and the period after the Kremlin had acquired a nuclear arsenal of its own. During the former period the Soviet leaders relied largely on their "ban-the-bomb" propaganda which insisted that atomic bombs were as evil and horrible as they were ineffectual. With the growth of the Soviet nuclear arsenal, and especially since the death of Stalin, threats of thermonuclear retaliation have alternated with proposals to eliminate nuclear weapons. The Soviet leaders no longer rely entirely on our inhibitions; they have sought also to play on our fears. But in doing so, nuclear power became better understood by the Soviet public, and this raised a host of problems with respect to doctrinal purity, militancy, and the perils of the nuclear age, which had been evaded in 1945.

II

The Soviet effort to minimize nuclear weapons was so consistent and was begun so early that it must have been planned long before the explosion of the first atomic bomb over Hiroshima. When President Truman informed Stalin, during the Potsdam Conference, that the United States possessed a new weapon of fearful power, he was startled by Stalin's nonchalance in acknowledging it: "The Russian Premier," wrote Truman, "showed no special interest. All he said was that he was glad to hear it and that he hoped we would make 'good use of it against the Japanese.' "[1] Against the background of the later disclosures of Soviet espionage, there can be no doubt that Stalin was well aware of the impact of what he was being told. It is almost certain, in fact, that Stalin learned of the possibility of nuclear explosions well before Truman, who was not informed of the existence of our Atomic Energy Program until he became President in April 1945. Stalin's behavior at Potsdam reflected a decision to minimize the importance of nuclear weapons in order to demonstrate the Kremlin's independence and the impossibility of intimidating it.

With the official Soviet attitude thus determined, the whole apparatus of Soviet propaganda and diplomacy went into action in support. The bombing of Hiroshima was mentioned in the Soviet press only briefly and with no further discussion or elaboration. The end of the Far Eastern war was attributed entirely to the intervention of Soviet armies. The bombing of Nagasaki was not reported when it occurred. Although the Soviet regime was soon to launch a world-wide campaign to "ban" the use of atomic bombs, the Soviet public had to wait for nearly ten years to find out precisely what the atomic bomb was.

Moreover, whatever the uncertainties and qualms of the power which did possess the atomic bomb, Soviet propaganda knew no such hesitations. As early as September 1, 1945, less than a month after the bombing of Hiroshima and Nagasaki, the Soviet *New Times* was ready with an official interpretation of the significance of nuclear weapons. Because the semblance of wartime harmony was still being maintained, the form chosen was one of those indirect methods so dear to the heart of Soviet strategists: an analysis of foreign press comments regarding the atomic bomb. After a brief summary of descriptions of the atomic bomb,

[1] Harry S. Truman, *Memoirs*, v. 1, *Year of Decisions* (New York: Doubleday, 1955), p. 416.

the article turned to an examination of its implications. The atomic bomb, argued the *New Times,* had not been the decisive weapon in the war against Japan. Such a proposition was advanced only by bankrupt Japanese militarists to obscure their ignominious defeat at the hands of the U.S.S.R., and by "semi-Fascist" commentators in the Western world: "The experience of the Second World War and the unsurpassed victories of the Red Army have clearly shown that success in war is not achieved by the one-sided development of one or the other weapon, but by the perfection of all arms and their skillful coordination."[2] In short, nothing of particular significance had happened at Hiroshima.

If the atomic bomb had not proved decisive against Japan, it could obviously not be used to intimidate the U.S.S.R. "Under the influence of the announcement of the atomic bomb, the reactionary circles [in the United States] . . . are inclined to stand forth unashamed in their imperialist nakedness. They demand that the United States should establish its domination over the world with the atomic bomb. Apparently the lessons of history mean nothing to those errant imperialists. They do not stop to ponder over the debacle of Hitler's plans of world dominion which, after all, were also based on the expectation of exploiting temporary advantages in the production of armaments."[3] But while nuclear weapons did not confer a basic advantage, their indiscriminate destructiveness made it all the more necessary for all "progressive" forces to unite against their use.[4]

In this manner the strains of subsequent Soviet nuclear policy emerged barely three weeks after the explosion of the first atomic bomb over Hiroshima: the relative unimportance of nuclear weapons, their special horror, and the Soviet Union as the defender of the peace appealing to all groups repelled by the prospect of atomic warfare. Stalin

[2] M. Rubinstein, "The Foreign Press on the Atomic Bomb," *New Times* (published in English by the newspaper *Trud,* Moscow), no. 7(17) (September 1, 1945), p. 14.

[3] Same, p. 15.

[4] Same, p. 17.

was merely ratifying official dogma when, a year after the first atomic explosion, he took his first public stand on nuclear matters: "I do not consider the atomic bomb as such a serious force as several political groups incline to think it. Atomic bombs are intended to frighten people with weak nerves, but they cannot decide the outcome of a war since for this atomic bombs are completely insufficient."[5]

This theme, once sanctified by Stalin, was henceforth repeated with tiresome regularity in Soviet literature and by the Communist parties all over the world. Under the heading "atomic bomb" the official Soviet encyclopedia confined itself simply to repeating Stalin's dictum quoted above.[6] And a Chinese Communist author, in assessing the significance of the new technology, did little more than paraphrase Stalin: "The atom bomb is one of the modern weapons which possess the greatest destructive power. . . . Except for causing effects of destruction bigger than those produced by ordinary bombs, however, such a weapon can produce no other effects. The final decisive force to destroy the enemy's fighting power is still not the atom bomb but strong and vast ground troops. . . . To countries with a fighting will and with vast territories such as the Soviet Union and China, the atom bomb's usefulness is even smaller."[7]

The Soviet leadership thus maintained rigidly the "pure" doctrine that no mechanical invention could possibly disturb the foreordained course of history. Accordingly the atomic bomb was increasingly treated as a Western propaganda trick designed as a means of blackmailing the "Socialist camp" into submission. The few Soviet discussions regarding nuclear matters which reached the public were entirely on the psychological level. Atomic warfare was not analyzed as a strategic problem. Instead, theories which

[5] *Pravda*, September 25, 1946.

[6] *Bol'shaia Sovetskaia Entsiklopediia* (2d. ed.; 1950), v. 3, p. 433.

[7] Teng Ch'ao, "Piercing through the Myth of Atomic War," *Mei-ti Chun-shih-shang ti Jo-tien* (The Military Weakness of American Imperialism) (Peiping: Shih-chieh Chih-shih, 1950), pp. 24–31.

had suggested that atomic warfare might change the course of history were derided. A Communist philosopher summed up the whole American discussion of nuclear matters as an effort to "frighten both imaginary opponents and one's own fellow citizens."[8] American writers were accused of exaggerating the effectiveness of the bomb, Lewis Mumford coming in for special ridicule for suggesting that after an atomic holocaust man would return to primitive conditions of life. The atomic bomb could have added little to the destruction of Stalingrad; yet still Russia had won the war.[9] And *Pravda* contributed its part to the campaign to deprecate the atom bomb by quoting unidentified reports from Tokyo that in Hiroshima only 8,481 individuals had been affected by the atomic explosion and only 7,967 in Nagasaki.[10]

The studied aloofness with respect to nuclear technology extended to the scientific achievement which had developed nuclear weapons. A book on atomic energy, published in 1952, disposed of the whole question of the military use of atomic energy in three pages out of four hundred, citing Stalin's dictum that nuclear weapons could not be decisive.[11] The study stressed the alleged contribution of Russian theorists like Dmitri I. Mendeleev to atomic research; it minimized the role of Western theorists and said practically nothing about the scientists who actually produced the bomb. Indeed, Lenin's alleged contribution to atomic science was given more prominence than that of any Western scientist. Lenin had taken note of the new theories of the "destructibility of the atom, its inexhaustibility, the changeability of all forms of matter and of its movement [which were, he continued] the foundation of dialectical

[8] O. V. Trakhtenberg, " 'Sotsiologiia' Atomnoi Bomby" (The "Sociology" of the Atom Bomb), *Voprosy Filosofii,* no. 3 (1948), p. 294.

[9] Same, pp. 294–5.

[10] *Pravda,* January 21, 1950.

[11] M. I. Korsunsky, *Atomnoe Iadro* (The Atomic Nucleus) (4th ed.; Moscow and Leningrad: Gos. Izd. Tekhniko-teoret. Lit., 1952), pp. 372–4.

materialism."[12] This general line was also followed in the Soviet encyclopedia's discussion of the scientific background of atomic energy.[13]

The effort to minimize nuclear technology was accompanied by a complete blackout on news regarding Western achievements. No mention was made in the Soviet press of the following events: the United States announcement of December 1951 regarding the possibility of peaceful applications of nuclear energy; the test of Britain's first atomic bomb in October 1952; or the explosions of the United States hydrogen bomb in November 1952. It was not until 1954 that the Soviet public was permitted to see a picture of the mushroom cloud which in the West had been a symbol of the nuclear age for nearly a decade. So loath were the Soviet leaders to acknowledge the role of atomic bombs in international politics that in attacking President Truman's statement of November 1950 that, if necessary, the United States might use nuclear weapons in Korea, they did not even mention the atomic bomb but charged him only with creating "new war hysteria."

The nonchalance toward atomic matters was maintained even with respect to Soviet accomplishments in the nuclear field. The Soviet press did not report the first Soviet atomic explosion, and the world had to hear of it through an American announcement. Even then the Soviet reaction was studiedly matter-of-fact. *Pravda* pretended surprise at the apparent excitement in the non-Soviet world about this turn of events, and Andrei Y. Vyshinsky at the United Nations emphasized its peaceful and not its military implications: "We want to harness atomic energy to carry out great tasks of peaceful construction, to blast mountains, change the course of rivers. . . ."[14]

The Soviet show of indifference to its own accomplish-

[12] Same, p. 61, quoted from V. I. Lenin, *Sochineniia*, v. 14 (Moscow: Gospolitizdat, 1947), p. 268.

[13] *Bol'shaia Sovetskaia Entsiklopediia*, cited, p. 417.

[14] A. Y. Vyshinsky, "Speech on Prohibition of Atomic Weapons and International Control of Atomic Energy," *Soviet News* (published by the Soviet Embassy, London), no. 2260 (November 14, 1949), p. 2.

ments in the nuclear field was probably caused in part by the fear that, if flaunted too much, the atomic bomb might cause a preventive attack by the United States before the Soviet retaliatory power was fully developed. It also reflected the predominant part played by doctrine in Soviet affairs. For better or worse, though more by necessity than by choice, the Soviet leadership had staked its survival as a militant revolutionary power on de-emphasizing nuclear weapons, at least through its period of maximum peril while the Soviet nuclear stockpile was small or nonexistent. It would not be deflected from this course even to celebrate its own achievements.

Moreover, the Soviet position had not been simply to deprecate nuclear weapons. Such a course, though useful to maintain morale, did not supply the rationale for the activism which, according to Soviet theory, alone can ensure the success of the revolutionary movement. And Soviet leadership required a doctrine of invincibility both for protection against imagined enemies and, even more importantly, in order to exert pressure on the peripheral powers of Eurasia. It was one thing, however, to assert that the atomic bomb could not be decisive by itself; it was another to maintain that the Soviet armed forces were basically superior to their opponents. But this is precisely what Soviet military doctrine set out to do. Concurrently with its campaign to minimize the implications of nuclear weapons, the Kremlin developed a strategic doctrine designed to demonstrate that it was the Soviet Union, not the United States, which possessed the decisive advantage should war break out. Soviet military doctrine found the key to its superiority in a distinction between what it defined as the "transitory" and the "constantly operating" factors of military science. The non-Soviet world might score advantages in the former category; the U.S.S.R. would nevertheless emerge victorious because of its superiority in the latter category.[15]

The distinction between transitory and permanently operating factors was not merely a dialectical quibble. It

[15] Raymond L. Garthoff, *Soviet Military Doctrine* (Glencoe, Ill.: The Free Press, 1953), p. 34 ff.

served as the basis of postwar Soviet military doctrine. It appeared in all military textbooks. It was taught at the military academies. It was repeated over and over again by all organs of Soviet propaganda. "Victory in war," wrote one Soviet author, "does not depend on 'transitory' factors, on one weapon or sudden invasion, but on certain constantly operating factors: durability of the rear, morale of the army and the people, the just character of the war and the superiority of the social and economic system."[16] In short, military superiority, according to Soviet military doctrine in the immediate postwar period, did not depend on technological supremacy.

It is remarkable that, at a time when most military thinking in the United States was centered around the notion that a new war would start with a surprise attack, such a course was explicitly rejected by Soviet theory and indeed ridiculed by it. At a period when the prevalent doctrine in the United States was concerned with an all-out war decided ultimately by the attrition of industrial potential, the Soviets never tired of emphasizing the virtue of the indirect approach and of the break-through at the enemy's weakest link. And the break-through could be achieved by psychological as well as military means. The same terminology was employed interchangeably for both political and military warfare.

It is possible, of course, that these arguments were advanced simply to deceive other powers about Soviet weakness. But it is one thing for the Soviet leaders to adopt a certain propaganda line in their relations with the rest of the world; it is quite another for them consciously to mislead their entire people, and above all their military services, on a matter of life and death. It can hardly be maintained that the Soviet leaders would teach their officer corps a doctrine they knew to be erroneous, write field regulations based on principles known to be fallacious, and train

[16] M. Gusev, *Bor'ba Sovetskogo Soiuza za sokrashchenie vooruzhenii i zapreshchenie atomnogo oruzhiia* (The struggle of the Soviet Union for the reduction of arms and the prohibition of atomic weapons) (Moscow: Gospolitizdat, 1951), p. 23.

and equip their military services for a war they knew to be suicidal simply to mislead the outside world. On the contrary, the consistency of Soviet behavior would indicate that on questions of doctrine the Kremlin generally does mean what it says.

III

The Soviet Union possessed another advantage in the immediate postwar period: the growing conviction of the non-Soviet world, assiduously fostered by Soviet propaganda, that a nuclear war would represent an unparalleled catastrophe. Thus the Kremlin was in the fortunate position that every increase in the power of its opponents caused a proportionate increase in the inhibitions against using it. The Soviet leadership set about systematically to exploit this. Domestically, the Kremlin attempted to maintain its militancy by minimizing the power of nuclear weapons. Internationally, it strove to increase hesitation by emphasizing the horror of the new technology.

In pursuance of this tactic, the Kremlin launched a world-wide campaign in favor of outlawing the atomic bomb but resisted all efforts to negotiate a system of international inspection. A United Nations Disarmament Commission, the majority of which was composed of non-Soviet states, was in Soviet eyes an inherently hostile organ. There was no point in making any sacrifices to an illusory good will, particularly as the first explosion of a Soviet atomic bomb was approaching and as an international inspection system would operate to perpetuate the position of the United States as the leading atomic power. Finally, there was not much symbolic value in technically complex negotiations about disarmament. It was much simpler and infinitely more effective to come out flatly for a program of "banning the bomb." This would serve the dual advantage of demonstrating Soviet independence of action and focusing attention on the horror of the weapon around which America's strategy was built.

Soviet persistence was not without effect. In every issue

under dispute, from the Berlin blockade to Korea, we made clear at the outset that we would not use our most powerful weapon, because we had become convinced, probably correctly, that world opinion would not condone its use, short of an extremity which Soviet strategy tried its best to avoid.

The principal tool to obtain world-wide support for the Soviet campaign to outlaw nuclear weapons has been the so-called "World Peace Movement." Starting with the Stockholm Peace Appeal in 1950, for which, according to Communist sources, more than 500 million signatures were obtained throughout the world,[17] the Peace Movement has been conducting a well-organized campaign to stimulate mass protests and mass action against the use of nuclear weapons. Its permanent organ is the World Peace Council, headed by the French atomic scientist, Frederic Joliot-Curie, a long-time Communist sympathizer. The World Council and the various national peace councils which exist in many countries on both sides of the Iron Curtain have been disseminating a steady stream of arguments about the horror of nuclear warfare and the necessity of outlawing it. Besides dozens of pamphlets they are publishing periodicals in twenty-five countries and in thirteen different languages.

It is tempting to dismiss the World Peace Movement and the strategy it represents as mere propaganda; it is also highly dangerous. The constant repetition of slogans and literature was directed at the psychological weak spots of the non-Soviet world. The West feels ambivalent about the role of force in international relations; a campaign against the horrors of nuclear warfare could only strengthen these inhibitions. The resentment against their colonial past causes many of the newly independent states to be almost desperately ready to believe the best of the Soviet Union and the worst of the West; an appeal which asked of them nothing more than to agree to the importance of peace and the horror of nuclear warfare was nearly irresistible. The Peace Movement thus enabled the Soviets to enlist the hopes and fears of many eminent men appalled by the pros-

[17] *New Times*, no. 23 (June 5, 1954), p. 5.

pect of nuclear war—men who were by no means Communist sympathizers. The task of psychological warfare is to hamstring the opponent through his own preconceptions, and this has been precisely the Soviet strategy with respect to nuclear weapons.

The Communist campaign, finely attuned to prevailing fears, almost imperceptibly shifted the primary concern away from Soviet aggression—the real security problem—to the immorality of the use of nuclear weapons, which happened to represent the most effective means for resisting it. Because of its skill in exploiting the inhibitions of the non-Soviet world, the Soviet bloc has discovered two forms of "atomic blackmail": the threat of its growing nuclear arsenal and an appeal to the West's moral inhibitions. In either case the consequence is a lowered will to resist. The purposeful employment of the two forms of "atomic blackmail" is illustrated by the boast of an East German newspaper that the World Peace Movement had restrained the United States from using atomic weapons in Korea while the development of the Soviet hydrogen bomb had tied our hands in Indochina.

While seeking to paralyze its opponents' will to resist through conjuring up the horrors of atomic war, the Kremlin did not propose to inhibit itself by such prospects. Too great an emphasis at home on the terrible consequences of nuclear war might give rise to the notion of a stalemate, as has indeed happened in the non-Soviet world. But a stalemate is as abhorrent to the dialectic as the admission that capitalism might save itself by means of a new technology. A stalemate implies that neither side can use force, and if acknowledged by the Kremlin, this would have come close to giving up the doctrinal basis of militant communism.

Starting in 1949, therefore, a refinement was added to the doctrine of inevitable and protracted conflict between opposing social systems. The next war, Moscow now claimed, would produce not the destruction of civilization as such, but the destruction of capitalism. This concept was first elaborated by Georgi Malenkov on the occasion of the thirty-second anniversary of the Communist revolution

(November 7, 1949); it was repeated in articles in the official party organ *Bolshevik* by Vyacheslav Molotov and Anastasy Mikoyan in subsequent months. Although it has been the subject of debate in the post-Stalin era, the idea that "only the imperialists will perish in an atomic war, but not civilization" has been explicitly reaffirmed and remains the official thesis today. Time and again the Kremlin has shown its confidence that it can afford to run more and greater risks than its opponents because it is less vulnerable; or, what amounts to the same thing, that its will to victory is greater than that of its declared victims.

IV

The Kremlin had brought off a tour de force. The Soviet Union had retained its militancy despite the United States atomic monopoly; indeed, it had transformed its relative weakness into an asset and solidified a position in the center of Europe denied the Tsars in centuries of striving. By its constant insistence that nuclear weapons were not decisive it had maintained flexibility of action and, perhaps more importantly, Soviet armed might had come to exert an increasingly powerful pressure on the consciousness of all the countries of Eurasia, even of those who most eagerly protested their belief in Soviet peaceful intentions—and perhaps particularly those. By its world-wide campaign about the horrors of atomic warfare the Kremlin had undermined the willingness to resist in many areas of the non-Soviet world and made very difficult the employment of the chief weapon in the Western arsenal.

All this had been accomplished, moreover, without losing sight of essential objectives. However the Soviet regime might minimize the importance of nuclear weapons for purposes of home consumption, all energies of the Soviet state were thrown behind a "crash program" to develop nuclear weapons and a strategic air force. In less than five years the United States atomic monopoly was broken, and the Soviet nuclear arsenal was growing hand in hand with the means to deliver it. The "lead-times" to accomplish this—

the time between conception and operational models—were in every case shorter than those of the United States. During the period of its greatest relative weakness, when it had infinitely more to lose from a major war than its opponents, the Soviet bloc, through its iron-nerved discipline, had expanded to the fringes of Eurasia. It thereby demonstrated that in the relation among states, strength of will may be more important than power.

For all its single-minded persistence, Soviet policy was making a virtue of necessity. As long as the U.S.S.R. did not possess a nuclear stockpile of its own it could find safety only by minimizing its importance or by conciliating powers which Soviet doctrine defined as inherently hostile. The course which was in fact adopted, while it required strong nerves, represented the sole option permitted by Communist orthodoxy. To take any other position would have been to give up the claim to invincibility on which depended so much of the domestic morale and the international prestige of the U.S.S.R. The doctrine of the "constantly operating factors" was the only means to retain militancy in the face of the United States atomic monopoly. And militancy, as Khrushchev emphasized in his speech to the Twentieth Party Congress in 1956, is what distinguishes communism from "opportunistic" socialism.

As long as nuclear weapons were difficult to manufacture and relatively scarce there was a measure of merit in the Soviet insistence on the superiority of the "constantly operating" factors. As the Soviet nuclear stockpile grew, however, and the hydrogen bomb was about to be added to the nuclear arsenal, it became necessary to integrate the new technology more positively into Soviet doctrine. Stalin's 1946 statement had seen the Soviet Union through its period of greatest peril without the admission of weakness which would have prevented it from filling the tempting vacuum opened by World War II. But in the approaching era of nuclear plenty atomic weapons could no longer be dismissed so cavalierly. Henceforth they would have to be integrated into Soviet theory as they were already being integrated into the Soviet armed forces. In October 1951, a few days after the Soviet Union had set off its second atomic explosion, Stalin made his first public pronouncement on nuclear matters since 1946.

Despite its characteristic obtuseness, Stalin's statement indicated a subtle shift of emphasis in familiar Soviet doctrine. The horror of atomic warfare was reiterated because the concept remained a useful instrument to paralyze resistance, but no more was said about nuclear weapons not being decisive. Stalin still advocated the outlawing of nuclear weapons, but the atomic bomb had ceased to be a "phantom" designed to "intimidate" and to "blackmail." It was so real, in fact, that the Soviets had felt "compelled . . . to have the atomic weapon in order to be fully armed to meet the aggressor."[18] Thus atomic weapons were officially declared a vital part of the equipment of a fully armed nation. For the first time Soviet military doctrine was free to discuss the role of nuclear weapons in strategy.

V

The growing Soviet self-confidence with respect to nuclear weapons began to emerge shortly after Stalin's death, coinciding with the first explosion of a Soviet thermonuclear bomb. In characteristic fashion the new emphasis on Soviet nuclear might was used to usher in the period of peaceful coexistence already foreshadowed by Stalin and made doubly necessary by the confusion produced by the death of the dictator. Heretofore, Soviet spokesmen had very rarely boasted of Soviet powers of retaliation, partly because they did not yet exist, partly because such boasts would have contradicted the policy of minimizing the role of nuclear weapons. But now the Soviets felt strong enough to threaten the United States openly and they possessed sufficient nuclear weapons to begin the adaptation of their military doctrine. When Malenkov, then Premier, announced on August 8, 1953, that the Soviets had set off a hydrogen bomb, he returned to the muted threat which

[18] *Pravda*, October 6, 1951.

had already been implicit in Stalin's 1951 interview. He warned that an atomic war against the U.S.S.R. would be folly, because the Soviet Union now possessed similar weapons for retaliation so that any aggressor was certain to suffer a decisive rebuff.

In the next six months the Soviet press showed a growing willingness to treat the problem of nuclear warfare in a more realistic manner. In October 1953, Ilya Ehrenburg admitted in an article that nuclear weapons did represent a danger to the world, although he branded Secretary Dulles's statements to that effect as "ludicrous" and "exaggerated." President Eisenhower's speech of December 10, 1953, appealing for extraordinary measures to save mankind from the holocaust of a hydrogen war was reprinted in part in *Pravda*. The continued Soviet desire to retain freedom of action by not frightening its own people was reflected in the deletion of several particularly ominous passages, such as the statement that the United States possessed hydrogen bombs of millions of tons of TNT equivalent. Nevertheless, the Soviet press and Soviet officials continued their references to the horrors of nuclear war on an ever increasing scale. An article in *Izvestia* (January 19, 1954) admitted that under modern conditions war "means colossal destruction." *Pravda* (January 30, 1954) welcomed the idea of a disarmament conference which would "contribute to the freeing of mankind from the terror of atomic bombing."

A fundamental change seemed in the offing, when Premier Malenkov on March 12, 1954, apparently overthrew the concept which he had himself announced five years previously that nuclear war would mean the end only of capitalist, not of Soviet civilization. "The Soviet Government," he said suddenly, ". . . is resolutely opposed to the policy of cold war, for this is a policy of preparation for fresh world carnage, which, with modern methods of warfare, *means the ruin of world civilization.*"[19] On March 27,

---

[19] "Speech by Comrade G. M. Malenkov," *Pravda* and *Izvestia*, March 13, 1954; cited from *Current Digest of the Soviet Press*, v. 6 (April 28, 1954), p. 8. [Emphasis added.]

1954, this theme was repeated by a Moscow radio commentator, who said that hydrogen bombs "would threaten the very existence of civilization."[20] The World Peace Council fell into line with a warning that the use of atomic weapons would result in the annihilation of man. Did this mean, then, that the power of the hydrogen bomb had shocked the Soviet leadership into giving up its militancy? Had the enormity of modern weapons forced it to accept the fact that war was now inconceivable? Was there now a balance between the inhibitions of the Soviet and of the non-Soviet world?

Malenkov's statement that a nuclear war would destroy civilization, that, in short, the Soviet Union was as vulnerable as its opponents, seemed to shock the Communist party into a renewed awareness of its orthodoxy. It had not prided itself on its "activism" for over a generation to give it up at the moment of its greatest technological achievement. It had not heaped scorn on the dangers of "passivity" for an equally long period to fall into it now by means of its own doctrine. On April 26, 1954, less than two months after propounding it, in a speech to the Supreme Soviet, Malenkov was obliged to repudiate his own statement and to assert that an atomic war would lead to the breakdown only of the capitalist system.[21] *Pravda* announced the Soviet position on nuclear weapons on February 26, 1955, with finality: "Only political adventurers can think that they will succeed with the help of atomic weapons in canceling the progressive development of mankind. Weapons have never altered or canceled the laws of social development; they have never created or abolished conditions which could alter social structures of entire countries."[22]

The Party Militant had triumphed. Henceforth Communist leaders all over the world repeated with pedantic regularity the doctrine that the U.S.S.R. possessed superior freedom of action because it was less vulnerable than the capitalist world. Molotov, Mikoyan, Shepilov, Zhukov and

---

[20] Moscow radio broadcast, March 27, 1954.
[21] *New Times*, no. 18 (May 1, 1954), Supplement, p. 9.
[22] *Pravda*, February 26, 1955.

Khrushchev defended the proposition at the Twentieth Party Congress in 1956. In France, Maurice Thorez warned his Communists not to be intimidated by American "atomic propaganda" because historical forces were on their side. In satellite East Germany, the Prime Minister, Otto Grotewohl, made the tactical advantages of the Soviet position explicit. "For us fighters against remilitarization it is *better and more correct* to draw from this fact [atomic destruction] the conclusion that a third world war will destroy not us, but the imperialist forces."[23]

Doctrinal purity had been maintained; the Soviet leadership had retained its freedom of action and defined its risks as smaller than those of its opponents. There is a tendency in the West to overlook Soviet doctrinal disputes, and their abstractness does not encourage closer examination. Yet they are the most profitable indication of Soviet intentions, far more rewarding than Soviet actions which are often deliberately designed to mislead or to lull. Since the Soviet leadership derives its claim to superiority from its theoretical insight, a doctrinal dispute in the U.S.S.R. has not only a philosophical, but an eminently practical significance. Throughout the history of Soviet communism, almost every dispute over doctrine has reflected a disagreement on policy, and almost every change of doctrine has sooner or later been translated into action.

And so it has been with the Soviet doctrine on nuclear weapons. Whether or not it was a conscious attempt to bring strategy into relationship with its willingness to take risks—and Grotewohl's statement would seem to indicate that it was—it has so worked out in practice. In every crisis, the non-Soviet world protests the horror of nuclear war and thereby reduces the strength of its negotiating position. By contrast, the Soviets do not seem so inhibited and feel free to threaten with rocket attacks on Britain and France or with dire consequences for countries accepting United States atomic support units.

[23] Speech to the Congress of Youth Against Remilitarization, *Neues Deutschland* (East Berlin), March 22, 1955. [Emphasis added.]

In fact, there seems to have grown up a tacit recognition of greater Soviet daring. When the Soviet Union was confronting difficulties in the satellite orbit, the West hastened to protest that it would neither use force against Soviet repressive efforts nor seek to enter into an alliance with any "liberated" satellite. These measures were justified with the argument that pressure by the West might cause a "desperate" Soviet Union to unleash nuclear war. But when the West confronted difficulties in the Middle East, the U.S.S.R. did not feel compelled to give similar assurances. On the contrary, it left no doubt that it was prepared to move into any vacuum; it spoke of "volunteers" and warned of rocket attacks. Obviously the Soviet leaders were less concerned that the West, in desperation, might unleash a nuclear war of its own. Thus Soviet leadership has been able to blackmail the West both with its strength and its weakness. We recoil before Soviet power but we also fear to exploit Soviet difficulties.

VI

No systematic attempt to integrate nuclear weapons into Soviet military doctrine was made until 1954. As the Soviet nuclear arsenal grew, however, it became important to find a rationale for its use. In the process of developing such a theory, Soviet strategic thought began to traverse the three seemingly inevitable stages which have characterized military thought in all countries seeking to come to grips with the strategic implications of nuclear weapons: (1) an initial period of learning the essential characteristics of the new weapons, which is accompanied by protestations of the still dominant traditionalists that nuclear weapons cannot alter the basic principles of strategy and tactics; (2) as the power of modern weapons becomes better understood, this is usually followed by a complete reversal: an increasing reliance on the most absolute applications of the new technology and on an almost exclusive concern with offensive retaliatory power; (3) finally, as it is realized that all-out war involves risks out of proportion to most of the issues

likely to be in dispute, an attempt is made to find intermediate applications for the new technology and to bring
power into harmony with the objectives for which to contend.

Once the strategic implications of nuclear technology became a fit subject for discussion in Soviet military journals,
the reaction of the Soviet military, as distinguished from the
political, leadership was not basically different from that of
their colleagues in the West, although it occurred later in
accordance with the time lag in the development of nuclear
technology. The big change, however, occurred in the period 1954–1957. From minimizing the role of nuclear
weapons it came to consider them an essential, if not the
primary, element of strategy. From deprecating the role of
surprise it elevated it almost to a "constantly operating factor." And it grew to accept strategic bombing and the possibility of a devastating, short war—all notions that had
heretofore been derided or rejected.

Soviet military doctrine does not seem as yet to have
reached the third stage of the evolution of strategic thought
with respect to nuclear weapons: that of finding subtler
uses for the new technology than all-out war. Nuclear
weapons have been integrated into Soviet strategic thought;
but after the initial period of denying that nuclear weapons
had brought about a fundamental change in strategy or
tactics, most Soviet discussions have concerned themselves
with the problems of all-out war. There has been practically no published discussion of limited nuclear war. This
may be due to the fact that the first priority of Soviet
weapons development has to be the acquisition of a strategic
arsenal and that fissionable material is not yet plentiful
enough to permit a large-scale production of "small" atomic
weapons. Whatever the reason, if the published discussion
reflects the actual state of Soviet military thinking—and on
the basis of the eminence of some of the authors it probably
does—this lag in Soviet doctrine may reveal a vulnerability
and a danger: a vulnerability because it may indicate Soviet
difficulties in mastering the tactics of limited nuclear war
and a danger because it may induce the Soviets to treat the

explosion of any nuclear weapon as the prelude to all-out war. Whether this Soviet vulnerability is exploited, whether this danger is intelligently countered depends importantly on our own strategic doctrine: on our ability to break away from our own preconceptions and on our readiness to face the prospects and opportunities of limited war.

Before turning to these matters, however, we must examine the probable nature of all-out war in a thermonuclear age. We shall examine it not so much in terms of its horrors, which are fairly well understood today, but in terms of its effectiveness as a deterrent and as an instrument of policy.

CHAPTER FIVE

The Esoteric Strategy—
Principles of
All-Out War

I

It is no longer necessary to labor the point that an all-out war with modern weapons will have consequences far transcending anything previously experienced. We know that blast and heat effects of thermonuclear and nuclear explosions can paralyze the intimate interrelationships of modern urban life. The immediate fall-out can reduce large areas to subsistence levels. The genetic effects of strontium 90 could threaten the whole human race.

In such a situation it is futile to speak of "purely" military considerations. From a purely military point of view nothing is more efficient for cratering airfields, destroying port facilities, or eliminating transportation centers than a megaton weapon. But the crucial problem of strategy, as we have seen, is to establish a reasonable relationship between power and the willingness to use it, between the physical and the psychological components of national policy. Faced with the knowledge of the consequences of a thermonuclear war, policy makers will be reluctant to engage in a strategy which may well bring social disintegration.

The new technology thus increases our dangers at the precise moment when our commitments have never been greater. For the first time in our history we are vulnerable to a direct hostile attack. No remaining margin of industrial and technological superiority can remove the consciousness of our increasing vulnerability from the minds of policy makers who have to make the decision of peace or war. But perhaps our dangers offer us at the same time a way out of our dilemmas. As long as the consequences of all-out thermonuclear war appear as stark to the other side as to us, we may avert disaster, not through a reconciliation of interests but through mutual terror. Is, then, our reliance on retaliatory power to achieve deterrence a valid basis for achieving a durable peace after all?

Stalemates have occurred frequently in the history of warfare. Normally they have been brought about by the emergence of a balance between offense and defense on the battlefield. The distinguishing feature of the current use of the term is that it refers not to a balance on the battlefield, but to a balance of terror. With each side possessing the capability of inflicting catastrophic blows on the other, war is said to be no longer a rational course of action. To be sure, even if a nuclear stalemate does exist, it would not make for stability in the present volatile state of technology, much less for a sense of harmony. The specter of a technological break-through by the other side would always loom large; it would give an apocalyptic quality to all internal relations.

It is important to be precise, however, about the meaning of nuclear stalemate. A great deal will depend on the correctness of our assessment of what the stalemate actually deters or does not deter and of whether the kind of war to which the term stalemate can properly be applied exhausts the strategic options of either side. In one sense, nuclear stalemate can be taken to mean that victory in all-out war has become meaningless. It is to the implications of nuclear technology for all-out war that we must now turn.

The renunciation of total victory is repugnant to our military thought, with its emphasis on breaking the enemy's will to resist and its reliance on the decisive role of industrial potential. Because we have thought of war more in moral than in strategic terms, we have identified victory with the physical impotence of the enemy. But while it is true that a power can impose its will by depriving the opponent of the resources for continued resistance, such a course is very costly and not always necessary. The enemy's decision whether to continue the struggle reflects not only the relation of forces but also the relationship between the cost of continued resistance and the objectives in dispute. Military strength decides the physical contest, but political goals determine the price to be paid and the intensity of the struggle.

Far from being the "normal" form of conflict, all-out war constitutes a special case. It comes about through the abdication of political leadership or when there exists so deep a schism between the contenders that the total destruction of the enemy appears as the only goal worth contending for. Thus war has been based on "purely" military considerations only during relatively brief periods: during the religious wars of the sixteenth and seventeenth centuries, when a religious schism induced both sides to seek to destroy their opponent; during the wars of the French Revolution, when an ideological schism caused the contenders to attempt to impose their notion of justice by force; and during the cycle of wars beginning with World War I, which started with an abdication of political leadership and has since turned into a revolutionary struggle.

In the intervals between these explosions of maximum violence, war was considered an extension of policy. Between the Congress of Vienna in 1815 and the outbreak of World War I, wars were limited by the political objectives of the opponents.[1] Because they were fought for specific goals which did not threaten the survival of any of the powers, a reasonable relationship existed between the force employed and the objective to be achieved. But with the outbreak of World War I, war suddenly seemed to become an end in itself. After the first few months of the war none of the protagonists would have been able to name an objec-

[1] The American Civil War was the only exception; it approached the status of a total war precisely because it was a revolutionary struggle.

tive other than the total defeat of the enemy—unless it were
such an objective as the German demand for the annexation of Belgium, which amounted to unconditional surrender. This was all the more remarkable because none of the
political leaders had prepared for anything but a war in the
nineteenth-century style, with rapid movements and quick
decisions, so that the stalemate of the first winter was due
primarily to the exhaustion of munitions supplies.

During World War I a gap appeared between military
and political planning which has not since been bridged.
The military staffs had developed plans for total victory,
because in such plans no political limitations interfere with
the full development of power and all factors are under the
control of the military. But the political leadership proved
incapable of giving these military objectives a political expression in terms of peace aims. It was forgotten that the
rapid decisions of nineteenth-century warfare had been due,
above all, to the willingness to acknowledge defeat. And
defeat was acknowledged with relative ease because its consequences did not threaten the national survival. When the
purpose of war became total victory, however, the result
was a conflict of ever increasing violence which petrified its
hatreds in a peace treaty which considered more the re-
dressing of sacrifices than the stability of the international
order.

The objective of nineteenth-century warfare was to create
a calculus of risks according to which continued resistance
would appear more costly than the peace terms sought to
be imposed. The more moderate the peace terms, the
smaller the required margin of superiority. The war ended
when a sovereign government agreed to the victor's terms
and thereby assumed responsibility for their execution. The
victor's task in these circumstances was to supervise the ful-
fillment of his conditions by a government which in turn retained control over its own population. The goal in total
war, on the other hand, has become, almost invariably, to
overthrow the enemy leadership. This has not only transformed every war into a variety of civil war, it has also increased the margin of superiority required to impose the

victor's will. Success in overthrowing the enemy government in effect forces the victor to assume responsibility for
the civil administration of the defeated. We could afford
to do so at the end of World War II, because neither our
social nor our material structure had been seriously impaired by the war; if anything, they had been strengthened.

At the scale of catastrophe produced by an all-out thermonuclear war, however, it is doubtful whether any society
will retain either the physical or psychological resources to
undertake the administration and rehabilitation of foreign
countries. And, in the absence of physical occupation, victory may prove illusory. It may create a vacuum which can
be exploited by powers whose position relative to the contenders has been improved by the devastation of all-out
war. The decline of Europe started with the exhaustion
produced by the First World War, for in it even the victors
were weakened in relation to the non-European powers.

The destructiveness of modern weapons deprives victory
in an all-out war of its historical meaning. Even the side
which inflicts a greater devastation than its opponent may
not retain sufficient resources to impose its will. And the
same exorbitant destructiveness has altered the significance
of the industrial potential on which we have traditionally
relied for victory. Since World War I our strategic doctrine
has always been built around the proposition that our
forces-in-being at the beginning of a war need only be large
enough to avoid disaster and that we could then crush the
enemy by mobilizing our industrial potential after the outbreak of hostilities. The strategic significance of our industrial potential has presupposed a fortuitous combination of
circumstances, however: our invulnerability to direct attack, the existence of allies to hold a line while we were
mobilizing, and, above all, a certain stage of industrial and
technological development.

If the stockpiles of weapons available at the beginning
of a war suffice to destroy the opponent's industrial potential, it is clear that industrial potential has lost a great deal
of its significance and that the side whose forces-in-being

are superior, whatever its industrial base, will gain a decisive advantage. And when weapons have become extremely powerful, there is an upper limit beyond which increased destructiveness pays diminishing returns. When both sides are capable of inflicting catastrophic losses on each other with their forces-in-being, an increment of destructive power may be strategically insignificant. Even superior quality may be overcome to some extent by the power of modern weapons. A more sophisticated delivery system will be meaningless as long as both sides can reach their targets. Thus an all-out war fought with modern weapons will be decided by the forces-in-being. We can no longer afford to count on a more or less prolonged period of mobilization. The only way we can derive an advantage from our industrial capacity is by utilizing it *before* the outbreak of a war.

An all-out war will be primarily an air war, or at least a war of strategic striking forces, and it will be decided by the forces-in-being. Our problem is complicated by the fact that we have explicitly rejected the use of surprise attack as an instrument of strategy. This is demonstrated not only by repeated statements of policy, but above all by our entire past behavior. If we refrained from utilizing our atomic monopoly at a time when the Soviet capability to retaliate was almost nonexistent, it is against all probability that we would do so now.

But the side which concedes the first blow in all likelihood also concedes the margin required to impose its will. As a result, unless our air defense is capable of reducing the enemy blow below the level of catastrophe—an unlikely situation—the strategic problem of all-out war must be stated for us not in terms of a strategy to achieve victory, but of a strategy to avoid defeat. The purpose of our capability for all-out war will be to deter Soviet aggression against us by developing a retaliatory force of a size which can inflict an unacceptable amount of damage on the enemy, no matter what level of destruction he may accomplish by a surprise attack.

II

A strategy which seeks to deter all-out war must prevent a situation from arising in which the U.S.S.R. can calculate that it possesses a sufficient margin of certainty to make a surprise attack on the United States seem a worth-while risk. To be sure, such a strategy presupposes a certain amount of rationality on the part of an enemy. But any strategy must count on a somewhat rational enemy; nothing can deter an opponent bent on self-destruction.

What is a sufficient degree of certainty, and how can it be achieved? Obviously the mere ability to inflict a greater amount of damage than the enemy will be meaningless if at the end of the war the victor does not retain sufficient resources to impose his will. An aggressor, in trying to decide whether to launch an all-out war, must therefore be able to count on a combination of the following factors: he must be certain that his surprise attack will reduce our forces-in-being to a level at which his defense can contain them, or at least at which they are no longer able to inflict unacceptable damage; he must be confident that our air defense will not reduce his attacking force to a level at which it will no longer be able to inflict the amount of damage he calculates as necessary to impose his will. The degree of certainty, moreover, must be almost foolproof: a slight probability will not be sufficient, for the attacker is staking not his chances of victory, but his national survival.

An all-out attack by the U.S.S.R. could, therefore, be impelled only by a consciousness of overwhelming power, of great United States vulnerability, or by the fear of an imminent United States attack. Can the U.S.S.R. count on the possession of an overwhelming superiority? Many witnesses before the Symington Committee argued as if military superiority depended almost entirely on numbers of airplanes, particularly of long-range bombers. ". . . the only thing I can say," testified General LeMay, "is that from 1958 on, he [the U.S.S.R.] is stronger in long-range air power than we are, and it naturally follows that if he is stronger, he may feel that he should attack."[2]

But this does not follow naturally at all. Superiority cannot be measured merely in numbers of offensive planes or rockets; it depends also on the capability for defense. The best strategic posture for an all-out war depends on the proper "mix" of offensive and defensive capabilities. If so many resources are devoted to defense that the offensive striking force can no longer inflict an unacceptable degree of damage on the aggressor, the enemy may be tempted to attack. If the defense is slighted, too great a demand is put on the powers of resistance of society. The ideal offense-defense relationship is one in which the defense can reduce the enemy attack to acceptable levels while the offense cannot be so contained by the enemy's defense.

The Soviet Union does not have a capability approaching this ideal. The vulnerabilities of the United States to nuclear attack, while extremely serious, are not likely to be so great as to tempt the Soviet leaders to undertake a surprise attack, either because the Soviet striking force is not yet sufficiently strong or because some of our vulnerabilities, as in the field of civil defense, are matched by similar deficiencies in the U.S.S.R. Thus if we behave effectively we have time to make good our shortcomings. We should press more vigorously the dispersal of our Strategic Air Force. We must bring into being a really effective civil defense organization. We must develop new antisubmarine capabilities. And, of course, we must press with special vigor to overcome the present Soviet lead in ballistic missiles. If we carry out these measures, all of which lie in our own control, all-out war should remain an unattractive course for the U.S.S.R.

The essence of the nuclear stalemate is that it keeps the two superpowers from launching an all-out war because each can force the other to pay an exorbitant price for vic-

[2] U. S. Senate, *Study of Airpower,* Hearings before the Subcommittee on the Air Force of the Committee on Armed Services, 84th Cong., 2nd Sess. (Washington: GPO, 1956), p. 213.

tory. Henceforth the only outcome of an all-out war will be that *both* contenders must lose. Under almost any foreseeable circumstances an upper limit of destruction will be reached before attrition of industrial potential can make itself felt, and long before that point is reached the forces-in-being on both sides will have inflicted losses completely disproportionate to any objective which is likely to be the original purpose of the war. Nuclear stalemate should, therefore, not be confused with nuclear parity. It comes about because, after a certain point, superiority in destructive power no longer pays strategic returns.

In such a situation deterrence becomes a complex problem. From now on the decision between peace and war, never an easy one, will be complicated by the consciousness that all-out war entails the risk of national catastrophe. It is likely to be employed, therefore, only as a last resort: an act of desperation to be invoked only if national survival is unambiguously threatened. And what constitutes an unambiguous threat will be interpreted with increasing rigidity as the risks of all-out war become better understood.

The capability for waging all-out war thus operates as a protection against a sudden onslaught on the territorial United States. It also poses risks which may make the decision to initiate war for any lesser objective increasingly difficult. The nuclear stalemate may prevent all-out war. It will not deter other forms of conflict; in fact it may even encourage them. The side which can present its challenges in less than an all-out form thereby gains a psychological advantage. It can shift to its opponent the agonizing choice of whether a challenge which explicitly stops short of all-out war should be dealt with by total retaliation.

All-out war has therefore ceased to be a meaningful instrument of policy. It cannot be used against the minor powers for fear of the reaction of world opinion and also because its intricate strategy is not appropriate to wars of limited objectives. And it cannot be used against a major power for anything except negative ends: to prevent the opponent's victory. Thus an all-out war which starts as an all-out war is the least likely contingency, although it is the only one for which we have an adequate doctrine. To be sure, an all-out war could come about as the result of an irrational decision or of a miscalculation or because a small war may gradually spread. There is no protection against irrational decision except to deprive the other side of the power to injure us—a possibility which ended with the loss of our atomic monopoly.

This is not to say that we can afford to be without a capability for fighting an all-out war or that it will be easy to maintain the conditions which will make such a war seem unattractive to an opponent. It does mean, however, that, if we behave effectively, we can always make the risks of all-out war seem prohibitive to an adversary. Whether we keep up in the technological race, whether our retaliatory force is well dispersed, whether our air defense exacts the maximum attrition and our civil defense is capable of preventing panics—all these decisions are within our exclusive control. But although these conditions are within our control they will not be easy to achieve. At the current rate of technological change the side which has conceded the first blow to its enemy will always live on the verge of catastrophe, for an adverse technological break-through is always possible. Thus the stalemate for all-out war is inherently precarious. It will impel a continuous race between offense and defense and it will require a tremendous effort on our part simply to stay even.

The dilemma which has been pointed up by the Symington hearings has been defined as the choice between Armageddon and defeat without war. The enormity of modern weapons makes the thought of all-out war repugnant, but the refusal to run any risks would amount to handing the Soviet leaders a blank check. We can overcome the paralysis induced by such prospects only if our strategy can pose less absolute alternatives to our policy makers. To be sure, we require at all times a capability for all-out war so great that by no calculation could an aggressor hope to destroy us by a surprise attack. But we must also realize that a capability for all-out thermonuclear war can only avert disaster. It cannot be employed to achieve positive ends.

We thus return to the dilemma which has plagued all our postwar military thinking. Does the nuclear age permit the establishment of a relationship between force and diplomacy? Is it possible to imagine applications of power less catastrophic than all-out thermonuclear war?

CHAPTER SIX

What Price Deterrence?
The Problems of
Limited War

I

Perhaps the basic problem of strategy in the nuclear age is how to establish a relationship between a policy of deterrence and a strategy for fighting a war in case deterrence fails. From the point of view of its impact on the aggressor's actions, maximum deterrence can be equated with the threat of maximum destructiveness. From the point of view of a power's readiness to resist aggression, the optimum strategy is one which is able to achieve its goals at minimum cost. The temptation of strategic doctrine is to seek to combine the advantages of every course of action: to achieve maximum deterrence but also to do so at minimum risk.

Ever since the end of our atomic monopoly, however, this effort has been thwarted by the impossibility of combining maximum destructiveness with limited risk. The greater the horror of our destructive capabilities, the less certain has it become that they will in fact be used. In such circumstances deterrence is brought about not only by a physical but also by a psychological relationship: deterrence is greatest when military strength is coupled with the willingness to employ it. It is achieved when one side's readiness to run risks in relation to the other is high; it is least effective when the willingness to run risks is low, however powerful the military capability. It is, therefore, no longer possible to speak of military superiority in the abstract. What does "being ahead" in the nuclear race mean if each side can already destroy the other's national substance? What is the strategic significance of adding to the destructiveness of the nuclear arsenal when the enormity of present weapons systems already tends to paralyze the will?

Given the power of modern weapons, a nation that relies on all-out war as its chief deterrent imposes a fearful psychological handicap on itself. The most agonizing decision a statesman can face is whether or not to unleash all-out war; all pressures will make for hesitation, short of a direct attack threatening the national existence. And he will be confirmed in his hesitations by the conviction that, so long as his retaliatory force remains intact, no shift in the territorial balance is of decisive significance. Thus both the horror and the power of modern weapons tend to paralyze action: the former because it will make few issues seem worth contending for; the latter because it causes many disputes to seem irrelevant to the over-all strategic equation. The psychological equation, therefore, will almost inevitably operate against the side which can extricate itself from a situation *only* by the threat of all-out war. Who can be certain that, faced with the catastrophe of all-out war, even Europe, long the keystone of our security, will seem worth the price?

As the power of modern weapons grows, the threat of all-out war loses its credibility and therefore its political effectiveness. Our capacity for massive retaliation did not avert the Korean War, the loss of northern Indochina, the Soviet-Egyptian arms deal, or the Suez crisis. Moreover, whatever the credibility of our threat of all-out war, it is clear that all-out thermonuclear war does not represent a strategic option for our allies. Thus a psychological gap is created by the conviction of our allies that they have nothing to gain from massive retaliation and by the belief of the Soviet leaders that they have nothing to fear from our threat of it.

This gap may actually encourage the Soviet leaders to engage in aggression. The destructiveness of nuclear weapons having made it unlikely that any responsible statesman will lightly unleash a general war, one of the gravest dangers of all-out war lies in miscalculation. This is the only war which it is within our power to avoid, assuming we leave no doubt concerning our capabilities and our determination. But even this "avoidable" war may break out if the other side becomes convinced that we cannot interfere locally and that our threats of all-out war are bluff. If that should happen, the Soviet bloc may then decide, as its nuclear arsenal grows, to absorb the peripheral areas of Eurasia by means short of all-out war and to confront us with the choice of yielding or facing the destruction of American cities. And because the Sino-Soviet leaders may well be mistaken in their assessment of our reaction to such a contingency, the reliance on "massive retaliation" may bring about the total war it seeks to prevent.

To be sure, a threat to be effective need not be *absolutely* credible. An aggressor may be reluctant to stake his national existence for a marginal gain even if he should have some doubts about whether a threat will in fact be implemented. It has even been argued that a reduction of our forces around the Soviet periphery would multiply Soviet hesitations because it would make clear to the Soviet leaders beyond doubt that *any* aggression may involve all-out war. And for purposes of deterrence, so the argument goes, what we *may* do will prove as effective as what we *will* do.

Such a strategy, however, would be highly risky and demoralizing. It is a strange doctrine which asserts that we can convey our determination to our opponent by reducing our overseas commitments, that, in effect, our words will be a more effective deterrent than our deeds. It overlooks that all Soviet and Chinese aggressive moves have occurred in areas where our commitment of resources was small or nonexistent: Korea, Indochina, and the Middle East. Above all, a strategy which sought to compensate for its lack of plausibility by posing ever more fearful threats would be demoralizing. It would place control over our survival entirely in the hands of another power; for any Soviet move, however trivial, would force us to respond, if at all, by what may amount to national suicide. It ignores the contemporary revolution which, as events in the Middle East and the satellite orbit have shown, may create its own tensions independent of the plans of the major powers and which may force the United States and the U.S.S.R. to contest certain areas themselves.

The power of modern weapons thus forces our statesmanship to cope with the fact that absolute security is no longer possible. Whatever the validity of identifying deterrence with maximum retaliatory power, we will have to sacrifice a measure of destructiveness to gain the possibility of fighting wars that will not amount to national catastrophe. Policy, it has been said, is the science of the relative. The same is true of strategy, and to understand this fact, so foreign to our national experience, is the task history has set our generation.

II

What strategic doctrine is most likely to enable us to avoid the dilemma of having to make a choice between all-out war and a gradual loss of positions, between Armageddon and defeat without war? Is limited war a conceivable instrument of policy in the nuclear period? Here we must analyze precisely what is meant by limited war.

It is a historical accident reflecting the nature of our foreign involvements that we should have come to consider limited war an aberration from the "pure" case and that we have paid little attention to its strategic opportunities. In a sense this is due too to the manner in which we have legitimized the limited wars which we *have* fought. Every war in which we have been engaged in the Western Hemisphere was a limited war, in the sense that it did not involve a mobilization of all our material resources. But since we generally justified them as expeditions, punitive or otherwise, they rarely entered our national consciousness as part of the phenomenon of limited war.

The debate which has raged since Korea on the subject of limited war has tended to confuse the issues, because it has not sufficiently distinguished between the various forms of limited war. Some wars are inherently limited because of the disparity in power between the protagonists. A war between the United States and Nicaragua would not require more than a fraction of our strength whatever the objectives we set ourselves. Such a war would be all-out in relation to Nicaragua but limited with respect to us. Another variation of this form of limited war occurs when the stronger power is restrained from exerting its full potential by moral, political, or strategic considerations. This was the case in the Korean War, in which the Chinese probably made the maximum military effort of which they were capable while we, for a variety of reasons, limited our commitments. Still another kind of limited war is one between major powers in which the difficulty of supply prevents one side from making a total effort. An example of this is the Russo-Japanese war of 1905, in which the Russian commitment was limited to the forces that could be supplied over a single-track railway. Finally there may occur limited wars between major powers which are kept from spreading by a tacit agreement between the contestants and not by difficulties of technology or of logistics.

If one inquires which of these types of limited war are possible in the present situation, four broad categories can be distinguished. The first includes wars between secondary powers, such as between Israel and Egypt, or between India and Pakistan, whether or not they involve the danger of the major powers joining in. The second type consists of wars involving either the Western powers or the Soviet bloc against countries which are clearly outmatched and under circumstances in which outside intervention is not likely. Examples of this would be Soviet intervention in the satellites, or United States military action in the Western Hemisphere. A third category is conflicts which begin as struggles between a major and a minor power but which may involve the prospect of spreading, as in the case of a Chinese move against South Vietnam or the Anglo-French "police action" against Egypt. Finally there is the problem of limited war which begins explicitly as a war between the major powers. This is obviously the most explosive situation. If a war between major powers can be kept limited, it is clear that the first three situations would also stand a good chance of being kept from expanding.

In the history of warfare limited wars between major powers have been a frequent occurrence. For a long time, however, they remained limited less by strategic choice than by considerations of domestic policy. In the seventeenth century Louis XIV employed almost his entire army for a period of close to twenty-five years. But his military establishment utilized only a small proportion of the national resources because of a domestic structure which prevented him from conscripting his subjects, levying income taxes, or confiscating property. France's armies were therefore limited by the availability of resources, and so were the wars it fought. On the other hand, the wars of Prussia, without exceeding those of France in scope, required a far greater mobilization of the national resources. Because of Prussia's limited resources it was able to survive as a major power only by organizing the entire state for war. But Prussia's exertions gave it only a precarious parity with the other powers; it did not force them to emulate it. Wars remained limited because the major powers were able to mobilize only a small proportion of their national resources for war and because Prussia, the one power which was not so restrained, did not thereby gain a decisive advantage.

Since the French Revolution the domestic restrictions on the capacity of governments to mobilize national resources have increasingly disappeared. And this has occurred simultaneously with an industrial revolution which has made it technically possible to devote a substantial proportion of the national product to war without imposing a degree of privation which would shake the social order. To be sure, there still exist differences in the *willingness* of governments to exact sacrifices. One of the sources of Soviet strength is the readiness to devote a much larger proportion of the national income to military expenditures than the United States. But for purposes of present strategy it is clear that no major power will be forced to adopt a strategy of limited objectives because of insufficient resources. With modern weapons, a limited war becomes an act of policy, not of necessity.

What, under modern conditions, is a limited war? One can think of many models. It may be a war confined to a defined geographic area or a war that does not utilize the entire available weapons system (such as refraining from the use of thermonuclear weapons). It may be a war which utilizes the entire weapons system but limits its employment to specific targets. But none of these military definitions seems adequate by itself. A war may be confined to a geographic area and yet be total in the sense of draining the national substance, as happened to France in World War I. The fact that the most destructive weapons are not employed or that the destructiveness of weapons used is small is no guarantee against excessive suffering. In the Thirty Years' War the power of weapons was negligible compared to modern armaments, and the number of men in each army was small by present-day standards—the Austrian Field Marshal Montecuccoli put at 15,000 the absolute maximum that could be commanded efficiently in one army. Yet it is estimated that the population of Germany was reduced by 30 per cent during its course. A new world war fought with what are now called conventional weapons would also produce appalling casualties, since the destructive power even of these weapons has increased between five- and tenfold since World War II. In short, there exists no way to define a limited war in purely military terms. The end result of relying on purely military considerations is certain to be all-out war: the attempt to render the enemy defenseless.

A limited war, by contrast, is fought for specific political objectives which, by their very existence, tend to establish a relationship between the force employed and the goal to be attained. It reflects an attempt to *affect* the opponent's will, not to crush it, to make the conditions to be imposed seem more attractive than continued resistance, to strive for specific goals and not for complete annihilation.

Limited war presents the military with particular difficulties. An all-out war is relatively simple to plan because its limits are set by military considerations and even by military capacity. The targets for an all-out war are clear, and the force requirements are determined by the need to assemble overwhelming power. The characteristic of a limited war, on the other hand, is the existence of ground rules which define the relationship of military to political objectives. Planning becomes much more conjectural, much more subtle, and much more indeterminate, if only because a war against a major enemy can be kept limited only if both parties so desire, and this desire in itself tends to introduce a factor which is outside the control of planning officers. Since the military can never be certain how many forces the opponent will in fact commit to the struggle and since they feel obliged to guard against every contingency, they will devise plans for limited war which insensibly approach the level of all-out conflict.

From a purely military point of view they are right, for limited war is essentially a political act. Its distinguishing feature is that it has no "purely" military solution. The political leadership must, for this reason, assume the responsibility for defining the framework within which the military are to develop their plans and capabilities. To demand of the military that they set their own limits is to set in motion a vicious circle. The more the military plan on the basis of crushing the enemy even in a limited area, the more the political leadership will recoil before the risks of taking *any* military action. The more limited war is conceived as a "small" all-out war, the more it will produce inhibitions similar to those generated by the concept of massive retaliation. The prerequisite for a policy of limited war is to reintroduce the political element into our concept of warfare and to discard the notion that policy ends when war begins or that war can have goals distinct from those of national policy.

To what extent can the nuclear age leave room for a policy of intermediate objectives? Do any of the factors apply today which in the past made possible a diplomacy of limited objectives and a military policy of limited wars?

In the great periods of European cabinet diplomacy, between the Treaty of Westphalia and the French Revolution and between the Congress of Vienna and the outbreak of the First World War, wars were limited because there existed a political framework which led to a general acceptance of a policy of limited risks. This political framework was based on several factors. There was, to begin with, a deliberate decision that the upheavals of the Thirty Years' War and the Napoleonic wars should not be allowed to recur. While most effective in the period immediately following these conflicts, this decision gave the newly established international order a breathing spell in which the major powers became convinced that none of the outstanding disputes involved their survival. More important was the fact that the international order did not contain a revolutionary power. No state was so dissatisfied with the peace settlement that it sought to gain its ends by overthrowing it, and no power considered that its domestic notion of justice was incompatible with that of the other states. Finally, in an era of stable weapons technology both the strength of the powers and the assessment of it were relatively fixed; the risks of surprise attack and of unforeseen technological developments were relatively small. All this did not make conflicts impossible, but it limited them to disputes within a given framework. Wars occurred but they were fought in the name of the existing framework, and the peace was justified as a better arrangement of a basically unchanged international order.

Today, as we have seen, we lack both stable power relationships and a legitimate political order on whose tenets all major powers are agreed. But these shortcomings may be outweighed by a third factor, the fear of a thermonuclear war. Never have the consequences of all-out war been so obvious, never have the gains seemed so out of relation to the sacrifices.

It is often argued that since limited wars offer no inherent guarantee against their expansion they may gradually merge into all-out war. On purely logical grounds the argument is unassailable. But it assumes that the major protagonists will be looking for an excuse to expand the war, whereas in reality both sides will probably grasp at every excuse, however illogical, to keep a thermonuclear holocaust from occurring. That, in fact, is what happened in the Korean War at a time when the weapons technology was much less horrendous. We refused to retaliate against the Manchurian air bases from which enemy planes were attacking our forces. And the Chinese made no effort to interfere with our aircraft carriers, or with our bases in Japan, or even to launch an attack against our only two big supply ports, Pusan and Inchon.

These limitations were not brought about by logic or agreement but by a mutual reluctance to expand the conflict. It is clear that war cannot be limited unless both sides wish to keep it limited. The argument in favor of the possibility of limited war is that both sides have a common and overwhelming interest in preventing it from spreading. The fear that an all-out thermonuclear war might lead to the disintegration of the social structure offers an opportunity to set limits to both war and diplomacy.

III

The conduct of limited war has two prerequisites: a doctrine and a capability. So long as we consider limited war as an aberration from the "pure" case of all-out war we will not be ready to grasp its opportunities and we will conduct the wars we do fight hesitantly and ambiguously, oscillating between the twin temptations to expand them (that is, to bring them closer to our notion of what war should be like) or to end them at the first enemy overture.

A doctrine for limited war will have to discard any illusions about what can be achieved by means of it. Limited war is not a cheaper substitute for massive retaliation. On the contrary, it must be based on an awareness that with the end of our atomic monopoly it is no longer possible to impose unconditional surrender at an acceptable cost.

The purpose of limited war is to inflict losses or to pose risks for the enemy out of proportion to the objectives under dispute. The more moderate the objective, the less violent the war is likely to be. This does not mean that military operations cannot go beyond the territory or the objective in dispute; indeed, one way of increasing the enemy's willingness to settle is to deprive him of something he can regain only by making peace. But the result of a limited war cannot depend on military considerations alone; it reflects an ability to harmonize political and military objectives. An attempt to reduce the enemy to impotence would surely lead to all-out war.

Nevertheless, a strategic doctrine which renounces the imposition of unconditional surrender should not be confused with the acceptance of a stalemate. The notion that there is no middle ground between unconditional surrender and the *status quo ante* is much too mechanical. To be sure, a restoration of the *status quo ante* is often the simplest solution, but it is not the only possible one. The argument that neither side will accept a defeat, however limited, without utilizing every weapon in its arsenal is contradicted both by psychology and by experience. There would seem to be no sense in seeking to escape a limited defeat through bringing on the cataclysm of an all-out war, particularly if all-out war threatens a calamity far transcending the penalties of losing a limited war. It simply does not follow that because one side stands to lose from a limited war it could gain from an all-out war. On the contrary, both sides face the same dilemma: that the power of modern weapons has made all-out war useless as an instrument of policy, except for acts of desperation.

The West has accepted several contractions of its sphere without resorting to all-out war. If the military position of the Soviet leadership became untenable and it were offered face-saving alternatives short of surrender, it too might accept local withdrawals without resorting to all-out war. Even if limited war offered no more than the possibility of local stalemates, it would represent a strategic improvement, for our current problem is our inability to defend major areas except by the threat of a thermonuclear holocaust which we should make every effort to avoid.

The development of a wide spectrum of capabilities is of crucial importance even if it is assumed that any war between us and the U.S.S.R. or China will inevitably be all-out. For unless the exchange of nuclear and thermonuclear blows leads to the social collapse of both contenders —a distinct possibility—the side which has in being superior forces for other forms of conflict may win in the end. If the Red Army, for example, should succeed in overrunning Eurasia during or after an exchange of all-out blows, we would probably not have sufficient resources remaining to undertake a reconquest. As stockpiles of the largest modern weapons are exhausted or delivery vehicles are used up, an increasing premium is placed on a diversified military capability, not only vis-à-vis the enemy but toward hitherto secondary powers as well. In the absence of forces for other forms of conflict, all-out war may merely pave the way for the dominance of the world by states whose social structure and forces-in-being have remained more or less intact during the struggle-to-death of the superstates.

There exist three reasons, then, for developing a strategy of limited war. First, limited war represents the only means for preventing the Soviet bloc, at an acceptable cost, from overrunning the peripheral areas of Eurasia. Second, a wide range of military capabilities may spell the difference between defeat and victory even in an all-out war. Finally, intermediate applications of our power offer the best chance to bring about strategic changes favorable to our side.

For while a balance can be maintained along existing lines on the Eurasian continent, it will always be tenuous. So long as Soviet armies are poised on the Elbe, Western Europe will be insecure. So long as Chinese might presses upon free Asia, the uncommitted powers are likely to seek safety in neutralism. The United States faces the task not only of stemming Soviet expansion, but also of reducing Soviet pressures and demonstrating the limitations of Soviet power and skills. The resolution of the free world, now assailed by a sense of its impotence, will improve to the extent that it realizes that the Soviet bloc, behind its façade of monolithic power, also shrinks from certain consequences. When we have achieved this capability and this understanding we may be in a position to reduce the Soviet sphere.

A strategy of limited war is more likely to achieve this objective than the threat of a total nuclear war. Either the threat of an all-out war will be considered a bluff or it will turn every dispute into a question of prestige, inhibiting any concessions. Actions short of total war, on the other hand, may help restore fluidity to the diplomatic situation, particularly if we analyze precisely what is meant by the concept of reducing the Soviet sphere. The Sino-Soviet bloc can be turned back short of general war in one of two ways: by a voluntary withdrawal or by an internal split. The former is unlikely and depends on many factors beyond our control, but the latter deserves careful study.

While it is impossible to predict the precise circumstances of a possible split within the Soviet orbit, its general framework can be discerned. The U.S.S.R. may be forced to loosen its hold on its European satellites if it finds that the effort to hold them in line absorbs ever more of its strength. And relations between China and the Soviet Union may become cooler if the alliance forces either partner to shoulder risks for objectives which are of no benefit to it. Tito's break with Moscow was caused at least in part by his disenchantment over the Soviet Union's lukewarm support on the Trieste issue, and that in turn was due to the unwillingness of the Kremlin to risk an all-out war for the sake of a peripheral objective. Similarly, it is not clear how much China would risk to rescue the U.S.S.R. from embarrassments in Europe or in the Middle East, or to what lengths the U.S.S.R. is prepared to go to increase the power of China in Asia. A test of our strategy is, therefore, its ability to bring about situations which accentuate potential differences within the Soviet bloc. In these terms, one of the basic indictments of an excessive emphasis on a strategy of all-out war is that its inability to differentiate and graduate its pressures may actually contribute to the consolidation and the unity of the Soviet bloc.

It is therefore misleading to reject a strategy of limited

war on the ground that it does not offer a military solution to our strategic problem. Its merit is precisely that it may open the way to a political solution. Had we defeated the Chinese Army in Korea in 1951, the U.S.S.R. would have faced the problem of whether the risk of expanding the war was worth keeping China from suffering a limited defeat. Had we followed up our victory with a conciliatory political proposal to Peiping, we could have caused it to reconsider the wisdom of being too closely tied to the U.S.S.R. Even if we had failed in our primary task of dividing the U.S.S.R. and China, we would have greatly improved our position toward our allies and even more toward the uncommitted nations in Asia. The best counterargument to the charge of colonialism is political moderation after a military victory. A military stalemate, on the other hand, always leaves open the question whether what is advanced as a proof of moderation is not in reality a sign of weakness or at least of irresolution. Thus, if limited actions are implemented as part of a policy which offers the other side a way out short of unconditional surrender, they may bring about local reversals. These in turn may set off chain reactions which will be difficult to control and which may magnify the tensions within the Soviet bloc. A strategy of limited war, then, would use our retaliatory power as a means to permit us to fight local actions on our own terms and to shift to the other side of the risk of initiating all-out war.

IV

Whatever the theoretical advantages of limited war, is it practical? Does not a policy of limited war run up against the geographic reality that the Soviet bloc possesses interior lines of communication and may therefore be able to assemble a superior force at any given point along its periphery? Can we afford a policy of limited war or will it not overstrain our resources just as surely as would all-out war? Does not the concern with local resistance mistake the real security problem which in major areas is political instability and a standard of living considered oppressively low by the majority of the population?

Admittedly, we alone cannot possibly defend the Soviet periphery by local actions, and the present period of revolutionary change will not be managed solely by reliance on a military doctrine. Our task also includes strengthening the will to resist among the peoples threatened by Communist expansionism. In the underdeveloped third of the world this means pursuing a variety of measures: a political program to gain the confidence of local populations and to remove the stigma of colonialism from us, together with a degree of economic assistance which will help bring about political stability. But such programs, although essential, will in the end be ineffective unless we improve our capacity for local defense. We have a weakness for considering problems as "primarily" economic or "primarily" military rather than as total situations in which political, economic, and military considerations merge, which is the way the Soviet leadership regards policy.

Thus one of the conditions of political stability is our capacity to react to local aggression at the place of its occurrence. Few leaders of threatened countries will wish to rely for protection on our strategic superiority in an all-out war. Victory in a general war will mean little to a country which meanwhile has undergone the moral and physical ravages of Soviet occupation.

Can the non-Soviet countries of Eurasia be defended, assuming the willingness of the threatened countries to resist and an ability on our part to help them? In support of a negative answer such factors are cited as the "unlimited" Soviet manpower and the vast distances of the threatened areas from the centers of our strength. Absolute numbers are important, but only the part of them that can be utilized effectively is strategically significant. The value of Sino-Soviet manpower is limited by the capacity of the Soviet bloc to equip and train it, and its effectiveness is reduced by the power of modern weapons and by difficulties of communications and supply.

The particular danger zone for limited wars is the arc

which stretches from the eastern border of Turkey around the periphery of Eurasia. Within that area the Indian subcontinent is protected by mountain barriers and by extremely difficult communications. Aggression against the Middle East would have to count on the flanking position of Turkey and, despite the Suez fiasco, Great Britain would probably join in resistance. An attack on Burma would antagonize India and would be difficult to supply, and the same would be true of the remainder of Southeast Asia. An attack in the Far East would have to take place either across water or against indigenous forces, as in Korea. Moreover, if we utilize nuclear weapons there will be an inherent upper limit to the number of troops that can be profitably employed in threatened areas. Thus if we could develop forces capable of conducting limited war and of getting into position rapidly, we should be able to defeat the Soviet Union or China in local engagements despite their interior position.

If we commit ourselves to a strategy of local defense, do we not run the risk of having our forces always at the wrong place? Cannot the Soviet bloc utilize its interior position to keep us constantly off balance? To be sure, the Soviet bloc is able to pick the initial point of attack, but the greater mobility of its interior position is illusory because of the difficulties of communication. Once the Soviet armies are committed in one area, they cannot be shifted at will against our air power or with greater speed than we can shift ours by sea or air. The Chinese Communists, for example, cannot draw us into Indochina and then attack in Burma with the same army. They can, of course, build up two armies, but we should be able to learn of this in time and then decide to defend one or the other area, or both, depending on the strategic situation.

V

It is often maintained that the call for forces capable of fighting local actions is a misreading of the nature of our military establishment. By building up forces for deterring all-out war, it is argued, we are also creating the capability to fight limited war.

Such an argument misunderstands the nature of our strategic problem. The strategic striking force is the prime deterrent against all-out war; it must therefore be reserved for this contingency. This is particularly important during a limited war, because to the extent that our retaliatory force suffers attrition in such a conflict, the enemy would lose his incentive for keeping the war limited. An aggressor who could tempt us to utilize our strategic striking force in a limited war would gain a strategic advantage, however military operations ended. To the extent that our retaliatory force declined in strength, our ability to deter all-out war would decline and therewith the sanction for keeping the war limited. To use our strategic striking force as a dual-purpose force would weaken the deterrent to all-out war at the precise time when it should be strongest. Or else it will in every crisis furnish arguments for conserving our strength for a "clearer" provocation or a principal enemy—as was demonstrated by General Hoyt S. Vandenberg's reluctance during the Korean War to commit our Strategic Air Force against Communist China.

Moreover, the nature of the weapons, the planning, and the concept of operations differ radically between forces useful for all-out war and those for limited war. The weapons system for all-out war is designed to inflict maximum destruction in the shortest time. The weapons system for a limited war, on the other hand, must be flexible and discriminating. In an all-out war the targets are known in advance, in fact each crew of the Strategic Air Command is training for a specific Soviet target all the time. Everything depends therefore on the efficiency with which the plan for all-out war can be implemented. In a limited war neither the locale of the conflict nor the targets can be determined in advance. Everything here depends on the rapidity with which planning can be adjusted to a developing situation. In an all-out war the chief problem is to eliminate the enemy's retaliatory force before it has done too much damage. In a limited war the problem is to apply graduated amounts of destruction for limited objectives and also to permit the necessary breathing spaces for political contacts.[1]

A weapons system for limited war is therefore basically different from a retaliatory force. Limited wars require units of high mobility and considerable firepower which can be quickly moved to trouble spots and which can bring their power to bear with discrimination. The capability for rapid deployment is crucial. Given the power of modern weapons and the speed of movement of military units, it will be very difficult to dislodge an enemy once he has become established. Since aggression is unlikely to occur unless the aggressor doubts either the capability or the willingness of his opponent to intervene, the ability to get into position rapidly even with relatively small forces can serve as a gauge of the determination to resist and contribute to the re-establishment of an equilibrium before either side becomes too heavily committed.

The biggest gap in our defense establishment is the lack of units capable of fighting local actions and specifically designed for this purpose. At present the Air Force is preoccupied with a doctrine of all-out war and of complete air superiority. The Army is small, relatively immobile, and its organization cumbersome. Only the Navy possesses a force capable to some extent of discriminating offensive operations.

In view of the fact that the Strategic Air Command is for all practical purposes the central core of the Air Force, the priority given to all-out war by air doctrine is understandable. It is only natural for the best crews, the best equipment, and the choicest bases to be assigned to our retaliatory force. The penalty for our preoccupation with the strategic striking force is that it turns the mode of operation which is necessary for all-out war into the pattern for the conduct of limited war as well. The "pure" air doctrine, the basis of the strategy of the Strategic Air Command, maintains that the air is indivisible, that wars can

[1] See below, Chapter 8, pp. 189–96, for the concept of "operations in phases."

be won only by dominating the skies completely. But, as we shall see later, complete command of the air will be possible, if at all, only in an all-out war.

The preoccupation with all-out war determines not only the doctrine of the tactical air forces but also their priorities for equipment and personnel and for mobility in case of conflict. Under present procedures many of the planes which have become obsolescent for strategic missions are assigned to the Tactical Air Command. Thus TAC took over the B-29 Superfortress when it was replaced by the B-47 medium jet bomber in the Strategic Air Command and it will receive the B-47 as it is replaced by the B-58. Some of the planes of the Tactical Air Command are therefore always at one stage of development behind those of the Strategic Air Command. The practice of assigning the obsolescent planes of our retaliatory force to the Tactical Air Command is a symptom of the tendency to consider the doctrines for limited and all-out war as essentially identical. This reduces the effectiveness of TAC against the latest types of enemy planes and affects its utility for tactical operations. The very characteristics which make planes of value for strategic air war may limit their usefulness for tactical operations. The B-47 is a high-altitude bomber of medium range. It was designed to deliver high-yield weapons over an area target, not to outmaneuver enemy fighters over a combat zone. It is therefore not the ideal plane for the flexible operations and relatively discriminating attacks required in limited warfare.

The same priorities which determine the assignment of weapons will also determine the availability of support from other commands within the Air Force. In case of a limited war, a considerable proportion of the tactical air forces will have to be moved from the United States to the theater of operations. Since most of the planes of the Tactical Air Command are of medium and short range, such an operation requires tankers for aerial refueling as well as an airlift to move supplies. But the TAC tanker fleet is composed of obsolescent B-29's, dangerous for the refueling of high-performance jet fighters and usable only in good weather. And the Strategic Air Command properly has first call on the available airlift. In case of limited war, competition between the requirements of the Strategic and the Tactical Air Commands is therefore inevitable. Since a war can be kept limited only through the maximum readiness of our retaliatory force, there will be a very understandable temptation to reserve the available airlift for its use. But since the tactical air forces will be ineffective unless they get into position quickly, existing priorities will hamper our Air Force in its deployment for a limited war.

This is not put forward as a criticism of Air Force policy. Given the present assignment of missions and budgetary levels, the current system of priorities is inescapable. It does suggest the importance of creating distinct forces for both all-out and limited wars, forces which will be as self-contained as possible, with their own training, supply, and equipment. Any other course will lead to a gradual merging of the forces designed for limited war into a reserve for the retaliatory force. It will either produce attrition of the retaliatory force in a limited war or will create pressures for inaction when the challenge does not seem to involve the national existence directly.

As for the Army's role in a limited war, it is handicapped by a doctrinal dispute with the Air Force, paralleling the difficulties already noted within the Air Force over the relative priorities for the Strategic and Tactical Air Commands. The strategic effectiveness of the Army is reduced further by the twin facts that its organization is in a state of transition and its force levels are too low. For the fiscal year 1958, the Army consists of seventeen divisions and a number of combat teams; since some of these units are training cadres, only fourteen divisions can be said to be ready for combat. It may be argued that a force of this size does not absolutely preclude our fighting limited wars. Valid as this contention may be from a purely military point of view, it is unrealistic psychologically. A limited war of any size would absorb so large a part of our strategic reserve that we would lose a great deal of flexibility for dealing with any other threat. The likelihood that any Chief of Staff would be unwilling to commit an army of the present size to a local war is shown by the hesitations of the then Chief of Staff General Matthew B. Ridgway with regard to both Indochina and the Chinese offshore islands. And the doubts of the military will reinforce the inhibitions of the political leadership.

Thus a vicious circle is set up. In deciding whether to engage in a limited war, the civilian leadership must depend on military advice, but the pressure of the military will in all good conscience have to be exerted against involvement, either because they do not possess adequate forces or because they lack an adequate doctrine or both. The circle is broken in practice only if a strong President assumes the responsibility for defining the limits of the conflict and the nature of our commitment, as happened in the Korean War.

The increasing power of modern weapons affects the Army's need for forces in two ways. On the one hand, it sets a limit to the number of troops which can be concentrated in a combat zone. On the other hand, the intricacy of the new tactics and the speed with which they must be executed place a very high premium on the readiness and mobility of the forces-in-being. It is no longer possible to count on a substantial mobilization of reserve forces to help redress the balance in case of local aggression, as was still the case in the Korean War. In any case, the training of reserve forces is not likely to be adequate for using the complicated weapons and applying the intricate tactics of modern war. Limited war, like all-out war, will have to be fought by the forces-in-being; it requires a highly professional force at instant readiness of training, doctrine, and equipment.

The introduction of modern weapons and the reorganization of the Army's cumbersome units make it possible to envisage a level of forces which would enable the Army to intervene effectively in threatened areas, particularly where there is a measure of local resistance. While these forces must be larger than the present Army strength, they are not so large as to be beyond the possibility of the economy to support them. The Chief of Staff of the Army, Maxwell D. Taylor, has estimated that twenty-eight modern divisions would be sufficient to meet all foreseeable dangers. And even an addition of four divisions to the present forces would greatly improve our posture for a limited war.

But an increase in Army strength by itself will avail little if we do not have the necessary mobility to intervene rapidly in case of aggression. We reacted to the frustrations of the Korean War with a determination never to be caught again in a predicament in which most of our forces were tied down in an exposed peninsula. Accordingly we set about reducing the deployment of our troops overseas and concentrating most of our strategic reserve in the United States.

As a concept this is reasonable. A strategic reserve is useless, however, unless it is able to bolster local resistance quickly. Otherwise it will be either too small for a general war or too immobile to redress the strategic balance locally. The importance of forces ready to intervene rapidly was surely one of the lessons of the Korean War. Whatever the state of our readiness, militarily or psychologically, the attack occurred in a fortuitous area, close to our only concentration of troops in Asia. And even these untrained troops, hastily assembled and under strength, managed to hold a line and restore the situation within a few months. Had we required even one more week to bring troops into Korea, it would have been too late, and Korea could probably not have been recaptured without an effort that would have materially increased the risk of a general war.

A strategic reserve must have mobility. In the past this mobility was assured by our command of the seas. But in modern warfare so leisurely a deployment is no longer possible, and in any case we have available sea transport for barely two divisions, either Army or Marine. We therefore have two choices: we can station ready forces in likely trouble spots or close to them, or we can keep the major portion of our strategic reserve in the United States but give it the mobility to move quickly to threatened areas. The first of these alternatives is politically difficult and strategically risky. The second presupposes two conditions: an Army organization less cumbersome than the present division, and an airlift which will enable us to intervene in threatened areas in time to be effective.

Our Army organization has been designed for wars of position and it has been geared to the speed of the internal-combustion engine and the availability of roads. But the traditional division, designed to cover a lineal front, may prove too large and too cumbersome to fight effectively in a situation which is not likely to provide a stabilized front in the usual sense. Above all, it is too complicated to be moved efficiently by air. The standard infantry division weighs approximately 28,000 short tons. It would require the entire available United States airlift, including the civil reserve fleet, over thirty days to move one division from the United States to the Middle East, provided all air-transport units were in position when the crisis occurred and provided they were not required for any other mission—two most unlikely contingencies.

One important means for improving the Army's mobility is to reduce the weight of its units, and substantial progress in this direction is taking place. The Army has given up its traditional divisional organization based on three regiments and is substituting a division composed of five combat teams. This change will increase the number of self-supporting commands and thereby enhance the flexibility of maneuver. It will permit the application of smaller and therefore more discriminating amounts of force. In addition, a new type of airborne division has been created, designed for rapid air transport. It weighs 14,300 short tons and its combat element weighs 5,000 short tons. This would halve the time required to move one division to the Middle East from the United States even with the existing airlift.

But the existing airlift places us in a precarious situation if we are called upon to wage a limited war. Unless the complete combat element of a division can be moved to a threatened area almost simultaneously, it may get there too late to affect events or it may arrive in driblets so small that it can be defeated in detail. According to the testimony of General Weyland, it would take the entire available airlift fifteen days to move even a streamlined Army division to the Middle East and at least ten days to move a regimental combat team of 7,000 men to Laos. But the entire airlift is unlikely to be available. In fact, no part of the airlift is presently earmarked for Army use, and its availability will depend on whatever priorities are in force upon the outbreak of a war.

Thus Army planning must of necessity take place in a vacuum or on the assumption of only a minimum availability of airlift. Indeed, any situation serious enough to require airlifting a division to the Middle East or to Laos is likely to be so serious as to cause the Strategic Air Command to exercise its first priority. Thus the Army faces exactly the same problem as the Tactical Air Command: it will have the greatest difficulty in utilizing the existing airlift at the very time when it is most needed.

To remedy this situation it will be necessary to create additional airlift capacity and to separate the airlift designated for all-out war from that part of it which is to be utilized for limited war. The same considerations which make an all-purpose military force inadvisable also counsel against creating an all-purpose airlift. The wisest course would, therefore, be to earmark most of the existing airlift for the Strategic Air Command and to create additional airlift reserved specifically for deployment in a limited war. Any other course will have the practical consequence that the first priority of the Strategic Air Command will cause the available air transport to be withheld from tactical use in case of a local aggression of any consequence.

To be sure, if the Navy develops the high-speed, nuclear-powered ships which are now being discussed, the requirements for airlift may decline. But until that time an adequate airlift remains our only means for attaining strategic mobility for a limited war. Surely one of the lessons of the fiasco of the British and French invasion of Suez was that the slowness of their moves, based on traditional concepts of logistics and sea transport, forfeited any chance for success. In the nuclear age the capability for rapid and limited action may prove as important a deterrent as the capability for a powerful and all-out response.

The objection may be raised that airlift, to be effective, must rely on our ability to use bases close to the combat zone. But for the foreseeable future we should be able to count on Okinawa or perhaps the Philippines as a staging area for the Far East, on Cyprus or Libya as staging areas for the Middle East, and on Great Britain as a staging area for Europe. And if our policy is at all far-sighted we should be able to create or hold other friendly areas close to likely danger zones.

If the Army and Air Force are handicapped by the doctrinal problem of distinguishing between all-out and limited war capabilities, the Navy faces a different challenge. The Navy task forces, built around fast aircraft carriers, are in some respects ideal supporting units for waging a limited war. They can provide air support in any area of the world and they supply us with a floating base structure immune to the political upheavals which may affect our ability to use our overseas bases. To be sure, in the face of the power of modern weapons the Navy task forces will not be able to operate very close to the shores of an enemy possessing substantial air power and modern weapons. And a carrier of the *Forrestal* class costing $189 million represents a heavy investment compared to the ninety-five planes it can carry, half of which are purely defensive. Nevertheless, in offensive operations in support of a limited war the Navy carrier task forces could play a major role.

But the effectiveness of the carrier task forces in a limited war is likely to be reduced by the growing Soviet submarine menace and by the fact that our strategy for dealing with that threat is essentially inconsistent with a policy of limited war. Our naval strategy proposes to defeat the submarine menace by destroying the opponent's port facilities and base installations. The Chief of Naval Operations has said that an attack on enemy bases is the primary task of antisubmarine warfare.

This strategy raises serious problems, however. Quite apart from the fact that atomic-powered submarines at sea can wreak considerable havoc before they must return to port, an attack with nuclear weapons on metropolitan Russia is not consistent with a policy of limited war. A nuclear or thermonuclear attack on the port cities of the U.S.S.R. is almost certain to unleash a retaliatory blow, if only because the Soviet staff will not know what our target is when they detect our planes on their radar screen. Thus, at a time when Soviet submarine forces are likely to be most active, our own antisubmarine strategy of destroying their home bases is likely to be most inhibited. Or else our retaliation against those bases will bring on an all-out war despite our intentions.

Like air doctrine, naval doctrine must distinguish between the strategy appropriate for an all-out war and that suitable for a limited war. It must not attempt to use the two concepts interchangeably. More emphasis will have to be placed on defeating submarines at sea. Thus each of the services must develop a distinctive strategy for waging limited war, as well as a spectrum of capabilities for the intermediate application of its power.

VI

Limited war is not simply a question of appropriate military forces and doctrines. It also places heavy demands on the discipline and subtlety of the political leadership and on the confidence of the society in it. For limited war is psychologically a much more complex problem than all-out war. In an all-out war the alternatives will be either surrender or unqualified resistance against a threat to the national existence. To be sure, psychological factors will largely determine the relative willingness to engage in an all-out war, and the side more willing to run risks may gain an important advantage in the conduct of diplomacy. However, once the decision to fight is taken, a nation's physical ability to conduct war will be the most important factor in the outcome.

In a limited war, on the other hand, the psychological equation will be of crucial importance, not only with respect to the decision to enter the war but throughout the course of military operations. A limited war among major powers can be kept limited only by the conscious choice of the protagonists. Either side has the physical power to expand it, and to the extent that each side is willing to increase its commitment in preference either to a stalemate or to a defeat, the war will gradually become an all-out one. The restraint which keeps a war limited is a psychological one: the consequences of a limited victory or a limited defeat or a stalemate—the three possible outcomes of a limited war—must seem preferable to the consequences of an all-out war.

In a limited war the choices are more varied than in an all-out conflict and their nature is more ambiguous. Victory offers no final solution, and defeat does not carry with it the penalty of national catastrophe. The side which is more willing to risk an all-out war or can convince its opponent of its greater readiness to run that risk is in the stronger position. Even when the willingness of both sides to run risks is equal at the beginning of the war, the psychological equation will constantly be shifting, depending on the course of military operations. Because the limitation of war is brought about by the fear of unleashing a thermonuclear holocaust, the psychological equation is, paradoxically, constantly shifting *against* the side which seems to be winning. The greater the transformation it seeks, the more plausible will become the threat by its opponent of launching an all-out war. The closer that the loser in a limited war is brought to the consequences which he would suffer by defeat in an all-out war, the less he will feel restrained from resorting to extreme measures.

At the same time, the winning side may become increasingly reluctant to test the opponent's willingness to resort to all-out war. The better its position, the more secure it will feel and the less it will be willing to take the risks of an all-out war. The more precarious the position of the losing side becomes, the more likely it will be to raise its commitment toward the level of an all-out war. Success in limited war requires, therefore, that the opponent be persuaded that national survival is not at stake and that a settlement is possible on reasonable terms. Otherwise the result is almost certain to be either stalemate or all-out war.

If an opponent attaches great importance to an area in dispute—or is thought to attach great importance to it—he will have a distinct psychological advantage in a limited war. This was the case with China's role in Korea. Some areas may be thought so important to one of the contenders that they will be protected by the belief of the opponent that any attack on them will lead to a general war. Protection for these areas will be achieved less by local defense than by the over-all strategic balance. This has been the case up to now with Western Europe with respect to the United States or with the satellite regions with respect to the U.S.S.R. As total war poses increasingly ominous prospects, however, the over-all strategic balance will be a less and less adequate protection to threatened areas, for ever fewer regions will seem worth this price. As the implications of all-out war with modern weapons become better understood, security for many areas will increasingly depend on the capability for local action. Limited war would thereby become a test of the determination of the contenders, a gauge of the importance they attach to disputed issues. If one side attaches greater importance to an area or an issue and is willing to pay a higher price, and if it possesses a capability for waging a limited war, it may well achieve a favorable shift in the strategic equation.

The key to a successful policy of limited war is to keep the challenge to the opponent, whether diplomatic or military, below the threshold which would unleash an all-out war. The greater the risk in relation to the challenge, the less total the response is likely to be. The more the challenge approximates the risks posed by all-out war, the more difficult it will be to limit the conflict. A policy of limited war therefore presupposes three conditions: the ability to generate pressures other than the threat of all-out war; the ability to create a climate in which survival is not thought to be at stake in each issue; and the ability to keep control of public opinion in case disagreement arises over whether national survival is at stake. The first condition depends to a considerable extent on the flexibility of our military policy; the second on the subtlety of our diplomacy; the third will reflect the courage of our leadership.

The problems posed by our military policy have been discussed earlier. But, assuming that it will be possible to create a spectrum of military capabilities to meet the widest range of Soviet challenges, will our diplomacy be able to bring about a framework in which national survival is thought not to be at stake? Pressures severe enough to cause withdrawal or stalemate may, after all, seem severe enough to threaten survival, especially to a regime like that of Soviet Russia. It must be admitted that the challenge to our diplomacy is formidable. It would be hopeless except against the background of a retaliatory capability which can make the Soviet leadership recoil from the prospect of an all-out war. As long as we maintain a powerful strategic striking force, an all-out conflict is likely in only two contingencies: if the Soviets see an opportunity to achieve hegemony in Eurasia by peripheral actions which we would be unable to counter except by all-out war; or if the U.S.S.R. should misunderstand our intentions and interpret each military move on our part as a prelude to a thermonuclear holocaust.

Provided our military policy equips us with a wide spectrum of capabilities, the task of our diplomacy will be to convey to the Soviet bloc what we mean by limited war. This is important, because Soviet reactions to what we do will depend not on what we intend but on what the Soviet leaders think we intend. The power and speed of modern weapons make too much obscurity dangerous. Unless there has been at least some degree of comprehension of the nature of limited war on both sides, it may be impossible to improvise it in the confusion of battle. As we shall discuss further, diplomacy should strive to insure that the opponent has the information he requires to make correct appraisals. To be sure, such a course will not restrain an enemy determined on a showdown. It may, however, prevent him from stumbling into an all-out war based on miscalculation or on misinterpretation of our intentions.

The same program which may reduce the danger of miscalculation by the enemy would also go a long way toward educating public opinion in the realities of the nuclear age. This may, of course, be less important in the Soviet bloc where dictatorship confers a much greater freedom of action. In the Western world, however, and particularly in the United States, a considerable change in the concept of war is required. It is important for our leadership to understand that total victory is no longer possible and for the public to become aware of the dangers of pressing for such a course.

A long history of invulnerability has accustomed us to look at war more in terms of the damage we can inflict than of the losses we might suffer. The American people must be made aware that with the end of our atomic monopoly all-out war has ceased to be an instrument of policy, except as a last resort, and that for most of the issues likely to be in dispute our only choice is between a strategy of limited war or inaction. It would be tragic if our government were deprived of freedom of maneuver by the ignorance of the public regarding the consequences of a course from which it would recoil if aware of all its implications. This is all the more true since the same ignorance which underlies the demand for all-or-nothing solutions might well produce panic if our people were unexpectedly brought face-to-face with the consequences of an all-out war. Conversely, a public fully aware of the dangers confronting it and forearmed psychologically by an adequate civil defense program will be better prepared to support a more flexible national policy.

Whatever aspect of our strategic problem we consider —mitigating the horrors of war, creating a spectrum of capabilities to resist likely Soviet challenges—we are brought to recognize the importance of developing a strategy which makes room for the possibility of limited war. Creating a readiness for limited war should not be considered a matter of choice but of necessity. It results from the impossibility of combining both maximum force and the maximum willingness to act.

A strategy which makes room for the possibility of fighting limited wars will not eliminate the precariousness of our situation. In the nuclear age the best strategy can provide only a relative security, for the threat of all-out war will always loom in the background as a last resort for either side. Moreover, as nuclear technology becomes more widely diffused, other and perhaps less responsible powers will enter the nuclear race. The fear of mutual destruction, today the chief deterrent to all-out war for the major powers, may prove less effective with nations who have less to lose and whose negotiating position might even be improved by a threat to commit suicide.

Even among the major powers the strategy outlined in this chapter will not be easy to implement. It presupposes a military capability which is truly graduated. It assumes a diplomacy which can keep each conflict from being considered the prelude to a final showdown. And it requires strong nerves. We can make a strategy of limited war stick only if we leave no doubt about our readiness and our ability to face a final showdown.

CHAPTER SEVEN

The Problems of
Limited Nuclear War

I

Some people assert that limited nuclear war is a contradiction in terms, that the only hope of keeping a war limited is to restrict ourselves to conventional weapons. If this is true, then the whole thrust of our military policy toward developing a diversified nuclear establishment is meaningless and dangerous. We should instead place our reliance on the most fearful application of our power to deter all-out war and on preparing conventional forces for limited wars. If, on the other hand, limited nuclear war is possible, it becomes important to determine whether it represents an advantageous strategy for us.

The arguments against limited nuclear war are persuasive. They call attention to the fact that nuclear weapons can now be made of all sizes, from less than one kiloton of TNT equivalent up to almost any desired explosive force. In the absence of a natural cutoff point, it is argued, the employment of any nuclear weapon may start a cycle of gradually expanding commitments ending in all-out war. Even if the war should be fought initially with so-called low-yield nuclear weapons, the losing side will always be tempted to redress the balance by resorting to weapons of greater power, thus inviting counterretaliation. Moreover, so the argument goes, limitations on the size of weapons to be employed cannot be enforced in practice, and each side will, therefore, seek to anticipate its opponent by using the largest practicable weapon. All-out war would thus occur in circumstances under which it would never be clear which side had taken the crucial step that caused the struggle to become total. A conventional war, on the other hand, has a clearly defined cutoff point; it can have a self-enforcing limit. If nuclear weapons of whatever power were employed, it would be clear which side had committed "atomic aggression."

Limited nuclear war is not only impossible, according to this line of reasoning, but also undesirable. For one thing, it would cause devastation within the combat zone approaching that of thermonuclear war in severity. We would, therefore, be destroying the very people we were seeking to protect. Moreover, the belief that nuclear weapons would permit economies of manpower is said to be an illusion. On the contrary, the technical complexity of modern weapons requires a heavy investment of manpower in all supporting services, and their destructiveness means that a large pool of trained replacements is called for. Finally, it is argued, a limited war fought with nuclear weapons would reduce the importance of our industrial potential. It would enable the Soviet bloc to concentrate its resources in a limited area of production and to bring about an equilibrium with a smaller investment of resources.

These arguments have great force. No one even generally familiar with the destructiveness of modern weapons can regard the prospect of any kind of nuclear war with equanimity. Yet the dilemma of nuclear war is with us, not by choice but because of the facts of modern technology. And before we can consider the problem of limited nuclear war we must discuss the tactics appropriate to the new technology.

Such an analysis is all the more important because the entire planning, procurement, research, and development of our defense establishment is built around nuclear weapons. A decision to refrain from using them would, therefore, place Eurasia at the mercy of the Soviet bloc, at least in an interim period while we were readjusting the planning of our military establishment and redirecting the equipping of our forces. Then too there are some applications of nuclear weapons that it will be very difficult to discard; for example, the employment of atomic warheads for antiaircraft missiles. Should this defensive employment of nuclear weapons be admitted, however, it will set in motion pressures for their offensive use. In short, as nuclear weapons become more varied conventional war becomes the most "unnatural" war and the most difficult to plan.

Moreover, in a war against a nuclear power the decision between conventional and nuclear weapons is not entirely up to us. An aggressor will always be able to shift to nuclear weapons, even in a war which starts out as a conventional war, perhaps by using initially weapons of very low yield. To be sure, such an action would make the identification of the "atomic aggressor" unambiguous, but the consequences which would follow are far from obvious. If the Soviet Union or Communist China is prepared to accept the onus of military aggression it may also be willing to accept the onus of "atomic aggression." It is not the onus attached to atomic aggression which would deter resort to nuclear weapons, but the consequences which would flow from using them.

What then would be our possible rejoinders to the introduction of nuclear weapons into a limited conventional war, particularly if it were accompanied by a Soviet announcement that they would be used only against "tactical" targets or that only weapons of a certain size would be utilized? Two reactions are possible. We can either resort to all-out war immediately in the face of *any* employment of nuclear weapons or we can respond by using nuclear weapons ourselves, but with the intention of keeping their employment limited.

Either course is subject to serious objections. The resort to all-out war would expose us to all the inhibitions of massive retaliation. Since an all-out war stakes the national substance, the decision to engage in it will depend less on the nature of the weapons employed by the enemy than on whether the provocation is considered "worth" a national catastrophe. And the judgment about whether the provocation warrants a final showdown will depend to a considerable degree on the importance which we attach to the area or the objective in dispute. Thus a Soviet attack on Western Europe may unleash an all-out war regardless of the weapons used, while Soviet repression of satellite revolts with nuclear weapons may not. Even if nuclear weapons were employed against United States forces, say, in the Middle East or Southeast Asia, a resort to all-out war by us would not be a foregone conclusion. It is difficult to believe that we would rush into the cataclysm of a thermonuclear war to prevent the defeat of a few conventional divisions, particularly if the Soviet leaders showed their usual skill in presenting their challenge ambiguously. Thus at the precise moment that decisive action would be most necessary, we might recoil before the implications of so absolute a strategy. At the very least we would be tempted, and rightly so, to ascertain whether all alternatives to an all-out struggle had been exhausted. And one of these alternatives is an effort to conduct a limited nuclear war.

A limited nuclear war which had to be improvised in the midst of military operations would be undertaken under the worst possible conditions, both psychological and military. A prerequisite for keeping a war limited is that both sides have correct intelligence about each other's intentions. Because of the need for rapid reaction which is imposed by the speed and power of modern weapons, a misinterpretation of the opponent's intentions is always possible and may well produce a cataclysm. The sudden introduction of nuclear weapons while military operations are taking place would force the powers to confront the problems of a limited nuclear war in the confusion of battle, at a time when correct intelligence is most difficult to come by. And their difficulties would be compounded by the fact that they would have had no previous experience to serve as a guide.

Moreover, if we concede the first nuclear blow, we can be certain that nuclear weapons will be used against us at a moment when we are most vulnerable, either physically or psychologically. In fact, the sudden introduction of nuclear weapons against a conventional force almost guarantees military success. Conventional forces must concentrate to be effective. The power of individual conventional weapons is so small, relatively, that they can hold a line or achieve a break-through only by massed firepower. But if troops are concentrated they may irresistibly tempt the opponent to use nuclear weapons. Thus, in a conventional war against a nuclear power, the choice is between employing ineffective formations which have been dispersed *as if* nuclear weapons might be used or courting disaster by concentrating forces. It may be argued that both sides will face the same problem and will labor under the same handicap. But the aggressor has the advantage of initiative, whether he uses conventional or nuclear weapons. Against a widely dispersed conventional defense, the task of even a dispersed conventional offensive is simplified, because the force required to overwhelm any given point is relatively small. And if the aggressor suddenly resorts to nuclear weapons, he may sweep all before him before effective retaliation can take place.

Any attempt to define the role of limited nuclear war will therefore have to start with the realization that a revolution in technology carries with it a revolution in tactics. With each new technological discovery, the temptation is strong to integrate it with what is familiar. Thus the first automobiles were built as much as possible like horse-drawn carriages. The first electric light was made to approximate the gas lamp it replaced. In each case, progress was impossible until a break was made with traditional patterns of thought and until the new discovery developed the forms appropriate for it.

The tactics of conventional warfare were based on the same principle of specialization of functions which has given such a strong impetus to industrial technology. The fighting units were designed to inflict the greatest amount of destruction at the lowest possible loss to themselves, but they were completely dependent on service organizations for their supply, maintenance, and equipment. Since the combat units had only a limited staying power when deprived of their logistic support, encirclement was the most efficient offensive tactic.

These tactics assumed that each side was in substantial control of the territory behind its battle zone and that the front was in effect a line without flanks. To be sure, in World War II deep thrusts by armored units were common. But they were in the nature of advancing the front line as far as the supply of fuel would carry the attacker. A tank force which lost contact with its supporting units or whose supporting units could not quickly catch up with it was totally vulnerable, as Germany learned during its Russian campaign. Because the supplies and ammunition for conventional war were too bulky to be stored in the immediate combat zone, a premium was placed on interdiction campaigns against cities, communication centers, and industrial installations.

But such tactics would produce appalling casualties in a nuclear war. Whatever the degree of dispersion, a linear concept of defense would invite the aggressor to step up the power of his weapons to achieve a break-through. Limited nuclear war is unthinkable as long as the reliance on traditional tactics causes the most profitable targets to be identical with the largest centers of population.

The tactics for limited nuclear war should be based on small, highly mobile, self-contained units, relying largely on air transport even within the combat zone. The units should be small, because with nuclear weapons firepower does not depend on numbers and because a reduction in the size of the target will place an upper limit on the power of the weapons it is profitable to employ against it. The units must be mobile, because when anything that can be detected can be destroyed, the ability to hide by constantly shifting position is an essential means of defense. The units should be self-contained, because the cumbersome supply system of World War II is far too vulnerable to interdiction. The proper analogy to limited nuclear war is not traditional land warfare, but naval strategy, in which self-contained units with great firepower gradually gain the upper hand by destroying their enemy counterparts without physically occupying territory or establishing a front line.

While it is impossible to hold any given line with such tactics, they offer an excellent method of depriving aggression of one of its objectives: to control territory. Small, mobile units with nuclear weapons can be extremely useful for defeating their enemy counterparts or for the swift destruction of important objectives. They are not an efficient means for establishing political control. The Hungarian revolution of October and November 1956 demonstrated the difficulty faced even by a vastly superior army in attempting to dominate hostile territory. The Red Army finally had to concentrate twenty-two divisions in order to crush a practically unarmed population. No such concentration is feasible in a nuclear war. Nuclear units of high mobility should, therefore, be used to make the countryside untenable for the invader. They should be supplemented by stationary defensive positions in deep shelters, immune to any but direct hits by the largest weapons.

A defense structure of this type would pose a very difficult problem for an aggressor. To defeat the opposing mobile units he would require highly mobile detachments of his own. To reduce nuclear strong points and control hostile territory, he would have to employ massive forces. Against determined opposition, it will prove very difficult to combine these two kinds of warfare. Well-protected fixed positions should force the aggressor to concentrate his forces and to present a target for nuclear attack. Mobile nuclear units should be able to keep the enemy constantly off balance by never permitting him to consolidate any territorial gains and by destroying any concentration of his forces. If these tactics were coupled with rapid offensive thrusts by units of the defensive force deep into the aggressor's territory, he might soon confront an untenable situation.

These tactics will require a radical break with our traditional notions of warfare and military organization. The Army has already made a start by reorganizing some of its divisions, each into five self-contained combat teams. It stresses the development of troop-carrying helicopters, and even the individual soldier in some units has been given a rudimentary ability to transport himself through the air by means of the "flying platform."

These measures, while useful, are only a beginning. The ultimate aim should be units which carry to its conclusion the analogy between limited nuclear war and naval strategy. Since the mobile units will not be able to rely on a logistics system of the traditional type, they should be able to carry all their supplies and maintain their own equipment. A great deal of thought will have to be given to measures for reducing the bulkiness of equipment, particularly to developing a substitute for the internal-combustion engine, whose demands for fuel and maintenance severely limit the range and staying power of mobile units. Such self-sufficiency may be very difficult to attain at a time when weapons generally are growing increasingly complex. But one reason for this complexity is that the emphasis of our research and development has been toward ever more powerful weapons and delivery systems for all-out war. A comparable effort may be necessary to apply the new technology to the requirements of limited war.

II

With proper tactics, nuclear war need not be as destructive as it appears when we think of it in terms of traditional warfare. The high casualty estimates for nuclear war are based on the assumption that the most suitable targets are those of conventional warfare: transportation centers and airfields—both of which are likely to be in or near cities. In conventional war, the cutting of supply lines is important because of the large numbers of troops involved, the insatiable need for materiel, and because of the reliance of combat troops on supporting units. As armies become both mobile and self-contained, however, the elimination of communication centers may lose its former significance.

Moreover, in nuclear war industrial potential will play a smaller role than heretofore. With conventional technology, a decisive victory on the battlefield could be achieved only by using quantities of arms too large to stockpile. Munitions and weapons had to be supplied out of current production. Under these circumstances, it made sense to attempt to achieve attrition by bombing industrial facilities. Under conditions of nuclear plenty, however, weapons may be more decisively employed against opposing military forces than against production centers. With cities no longer serving as key elements in the communications system of the military forces, the risks of initiating the bombing of cities may outweigh the gains that can be achieved.

The same applies to the traditional doctrine of the need for control of the air. The concept that air supremacy is the prerequisite of victory and that it is achieved by bombing enemy airfields will soon be outstripped by technological developments. So long as planes had to be concentrated on a relatively few bases for efficient operation, it was more economical to destroy them on the ground than in the air. But the concurrent development of missiles and of vertical take-off aircraft, which require little or no runway, are altering this relationship. Within ten years most tactical air support will be accomplished by these two weapons. It will then become meaningless to speak of air supremacy in the traditional sense. Against vertical take-off aircraft there will be no airfields left to crater, and launching sites, especially for short- and medium-range missiles, can be so dispersed and concealed that they will be hard to locate and even more difficult to destroy.

Even before missiles and vertical take-off aircraft are available in quantity, the concept of complete air supremacy will have become inconsistent with a policy of limited war. As the range of planes increases, complete air superiority can be achieved only by deep penetrations into enemy territory. But deep penetration of the territory of a major nuclear power may unleash a retaliatory blow. The enemy, observing a flight of planes on his radar screen, cannot know whether a "tactical" or a "strategic" target will be attacked and, faced with the risk of having his strategic striking power caught on the ground, he may launch his retaliatory blow. At least as long as the strategic striking force is composed of airplanes, sanctuary areas immune to attack are almost essential in a limited war between major powers, because any threat to the opponent's strategic striking force will invite a thermonuclear holocaust. Even in a limited conventional war, deep penetration into the airspace of a major nuclear power will have to be avoided. For when the enemy's early-warning line is crossed, he cannot know whether the attacking planes are carrying nuclear or conventional weapons. He may, therefore, assume the worst contingency and start his counterblow.

The corollary of these propositions is that for destroying targets deep within enemy territory, it is necessary to develop forms of attack as distinguishable as possible from an all-out strategic blow. Mobile units may be able to attack selected enemy targets at a considerable distance from the combat zone without unleashing all-out war, so long as their intentions are sufficiently clear: they should, therefore, be transported to their target by means which are least likely to be mistaken for the precursor of total war. A great premium will be placed on small, low-flying aircraft, on mobile tactical units, and even on unorthodox forms of attack, such as sabotage and partisan activity.

In these circumstances, it is possible to conceive of a pattern of limited nuclear war with its own appropriate tactics and with limitations as to targets, areas, and the size of weapons used. Such a mode of conflict cannot be improvised in the confusion of battle, however. The limitation of war is established not only by our intentions but also by the manner in which the other side interprets them. It therefore becomes the task of our diplomacy to convey to our opponent what we understand by limited nuclear war, or at least what limitations we are willing to observe. Unless some concept of limitation of warfare is established in advance, miscalculation and misinterpretation of the opponent's intentions may cause the war to become all-out even should both sides intend to limit it. If the Soviet leadership is clear about our intentions on the other hand, certain limitations may be established on the basis of self-interest—on the fear of all-out thermonuclear war and on the realization of the fact that new tactics make many of the targets of traditional warfare less profitable.

There remains the objection, that whatever the theoretical feasibility of limiting nuclear war, it will be thwarted in practice by the new tactics themselves and by the tendency of the losing side to redress the balance by expanding the area of conflict or by resorting to bigger weapons. The new tactics, it may be argued, will themselves complicate the limiting of war. The very mobility of units and the uncertainty about their location may tempt one side or the other to saturate an area with the highest-yield weapons. It is important, however, to distinguish between the difficulties of limiting war in general and those peculiar to nuclear war. If it is true that the losing side will invariably resort to every weapon in its arsenal and will disregard all restrictions as to targets and depth of the combat zone, then the only possible outcome of limited war is either stalemate or all-out war. Nor would these alternatives be avoided by a strategy of conventional war. A power which is prepared to unleash an all-out holocaust in order to escape defeat in a limited nuclear war would hardly be more restrained by an initial distinction between conventional and nuclear weapons. The argument that neither side will accept defeat amounts to a denial of the possibility of limited war, nuclear or other, an argument which is valid only if nations in fact prefer suicide to a limited withdrawal.

As to the contention that limited nuclear war would spread by slow stages into an all-out war, it is necessary to examine what these stages might be. One of the most persuasive opponents of limited nuclear war has admitted that even a conventional war is unthinkable without some limitations and that unrestricted conventional war in the age of nuclear plenty is a contradiction in terms.[1] These limitations, presumably defined in terms of targets and the depth of the combat zone, are essentially independent of the nature of weapons used. If they can be made to stick in a conventional war they can be made to stick in a nuclear

[1] James E. King, Jr., "Nuclear Plenty and Limited War," *Foreign Affairs*, v. 35 (January 1957), p. 244.

war as well. The distinguishing feature of nuclear war, which is said to make any effort at limitation illusory, is the variety of available weapons which would invite the losing side to resort to weapons of ever greater explosive power.

It must be admitted that the wide spectrum of nuclear explosives makes restrictions as to the size of weapons impossible to control, at least below the level which would produce significant fall-out, or about 1 megaton. Assuming, however, that both sides are eager to avoid all-out war—the prerequisite for *any* kind of war limitation—there exist some "built-in" restrictions which can form the basis of self-restraint. As long as both sides retain a retaliatory force capable of devastating the opponent, they will not look for an excuse to expand the war; rather they will have a powerful incentive to work out some set of limitations, however tenuous its logic. This, at least, was the experience of the Korean War, even at a time when nuclear stockpiles and delivery systems were still in a relatively elementary state.

The "built-in" restrictions rest on the assumption that high-yield weapons are not employed for their own sake but to achieve a military advantage. Much of the argument about the indiscriminate use of high-yield weapons in limited nuclear war supposes that there will be a stabilized front, with both sides pulverizing everything behind the enemy lines. But such a situation is most unlikely; rather, as we have seen, the combat zone in a limited nuclear war is likely to be highly fluid. When small mobile detachments are operating deep in each other's territory, there will be greater rewards for weapons with relative discrimination than for those which may destroy friendly troops and friendly populations together with a small number of the enemy.

Thus, in a limited nuclear war, it is difficult to conceive of many suitable targets for really high-yield weapons or of an advantage to be gained by using them which cannot be offset by retaliation. High-yield weapons cannot be used in proximity to friendly troops, or on territory expected soon to be occupied by friendly troops, or against friendly populations. Moreover, if each destruction of an area target by one side leads to the destruction of an area target in retaliation, the risks involved in stepping up the power of weapons may outweigh the gains to be achieved. It would seem much more effective to utilize weapons suitable for destroying the enemy mobile units, whose success or failure will ultimately decide the control of territory.

But won't the losing side use high-yield weapons in order to stave off defeat? Yes, if the winning side pursues its advantage to the point of threatening the opponent's survival or most vital interests. But if the side which has the upper hand uses its advantage to offer peace on moderate terms—an indispensable condition for limited war, nuclear or otherwise—its opponent may prefer local adjustments to total devastation.

This is not to say that every limited war should necessarily be fought as a nuclear war. It does indicate that, as long as we are confronted by an opponent capable of initiating nuclear war against us, we require a continuous spectrum of nuclear and nonnuclear capabilities. Nor should we be defeatist about the possibility of limiting nuclear war or about the casualties it might involve. It is far from certain that a conventional war involving fixed positions would produce less devastation than a nuclear war, and in certain circumstances it may produce more. Among combat units the absolute number of casualties in nuclear war will almost certainly be smaller than those of conventional war, although they may be higher in proportion to the number of troops involved.

III

Is limited nuclear war an advantageous strategy for us? It is important to define what is meant by an advantageous strategy in the nuclear age. It emphatically does not mean that limited nuclear war should be our *only* strategy. We must maintain at all times an adequate retaliatory force and not shrink from using it if our survival is threatened. In a conflict with a nonnuclear, minor power, in a civil war in which the population must be won over, the use of nuclear weapons may be unnecessary or unwise. *As a general rule, in a limited war the smallest amount of force consistent with achieving the objective should be used.* The problem of limited nuclear war arises primarily in actions against nuclear powers or against powers with vast resources of manpower.

By an advantageous strategy we certainly do not mean that limited nuclear war is desirable; the nuclear age permits only a choice among evils. It is important also to distinguish among the various senses in which a strategy may be deemed advantageous. It can apply to a strategy under which our relative superiority over our opponent is greatest. It can refer to a strategy which is most likely to avoid general war. It can mean the strategy which is least costly. It can imply the strategy which is most suitable for purposes of deterrence.

In terms of deterrence, the ability to wage limited nuclear war seems more suitable than conventional war because it poses the maximum *credible* threat. If we possess a wide spectrum of nuclear weapons the aggressor's risks are increased, and because limited nuclear war greatly complicates the problem of controlling territory, aggression may seem less attractive.

As compared to conventional war, does limited nuclear war reduce the credibility of the threat? Will it lower our willingness to resist a nuclear power? To be sure, limited nuclear war poses greater risks for both sides than conventional war. But it is a mistake to assume that the risks of nuclear war can be avoided by a decision to resist aggression with conventional weapons. Conventional war carries with it almost the same risks as nuclear war, for the side which engages in a conventional war against a nuclear power, without being willing to accept the risks of nuclear war, is at a hopeless disadvantage. Such an effort to hedge the risks would enable the opponent to gain his ends either by the threat or by the reality of nuclear war. Against a nuclear power, the decision to fight a conventional war can be justified only on the grounds that it represents an advantageous strategy; the over-all risks are not substantially less.

Does a strategy of limited nuclear war increase or decrease the risks of all-out war? The previous discussion has shown that there need not be an inevitable progression from limited nuclear war to all-out thermonuclear conflict. It remains to demonstrate that under most circumstances limited nuclear war may actually be less likely than conventional war to produce an all-out showdown.

Whether a limited war, nuclear or otherwise, may remain limited will depend on the working out of a subtle equation between the willingness of the contenders to assume risks and their ability to increase their commitments. By definition, a limited war between major powers involves the *technical* possibility that either side will be able to raise its commitment. If both sides are willing to do so in preference to accepting a limited defeat, a limited victory, or a stalemate, the result will be all-out war. If one side is willing to run greater risks, or, what amounts to the same thing, is less reluctant to engage in an all-out war, it will have a decisive advantage. If both sides are willing to run the same risks and are able to make the same commitments short of all-out war, the result will be a stalemate or a victory for the side which develops the superior strategy.

Assuming that our determination is equal to that of our opponent—and no strategy can be productive without this —the crucial question is whether a conventional war or a nuclear war is the more likely to stay limited. Obviously, a nuclear war involves a larger initial commitment than a conventional war. Is it safer, then, to begin a limited war with an initial commitment so large that any addition involves the danger of merging into all-out war, or is it wiser to begin it with a commitment which it is possible to raise at smaller risk?

Paradoxically, in a war which begins with a smaller investment it may prove much more difficult to establish an equilibrium. The consciousness that the opponent is able at any moment to increase his commitment may tempt the other side to raise its commitment in anticipation. In a war fought with conventional weapons, the detonation of any nuclear device would quite possibly set off an all-out holocaust. For if reliance is placed on conventional war, it follows almost inevitably that the nature of limited nuclear conflict will not be fully explored either in staff planning or in diplomacy, and hence the two sides will be less clear about each other's intentions. The fact that there exists a clear cutoff point between conventional and nuclear war may turn into a double-edged sword: the limitation may be more easily defined, but once breached, a vicious spiral may be set off. At best it will force the contenders to confront the problem of limited nuclear war under the most difficult circumstances; at worst it might unleash a thermonuclear holocaust.

A war which began as a limited nuclear war would have the advantage that its limitations could have been established—and, what is more important, understood—well in advance of hostilities. In such a conflict, moreover, the options of the aggressor are reduced in range. Whereas in a conventional war the choice is between continuing the war with its existing restrictions or risking an expanded *limited* war, in a nuclear war the choice is the much more difficult one between the existing war and all-out conflict. To be sure, even in a nuclear war it is possible to step up the commitment by resorting to higher-yield weapons. But given the proper tactics, such a course may not drastically alter the outcome, and if carried beyond a certain point it will unleash all-out war. As long as both sides are eager to avoid a final showdown, a nuclear war which breaks out after diplomacy has established a degree of understanding of the possibilities of the new technology would probably stand a better chance of remaining limited than would a conflict that began as a limited conventional war in an international environment which was unsure about the significance of nuclear weapons and which has come to identify any explosion of a nuclear device with total war.

The remaining question to be asked is: In the event of war, which side is likely to gain by fighting a limited nuclear war? Here our superior industrial potential, the broader range of our technology, and the adaptability of our social institutions should give us the advantage. When the destructiveness of individual weapons is small, manpower can substitute for technology, as was the case with Communist China in Korea. If weapons are too destructive, the importance of industrial potential is reduced because a very few weapons suffice to establish an equilibrium. For a nation with a superior industrial capacity and a broader base of technology, it will be strategically most productive to use weapons sufficiently complex to exploit its industrial advantage, sufficiently destructive so that manpower cannot be substituted for technology, yet discriminating enough to permit the establishment of a significant margin of superiority.

It would seem that the weapons systems appropriate for limited nuclear war meet these requirements. The Soviet Union has shown an extraordinary ability to produce results by concentrating its effort on a few strategic armaments, as it did in developing nuclear weapons and ballistic missiles. It is much less certain that with its inferior industrial plant it could compete with us in developing the diversified capability for a limited nuclear war—the wide spectrum of weapons, means of transportation, and elaborate systems of communication. In this respect the difficulties of the Soviet Union would be compounded by the backwardness of Communist China. While it is possible for China to develop a rudimentary nuclear technology within a decade, it would remain completely dependent on the U.S.S.R. for the sophisticated equipment needed for a limited nuclear war. And mere possession of complicated equipment by a backward nation offers no guarantee that it can be used effectively, as was demonstrated by Egypt's incapacity to use Soviet arms. When manpower can no longer be substituted for materiel, the strategic significance of Communist China may be much reduced and in certain circumstances it may even constitute a drain on the resources of the U.S.S.R.

Even should the Soviet Union overcome its difficulties in producing the required variety of weapons—and over a period of time it undoubtedly can do so—it will still be handicapped by the nature of its institutions and by its historical experience. The introduction of nuclear weapons on the battlefield will shake the very basis of Soviet tactical doctrine. No longer will the Soviet bloc be able to rely on massed manpower as in World War II and in Korea. In a limited nuclear war, dispersal is the key to survival, and mobility the prerequisite to success. Everything depends on leadership of a high order, personal initiative, and mechanical aptitude, qualities more prevalent in our society than in the Soviet bloc. To be sure, the Soviet forces can train and equip units for nuclear war. But self-reliance, spontaneity, and initiative cannot be acquired by training; they grow naturally out of social institutions or they do not come into being. And a society like that of the Soviet Union, in which everything is done according to plan and by government direction, will have extraordinary difficulty inculcating these qualities.

Soviet military doctrine prides itself on its centralized control. In World War II, Soviet commanders were permitted only the barest minimum of initiative; their primary task was implementing plans which prescribed not only the general objective—as in American field orders—but the detailed methods for attaining it. Soviet military literature, in fact, prides itself on the "single, monolithic strategic design" of the Soviet High Command. In World War II, the Soviet insistence on rigid centralization made for great flexibility at the top but extraordinary rigidity at the lower echelons. And this theory of command has been embodied also in the field regulations of 1946.

Again, in a limited nuclear war initiative is of cardinal importance because the fluidity of operations makes it impossible to predict all contingencies in advance. Soviet military doctrine, however, while paying lip service to initiative, discourages it in practice. Soviet doctrine distinguishes between two kinds of leadership: the first, inspiring, initiating, and directing; the other, implementing and directing according to plan.

As a result, the operations of the Soviet armed forces in

World War II, while often displaying great flexibility strategically, ran to stereotype tactically. Field regulations prescribed the exact location of company commanders in the rear of their troops. Field orders determined not only the direction of the attack but the precise form it was to take. The sphere of initiative of division commanders could not have been more restricted. Divisions were prohibited from crossing divisional boundaries, and commanders carried out this order even if it meant the destruction of a neighboring unit before their eyes. Regiments advanced on prescribed lines even into their own artillery fire. To deviate from orders was an offense punishable by court-martial if it did not succeed. To carry out even suicidal orders did not involve any stigma. "American lieutenants," wrote General Bradley, "were delegated greater authority on the Elbe than were Russian division commanders."[2]

It would, therefore, seem to the United States' advantage to adopt a strategy which places a premium on initiative and decentralized control. The more decisions Soviet commanders can be forced to improvise, the less they will be able to profit from their military tradition. The most effective means for taking advantage of the lack of initiative of subordinate Soviet commanders is by fluid operations. The best strategy for exploiting the rigidity of the Soviet command structure is that of limited nuclear war. An all-out war can be carried out according to a centralized plan with target systems and attack patterns carefully prepared in advance; this is, indeed, the only possible way of conducting such a conflict. A conventional war permits the massing of troops and the adoption of a rigid command structure. In limited nuclear war, on the other hand, everything depends on daring and leadership of a higher order—qualities in which both by tradition and training our armed forces are likely to excel those of the U.S.S.R.

It will not be easy for the Soviet leadership to develop in the subordinate commanders those qualities that will be at a premium in a limited nuclear war. Self-reliance cannot

[2] Omar N. Bradley, *A Soldier's Story* (New York: Holt, 1951), p. 551.

be improvised. It exists in the American officer corps because it is drawn from a society in which individual initiative has traditionally been encouraged. By the same token, these qualities will be difficult to realize in the Soviet armed forces because nowhere in Soviet society can models for them be found. Where everything is done according to plan, there may be a tendency to reduce even initiative to stereotype. It is no wonder that Soviet propaganda has been insistent on two themes: there is "no such thing" as limited nuclear war, and "ban the bomb." Both themes, if accepted, deprive us of flexibility and undermine the basis of the most effective United States strategy.

It may be objected that if a strategy of limited nuclear war is to our advantage it must be to the Soviet disadvantage, and the Kremlin will therefore seek to escape it by resorting to all-out war. But the fact that the Soviet leadership may stand to lose from a limited nuclear war does not mean that it could profit from all-out war. On the contrary, if our retaliatory force is kept at a proper level and our diplomacy shows ways out of a military impasse short of unconditional surrender, we should always be able to make all-out war seem an unattractive course.

What about nuclear weapons in the hands of what are now secondary powers? Within a decade the diffusion of nuclear technology through its peaceful uses will give many powers the wherewithal to manufacture nuclear weapons. And to the extent that nuclear weapons are thought to confer an advantage, they may be used regardless of what strategy we propose to follow. We, therefore, have no choice but to base our strategy on the assumption that a war between nuclear powers, even of the second rank, *may* involve the use of nuclear weapons.

It is important to distinguish, however, between the possession of nuclear weapons and their strategic effectiveness. By themselves, nuclear weapons have a considerable nuisance value. But unless they are coupled with sophisticated delivery means, highly complex communication systems, and appropriate tactics, it will be difficult to utilize them effectively. Unless the whole military establishment is geared to nuclear tactics, nuclear war becomes a highly dangerous adventure. What has been said above about Communist China would be even more true in many other underdeveloped regions. The only area where nuclear weapons would represent a significant increase in real strength is Western Europe, where technical skill is coupled with the industrial resources to maintain, with United States assistance, a diversified capability. In the rest of the world it will be difficult for the foreseeable future to provide either the equipment or the training required for sustained nuclear war.

For some time to come the underdeveloped regions will lack the fissionable material and the industrial base to bring about a capability for limited nuclear war and they will be even less able to create a meaningful capability for all-out war. A few nuclear weapons will not be strategically significant against a well-equipped enemy trained for nuclear war. They may merely serve to emphasize further the imbalance between weapons, training, and industrial potential which already besets the military establishments of so many countries.

The possession of nuclear weapons by our European allies, on the other hand, will improve the over-all position of the free world. It will make an attack by the Soviet Union on Western Europe an increasingly hazardous undertaking and it may improve the ability of the free world to hold other areas around the Soviet periphery. On balance, therefore, the diffusion of nuclear weapons technology will be to our net strategic advantage.

This is not to say that we should be complacent about the prospect of a world armed with nuclear weapons. The possession of nuclear weapons will create tense situations among the secondary powers themselves, and acts of desperation against stronger states, while militarily inconclusive, may set off a cycle of violence difficult to control. Of these dangers we shall say more later, but meanwhile it can be asserted that the Soviet Union probably has more to lose from the spread of nuclear technology than does the Western world.

I V

The discussion in this chapter has led to these conclusions: War between nuclear powers has to be planned on the assumption that it is likely to be a nuclear war. Nuclear war should be fought as something less than an all-out war. Limited nuclear war represents our most effective strategy against nuclear powers or against a major power which is capable of substituting manpower for technology.

Such a strategy is not simple or easy to contemplate. It requires an ability to harmonize political, psychological, and military factors. It presupposes a careful consideration of the objectives appropriate for a limited war and of the weapons systems which have a sufficient degree of discrimination so that limited war does not merge insensibly into an all-out holocaust.

Nor should a policy of limited nuclear war be conceived as a means to enable us to reduce our readiness for all-out war. None of the measures described in this chapter is possible without a substantial retaliatory force; it is the fear of thermonuclear devastation which sets the bounds of limited war. It may be argued that a strategy based on what Sir Winston Churchill called a balance of terror is inherently tenuous, and that one side or the other will find the temptation to resort to all-out war irresistible. In the past, so this argument goes, new discoveries often have been greeted with prophecies of impending doom or assertions that they made war impossible, and in every case they were nevertheless used to the limit of their effectiveness.

It cannot be denied, of course, that many inventions have been taken to augur the end of war and have instead added to the horror of war. Yet it is equally true that no discovery has ever added so much destructive power so suddenly as have nuclear weapons. Gunpowder, for example, was introduced gradually over a period of centuries. In the early sixteenth century—more than a hundred years after it became widely known—Machiavelli could still argue that it was less efficient than the then "traditional" armaments. As late as 1825, the British War Office could still seriously discuss a proposal to reintroduce the crossbow to replace the musket. Nuclear weapons, on the other hand, represent an increase in the scale of destructiveness which cannot be misunderstood.

The employment of shrapnel or dum-dum bullets, despite international prohibitions against their use, demonstrated that treaties will not restrain antagonists engaged in a mortal struggle unless the international agreements are reinforced by considerations of self-interest. These weapons were used because one side or the other foresaw a net advantage. The essence of the nuclear era, on the other hand, is that neither side can gain from all-out war unless one side achieves a clear superiority in its capacity to conduct an all-out war. If we make sure that this does not happen, then all-out war can be rationally employed only to escape unconditional surrender.

The strategy described in this and the preceding chapters must be considered not against the background of nostalgia for a more tranquil past, but against the perils of an all-out thermonuclear catastrophe. To be sure, this strategy offers no final solutions, and stalemates are more likely than complete victory. But in many areas now overshadowed by the Soviet threat the possibility of a stalemate represents a strategic advance. Moreover, both the risks and the frustrations of limited nuclear war are the penalties we pay for living in the nuclear period, penalties which we consciously accepted when we permitted our atomic monopoly to be broken without having first achieved a workable system of international control.

The American strategic problem can, therefore, be summed up in these propositions:

1. Thermonuclear war must be avoided except as a last resort.

2. A power possessing thermonuclear weapons is not likely to accept unconditional surrender without employing them, and no nation is likely to risk thermonuclear destruction except to the extent that it believes its survival to be directly threatened.

3. It is the task of our diplomacy to make clear that we do not aim for unconditional surrender, to create a framework within which the question of national survival is not involved in every issue. But equally, we must leave no doubt about our determination to achieve intermediary objectives and to resist by force any Soviet military move.

4. Since diplomacy which is not related to a plausible employment of force is sterile, it must be the task of our military policy to develop a doctrine and a capability for the graduated employment of force.

5. Since a policy of limited war cannot be implemented except behind the shield of a capability for all-out war, we must retain a retaliatory force sufficiently powerful and well protected so that by no calculation can an aggressor discern any benefit in resorting to all-out war.

Nevertheless, it would be risky to rely too much on the self-evidence of the horrors of nuclear war. Limited nuclear war is impossible unless our diplomacy succeeds in conveying our intentions to the other side. It may even have to make up for any lack of imagination on the part of the Soviet leaders by indicating to them our understanding of the nature and the limits of nuclear war. To be sure, such a program will not deter an opponent determined to force a final showdown. No diplomatic program can be a substitute for an adequate retaliatory power. But diplomacy can help to avoid miscalculation of our intentions or misunderstanding of the nature of nuclear warfare. This is all the more important because, whatever the possibilities of limited nuclear war, they cannot be improvised under the pressure of events. In seeking to avoid the horrors of all-out war by outlining an alternative, in developing a concept of limitation that combines firmness with moderation, diplomacy can once more establish a relationship with force, even in the nuclear age.

CHAPTER EIGHT

Diplomacy, Disarmament, and the Limitation of War

I

It may seem wholly unreasonable to ask that diplomacy rescue mankind from the horrors of a thermonuclear holocaust. How can there be an agreement on the limitation of war when all negotiations with the Kremlin have proved that the two sides have rarely been able to agree even on what constitutes a reasonable demand? As we have seen, almost everything conspires today against the subtle negotiation, the artful compromise, of classical diplomacy. Diplomacy, the art of settling disputes by negotiation, presupposes that all the major powers accept a framework which recognizes the necessity of both change and continued harmony. But negotiations can be successful only if all parties accept some common standard transcending their disputes. They must agree either that the maintenance of the international system is more important than their disagreements or that the consequences of not making concessions will be more serious than those of doing so, or both. In the past, settlements have come about because the realization of the advantage of harmony was combined with the fear of the consequences of proving obdurate. The greater the interest of the major powers in maintaining good relations, the less necessary it has been to resort to force or the threat of force.

The result has been that diplomacy has proved most ef-

fective when disagreements did not concern issues considered vital by the contenders. No nation can negotiate about
its survival and no nation will give up conditions which it
considers essential to its survival for the sake of harmony.
An international order that does not protect the vital interests of a particular power, as it conceives them, will not
seem to that power worth preserving, and its relations with
the remainder of the international community will become
revolutionary. And wherever there appears a revolutionary
power or group of powers, the emphasis of diplomacy
changes. The need for harmony will no longer seem a sufficient motive for the settlement of disputes. Vital interests
will constantly seem in conflict, and negotiations will become increasingly futile. Disagreements tend to be pushed
to their logical extreme, and relations come to be based on
force or the threat of force.

Contemporary diplomacy is taking place in unprece-
dented circumstances. Rarely has there been less common
ground among the major powers, but never has recourse to
force been more inhibited. This brings about a dual frustration: with respect to power and with respect to diplomacy. Were weapons technology stable, the fear of war
might be counted on to counterbalance the antagonisms of
a revolutionary period. But weapons systems are changing
at an ever accelerating rate, and every major power believes that its survival may be at the mercy of a technological break-through by its opponent. The inhibitions with
respect to the use of force, therefore, do not end the revolutionary contest between us and the Soviet bloc; they
transform it into an armaments race.

At the same time the more absolute the sanctions of modern war, the more extreme have been the demands made
on diplomacy. The fear of total war has had as its counterpart the call for total diplomacy. Diplomacy is asked to
solve two major concurrent revolutions, that of the Soviet
bloc and that of the newly independent states, at a moment when many of the pressures traditionally available to
it have lost their potency. In a situation which has never
been more tense, diplomacy has never had fewer tools at

its disposal. It is said that, force having abdicated, diplomacy must take over. But diplomacy may be handicapped in taking over precisely because force has abdicated.

It is, therefore, asking too much of diplomacy that it should *resolve* present-day conflicts. Diplomacy can provide a forum for the settlement of disputes which have become unprofitable for both sides. It can keep open channels for information. Most importantly, it can enable each side to convey its intentions to the other.

For the primary bridge between the two sides is a common fear. The Soviet bloc and the free world may not agree on any positive goals but they have at least one interest in common: given the horror of thermonuclear weapons, neither side can be interested in an all-out war. In these circumstances, all-out war is more likely to arise out of a misunderstanding of the opponent's intentions than out of conviction in an ability to destroy the opponent at acceptable cost. To prevent such miscalculation or misinterpretation of our intentions by the Soviet Union should be a principal task of our diplomacy. It must make sure that the other side obtains the information it requires to make correct decisions; it must convey what we understand by limited war and to some extent how we propose to conduct it.

The task will not be easy. The same suspicions which cause our arguments to lack persuasion in diplomatic conferences may lead the Soviets to mistrust an effort to convey our intentions with respect to military strategy. Nevertheless, the catastrophe of all-out war is so frightful that it should provide a strong incentive for the Soviet leaders at least to test the sincerity of American professions. If diplomacy cannot give effect to the one interest both sides have overwhelmingly in common—the avoidance of an all-out holocaust—it is futile to expect that it will settle the more fundamental issues of ideological conflict and revolutionary upheaval.

II

Unfortunately, diplomacy has addressed itself to the problem of eliminating the use of nuclear weapons almost to the exclusion of measures to mitigate their consequences. It is unfortunate, not because the goal is undesirable but because disarmament negotiations as heretofore conceived may have addressed themselves to the most insoluble problem. Just as our military policy has been preoccupied with all-out war so our diplomacy has been primarily concerned with all-out peace. In their quest for total remedies, both our diplomacy and our military policy have inhibited the consideration of more attainable goals: an understanding of some principles of war limitation which may not prevent war but which could keep any conflict that does break out from assuming the most catastrophic form.

The notion that armaments are the cause rather than the reflection of conflict is not new. It has been the basis of schemes of disarmament throughout history; it was the rationale for all the disarmament conferences in the Twenties and Thirties. Nevertheless it is open to serious doubt. Between the Congress of Vienna and the unification of Germany, the standing armies were very small because the outstanding disputes did not involve, or were not thought to involve, matters of life and death. After 1871 there started an armaments race which has not ended to this day. Between the unification of Germany and World War I Europe was torn by two schisms which, to the powers concerned, seemed to involve "vital" interests: that between France and Germany over Alsace-Lorraine and that between the Austro-Hungarian Empire and Russia over the fate of the Balkans. After the First World War the rebellion of Germany and the U.S.S.R. against the Treaty of Versailles and the rise of the dictatorships created a climate of insecurity which doomed all disarmament efforts to futility. And after the Second World War the intransigence of the Soviet bloc forced the free world to restore a measure of its strength even after it had disarmed unilaterally almost to the point of impotence.

There is little indication that the level of armaments itself produces tension. Great Britain has a strategic air force and a nuclear stockpile capable of inflicting serious, although perhaps not fatal, damage on the United States. But this fact has caused no uneasiness in the United States and no increase in our defense effort. Conversely, Great Britain did not seek to forestall the development by the United States of a navy superior to its own—something it had fought innumerable wars to prevent in the case of other powers. This was because the "vital interests" of both powers are in sufficient harmony so that they can have a large measure of confidence in each other's intentions. Each can afford to permit the other to develop a weapons system capable of imperiling its security and perhaps even its survival because it knows that this capability will not be so used.

To be sure, the degree of confidence between the United States and Great Britain is exceptional. More usually, powers are conscious of some clashing "vital interests." As a result, a rise in the level of armaments of one major power may set in motion a vicious circle. Increased military preparedness serves as a warning of an increased willingness to run risks. The other powers can escape the pressure implicit in a stepped-up defense effort only by making concessions (a dangerous course, for it may whet appetites and establish a method for settling future disputes) or by entering the armaments race themselves. But while the vicious circle of an armaments race is plain, it is not nearly so obvious that it can be ended by an international convention. If disagreements on specific issues had been tractable, the armaments race would never have started. Since negotiations on outstanding disputes have proved unavailing, it is improbable that a disarmament scheme acceptable to all parties can be negotiated.

A general disarmament scheme, to be successful, must deprive each party of the ability to inflict a catastrophic blow on the other; at the very least it must not give an advantage to either side. A meaningful agreement is, therefore, almost impossible under present circumstances. For the same mistrust which produced the armaments race will reduce confidence in any agreement that may be negotiated and it will color the proposals which may be advanced. Each side will seek to deprive the other of the capability it fears most as a *prelude* to negotiations, while keeping its most effective weapon under its control until the last moment. Thus, the phasing of disarmament has proved almost as difficult a matter to negotiate as the manner of it. During our atomic monopoly, the Soviet Union insisted that the outlawing of nuclear weapons precede any negotiations on disarmament, while we in turn refused to discuss surrendering our atomic stockpile until an airtight control machinery had first been put into operation. With the growth of the Soviet nuclear stockpile, both sides have continued to strive to neutralize the other's strongest weapon. The Soviet Union has attempted to expel our troops and particularly our air bases from Eurasia. We have striven for means to neutralize the Soviet ground strength. Each side wishes to protect itself against the consequences of the other's bad faith; each side, in short, brings to the disarmament negotiations the precise attitude which caused the armaments race in the first place.

A reduction of forces is all the more difficult to negotiate because it seeks to compare incommensurables. What is the relation between the Soviet ability to overrun Eurasia and American air and sea power? If the United States weakens its Strategic Air Command, it would take years before it could be reconstituted. If the Soviet Union reduces its ground forces, the strategic impact would be much smaller, and, given the structure of Soviet society, the troops could be reassembled in a matter of weeks. A substantial reduction of Soviet forces would not deprive the Kremlin of its large reserves of trained and rapidly mobilizable manpower. That such thoughts were not far from Soviet minds is shown by Marshal Georgi Zhukov's speech to the Twentieth Party Congress in February 1956, explaining the Soviet arms reduction: "As a result of the reduction of the armed forces, a certain proportion of the draft group will not enter the forces. We must take steps to see that the young people who are released from the draft can receive, even outside the army, the military training necessary to fulfill their duty to defend the homeland."[1]

In such circumstances a reduction in forces would not contribute a great deal to a lessening of tensions. Even if a scale of comparison between different weapons systems could be agreed upon it would still not remove the real security problem: the increasingly rapid rate of technological change.

Disarmament plans of the past were based on a reasonably stable weapons technology. Once the proposed reduction of forces was implemented, strategic relationships remained fairly constant. But under present conditions, the real armaments race is in the laboratories. No reduction of forces, however scrupulously carried out, could protect the powers against a technological break-through. Even were strategic striking forces kept at fixed levels and rigidly controlled, an advance in air defense sufficient to contain the opposing retaliatory force would upset the strategic balance completely. The knowledge by each side that the other is working on ever more fearful means of destruction or on means of attacking with impunity would cause current international relations to be carried on in an atmosphere of tenseness and imminent catastrophe, whatever agreements may be concluded about reduction of forces.

In addition to the technological problems, the structure of international relations will prevent a reduction of forces from going beyond a certain point. None of the major powers, certainly not the U.S.S.R., will accept a disarmament scheme which impairs its relative position vis-à-vis secondary states. Nothing is likely to induce the U.S.S.R. to accept a level of armaments which reduces its ability to control the satellites or to play a major role in contiguous areas such as the Middle East. But forces sufficient to accomplish this task are also sufficient to imperil all the peripheral pow-

[1] *Current Digest of the Soviet Press*, v. 8 (April 18, 1956), p. 37.

ers of Eurasia. A reduction of forces which does not affect the relative Soviet position vis-à-vis the secondary powers will not diminish the basic security problem of the non-Soviet world.

Nor is it a foregone conclusion that a reduction of forces would inevitably be beneficial. A reduction of nuclear stockpiles might well increase the tenseness of international relationships. Given the diffusion of nuclear technology, a reduction of stockpiles would be almost impossible to verify. Thus each power would probably seek to keep back part of its stockpile to protect itself against the possibility that its opponent might do so. An attempt to reduce nuclear stockpiles, far from removing existing insecurity, may merely serve to feed suspicions.

Moreover, to the extent that nuclear stockpiles are in fact reduced, any war that does break out is likely to assume the most catastrophic form. The technical possibility of limiting nuclear war resides in the plentifulness of nuclear materials. This makes it possible to conceive of a strategy which emphasizes a discriminating use of modern weapons and to utilize explosives of lesser power which, from a technical point of view, are really "inefficient" high-yield weapons. But if the quantity of weapons decreases, a premium will be placed on engineering them to achieve maximum destructiveness and to use them on the largest targets. The horrors of nuclear war are not likely to be avoided by a reduction of nuclear armaments.

III

Because a reduction of forces has proved so nearly impossible to negotiate and because its rewards would be so questionable even if achieved, the major emphasis of disarmament efforts has turned to the problems of inspection and control and to the prevention of surprise attack. However, for a variety of reasons, every inspection scheme that has proved acceptable to the free world has been objectionable to the U.S.S.R. As a result, the negotiations about control and inspection have produced the same vicious circle as the efforts to bring about a reduction in armaments: were it possible to agree on an inspection and control machinery, it would also be possible to settle some of the disputes which have given rise to existing tensions. As long as specific issues prove obdurate, there is little hope in an over-all control plan.

In addition to the psychological and political problems, the technological race makes it difficult to negotiate a control plan. For the rate of change of technology has outstripped the pace of diplomatic negotiations, so that control plans change their meaning while they are being debated. The control scheme of the first United States disarmament proposal (the Baruch plan) assumed that an international authority with powers of inspection and in control of mining, processing, and producing fissionable materials would be able to eliminate nuclear weapons from the arsenals of the powers. The United States contribution was to be the destruction of our nuclear stockpile as the last stage of the process of disarmament. Even this scheme would not have been "foolproof." Within the United States atomic energy program, with every incentive to achieve an accurate accounting and no motive for evasion, the normal "slippage" in the handling of fissionable materials due to error and mechanical problems of handling is several per cent. A nation determined on evasion could easily multiply this percentage without being in obvious violation of international agreements and utilize the "saved" slippage slowly to build up a nuclear stockpile of its own. Their awareness of this possibility would in turn give other powers a motive for evasion.

Nevertheless, at the early stages of the atomic energy program the stockpiles were still so small and the possibility of building them up to substantial proportions through evasions was so slight that an inspection program would have contributed materially to reducing the danger of nuclear war. Any power determined to produce nuclear weapons would have had to break existing agreements flagrantly and thereby bring down on itself either the international enforcement machinery or war with the United

States. But in the age of nuclear plenty, the control machinery envisaged by the Baruch plan would prove futile as a means to eliminate stockpiles. So many nuclear weapons of so many different sizes have been produced and they are so easy to conceal that not even the most elaborate inspection machinery could account for all of them. Control machinery cannot effectively prevent the accumulation of nuclear weapons at this stage of their development, even assuming the desirability of doing so.

And so it is with each new technological discovery. In the very early stages of development, a scrupulous control system may forestall its being added to the weapons arsenal. But by the time disarmament negotiations have run their tortuous course, the weapon will have become so sophisticated and the production of it will have reached such proportions that control machinery may magnify rather than reduce the existing insecurity: it may compound the fear of surprise attack with fear of the violation of the agreement by the other side.

The inconclusiveness of negotiations about inspection machinery reflects also the difficulty of controlling the development of new weapons. And without such control disarmament schemes will be at the mercy of a technological break-through. Since each scientific discovery opens the way to innumerable other advances, it is next to impossible to define a meaningful point to "cut off" weapons development. At the beginning of the atomic age, a strict inspection system might have succeeded in stopping the elaboration of nuclear weapons. By 1952 it might still have been possible to "control" the development of thermonuclear weapons, albeit with great difficulty. For the hydrogen bomb developed so naturally out of research on nuclear weapons that the definition of a meaningful dividing line would have been exceedingly complicated. By 1957 the production of thermonuclear devices had so far outstripped any possible control machinery that the emphasis of disarmament negotiations turned from eliminating stockpiles to methods of restraining their use. And with the diffusion of nuclear technology among other powers, effective control of the development of nuclear weapons even by smaller states will be almost out of the question.

Moreover, once a weapon is developed its applications are elaborated until ever wider realms of strategy become dependent on it. A nation may be willing to forego the offensive uses of nuclear weapons but it will be most reluctant to give up its defensive applications in, for example, the form of antiaircraft or antimissile devices. But in advanced stages of their elaboration weapons find a dual purpose: the launching site for antiaircraft missiles can be used as well for attacking ground targets; a nuclear weapon launched from a plane against enemy bombers will be equally effective against enemy supply centers. Thus weapons can be kept from being added to stockpiles only at their inception, when their implications are least understood. By the time their potential is realized, the possibility of preventing their addition to existing arsenals by means of inspection or control has usually disappeared. Hence it may already be too late to control missiles, many of which have entered production with others soon to follow.

IV

The difficulty of devising effective machinery to control the development of ever more destructive weapons has caused most disarmament negotiations since 1955 to concern themselves with means to prevent surprise attack. Since one of the causes for present tensions is the insecurity caused by the fear of imminent catastrophe, so the argument goes, an inspection system which would reduce the danger of surprise attack would also remove some of the urgency from international relationships. This reasoning produced President Eisenhower's proposal at the Geneva summit conference, in July 1955, to exchange military blueprints with the Soviet Union and to permit aerial reconnaissance of each other's territories. The principle of inspection to prevent surprise attack has been accepted in the Soviet counterproposal for stationing ground observers at strategic points in the territory of the other nations.

It cannot be denied that the danger of surprise attack contributes to the tensions of the nuclear age even if it does not cause them. It is less clear, however, that inspection schemes so far proposed would add a great deal to existing warning methods and intelligence information or that they would significantly reduce the element of surprise.

The relative ineffectiveness of inspection in preventing surprise in an all-out war is due to the nature of strategic striking forces. Because it cannot afford to be caught on the ground a strategic striking force must be prepared to attack from its training bases at a moment's notice. If properly prepared, it should require no noticeable mobilization to launch its blow. Since "normal" peacetime maneuvers of a strategic striking force should approximate as nearly as possible its behavior in case of emergency, an enemy should not be able to tell whether a given flight is a training mission or a surprise attack until his early-warning line is crossed. Unless most planes are grounded all the time, there is no guarantee that planes on so-called training missions will not be used for a surprise attack.

Even filing flight plans in advance will not eliminate this danger. Given the speed of modern planes, by the time inspectors are aware of a violation of a flight plan and can communicate this information to their government the planes will probably have reached the opposing early-warning lines. If flight plans are cleverly arranged—and every incentive would seem to exist for doing this—it will be very difficult to discover whether a given flight is a move to advanced bases or a prelude to an all-out attack.

Inspection could, of course, be coupled with the grounding of all planes, except perhaps a very small number insufficient to inflict a catastrophic blow. Such a course would be highly dangerous, however. Without constant training it is difficult to maintain the readiness or the morale of the retaliatory force. Since our strategy is more dependent on its strategic striking forces than that of the Soviet Union, the grounding of all planes would be to our disadvantage. Even should we develop a capability for limited war equal to that of the Soviet Union, the grounding of our Strategic

Air Force would stand to benefit our opponent. It would tell him our precise deployment and enable him to concentrate his attack and his defenses against it. To be sure, we would have the same information about the Soviet Long-Range Air Force. But since we concede the first blow, it would be much less useful to us: the Soviet planes presumably will have left their bases by the time we become aware that an attack is imminent.

Even when all planes are grounded, the maximum warning achievable by inspection is the interval between the time when planes leave their bases and the time when they would have been detected by existing warning systems. With the present family of airplanes, an inspection system at best would add perhaps three hours' warning to the side which is being attacked. To be sure, three hours' additional warning is not negligible; it may indeed spell the difference between survival and catastrophe. But since the victim of aggression cannot be certain what the apparent violation of inspection signifies, he may have difficulty in utilizing the additional warning effectively. And if inspection is coupled with the grounding of the strategic striking force, the gain in warning time may be outweighed by the aggressor's knowledge of the opponent's deployment.

As the speed of planes is increased the warning time afforded by even a perfect inspection system, correctly interpreted, is progressively reduced. In the age of the Intercontinental Ballistic Missile the maximum warning time, assuming perfect communication between the inspector and his government, would be thirty minutes, the period of time the missile would be in transit. In the age of the missile and the supersonic bomber, even a foolproof inspection system will tell the powers only what they already know: that the opponent possesses the capability of launching a devastating attack at a moment's notice and with a minimum of warning.

The proposals for inspection as a bar to surprise attack in fact reflect the thinking of a period when forces-in-being could not be decisive and when their power and speed were of a much lower order. As long as the forces-in-being were relatively cumbersome and had to be concentrated before an attack could be launched, the warning afforded by an inspection system might have been strategically significant. As late as 1946, had the Baruch plan been accepted, a nation determined on nuclear war would have had to wait several months or even years after a violation until its stockpiles had been built up to respectable levels. The existence of a control system in such conditions afforded a breathing spell to all powers. With the power and speed of current weapons, however, even an airtight inspection system would not supply such guarantees. When wars can be fought by the forces-in-being and when striking forces are designed to be able to attack with no overt preparation, warning can be attained under optimum conditions only for the time the delivery vehicles, whether planes or missiles, are in transit. At present this is a maximum of ten hours, a substantial proportion of which is already under surveillance by existing warning methods.

The extreme readiness of the forces-in-being also reduces the value of aerial reconnaissance. Since flying time from the interior of Russia to our Early Warning Line is less than five hours with the present family of airplanes, air bases of the Soviet Long-Range Air Force would have to be photographed at least every five hours. If the reconnaissance occurred at longer intervals, the Early Warning Line would provide a better indication of a surprise attack because an attack launched immediately after an aerial inspection would reach our Early Warning Line before the next reconnaissance sortie discovered that the opposing force had left its base. As the speed of planes increases, the frequency of reconnaissance missions would have to be increased so that, in practice, reconnaissance planes would probably have to hover over enemy airfields almost constantly. And in the missile age aerial reconnaissance would be fortunate if it could discover launching sites: it would not be able to furnish an indication of impending attack.

It is, therefore, difficult to imagine that present vigilance could be reduced or that insecurity would be removed by any inspection system now in prospect. The machinery required would be so formidable and the benefits relatively so trivial that an inspection system may actually have pernicious consequences. It may give a misleading impression of security and, therefore, tempt us to relax our preparedness. More likely, given the prevailing distrust, it will induce both sides to place their striking forces in an even greater state of readiness in order to compensate for the loss of secrecy by a demonstration of power.

Indeed, unless designed with extraordinary care, a system of inspection may well make a tense situation even more explosive. The value of an inspection system depends not only on the collection but also on the interpretation of facts. But the information produced by inspection is of necessity fragmentary and it is likely to be most difficult to obtain when it is most needed, when international tensions are at their height. On the other hand, the only meaningful reaction to an apparent violation of the inspection system is to launch an immediate retaliatory attack, because negotiations or protests could not begin to be effective before the enemy force has reached its targets. The knowledge that all-out war is the sanction for seeming violations may well add to the tenseness of relationships. Instead of reducing the danger of all-out war, inspection systems may make more likely a showdown caused by a misunderstanding of the opponent's intentions.

V

The technical complexity of inspection and its futility in the present climate of distrust has induced some thoughtful individuals, appalled at the prospect of nuclear war, to advocate an international disarmament authority as the only solution. As long as both sides possess thermonuclear weapons and the means to deliver them, it is argued, a vicious spiral of constantly growing insecurity is inevitable. The only solution, this school of thought maintains, is the surrender of all strategic weapons to a world authority which would be the sole agency to possess heavy armaments and the means for delivering them. The disarmament executive should be composed of minor powers which are not part of the East-West struggle. With a preponderance of force, it could play the role of a world policeman and enforce peace if necessary. The United Nations Emergency Force for Egypt was greeted in some quarters as the forerunner of such an international agency.

The idea of escaping the tensions of international relations by an analogy to domestic police powers has come up repeatedly in the past and usually at periods when international schisms made it least realizable. It is true, as the advocates of the plan of world government contend, that the system of sovereign states produces international tensions because a sovereign will can be ultimately controlled only by superior force. But it is hardly realistic to expect sovereign nations, whose failure to agree on issues of much less importance has brought about the armaments race, to be able to agree on giving up their sovereignty. History offers few examples of sovereign states surrendering their sovereignty except to outside compulsion. To be sure, the lessons of history are no more conclusive than the unparalleled destructiveness of modern weapons; still it is difficult to imagine any motive which could induce the Soviet Union to give up its thermonuclear stockpile to an international body. And the reaction of the United States Congress will hardly be more hospitable.

The various proposals for a world authority would, therefore, scarcely warrant extensive consideration were they not such an excellent illustration of the prevailing notion that the United Nations somehow has a reality beyond that of the powers comprising it. It is a symptom of our legalistic bias that so many consider a legal entity, the United Nations, as somehow transcending the collective will of its members. For as long as the United Nations is composed of sovereign states it will reflect the precise rivalries that animate these powers outside that organization. To be sure, the United Nations offers a convenient forum for the settlement of disputes and it can give symbolic expression to the consensus of world opinion on particular issues. But the gap between the symbolic acts of the United Nations and its willingness to run substantive risks is inherent in its structure. The delegates represent not a popular constituency but sovereign governments and they vote not according to their convictions but in pursuance of the instructions they receive. The effectiveness of the United Nations can be no greater than the willingness of its component governments to run risks. The United Nations Emergency Force would never have entered Egypt had not both parties to the dispute accepted it and had not both parties sought a device to liquidate military operations. The United Nations Emergency Force did not cause the cessation of the war; rather it ratified a decision already made. For this reason it does not offer a particularly hopeful model for what will be the real security problem of our period: the growing Soviet power coupled with a refusal to yield to anything except superior force.

The argument that a supranational authority composed of neutral minor powers will be able to resolve tensions which have proved intractable to direct negotiations and that it can be entrusted with the exclusive custody of weapons capable of encompassing the destruction of humanity reflects two related beliefs: that the nature of aggression is always unambiguous and that weakness somehow guarantees responsibility and perhaps even superior morality. But in the nuclear age, recognizing aggression has proved as complicated as resisting it. Were a supranational disarmament executive charged with enforcing the peace, it is predictable that its major problem would be to define a meaningful concept of aggression. It is significant that in 1957 the United Nations had to give up a prolonged effort to achieve such a definition.

Moreover, it would be difficult to find powers clearly recognized as neutral to act as custodians of the thermonuclear stockpile or with sufficient technical competence to administer it were they so recognized. And the very quality which would make powers acceptable as members of a disarmament authority—their neutrality—will reduce their willingness to run risks. In the face of a dispute between the United States and the U.S.S.R. these states will lack the power to impose their will or the will to use their power.

Nor is it clear why a monopoly of power in the hands of states dependent for equipment, training, and facilities on the two superpowers should bring about stability. It is not at all obvious that weakness guarantees responsibility or that powers which have difficulty playing a role in their own regions will be able to judge global problems with subtlety and discrimination. And this still overlooks the dilemmas of where to store the international stockpile of bombs, and where to locate the bases of the international air force—all of which will become matters of life and death to the nations of the world. In short, there is no escaping from the responsibilities of the thermonuclear age into a supranational authority, for, if all its complicated problems could be negotiated, the substantive issues now dividing the world would be soluble too.

VI

Our disarmament efforts have been directed to the most intractable element of the problems posed by nuclear weapons. By leaving no middle ground between total peace and total war, they require the major atomic powers to stake their survival on the observance of an international agreement in an international order where the breach of agreements has become commonplace and where one of the great power blocs explicitly rejects the observance of agreements if they do not reflect a relation of forces.

A more productive, less absolute, solution might be an endeavor to mitigate the horrors of war. There has been a reluctance to advance such a program, as if the admission that war may occur could itself be a factor in bringing it on, or perhaps because of lack of clarity about the possibilities of limiting war in the nuclear age.

But we have little reason to assume that war will soon be banished from the earth. Even if the good faith of the major protagonists were assured, the possibility of war would remain. The revolution taking place in so many parts of the globe will provide its own impetus; it will create its own tensions, not necessarily sought by any of the major powers. The conflict over the Suez Canal was hardly foreseen by the Western powers and perhaps not even by the Soviet Union. And the Hungarian revolution came as a rude shock to the Kremlin. Both situations resulted in military actions which, with the prevailing strategic doctrines, might easily have turned into all-out war. Similar Soviet moves in East Germany or Poland would be fraught with even more serious danger. In turn, the absence of any generally understood limits to war undermines the willingness to resist Soviet pressures. A gap is thus opened between the quest for total peace and the military doctrine of total war, a gap within which the Soviet Union can operate with relative impunity.

A program to mitigate the horrors of war would have the advantage of focusing thinking on things to accomplish rather than on those which should be prohibited. It would relate disarmament to strategy and thus help to bridge the gap between force and diplomacy. It would overcome a situation in which the Soviet leaders can conduct atomic blackmail in the guise of disarmament negotiations and transform conferences into a fertile ground for paralyzing the will to resist by evoking the most fearful consequences of such a course. Above all, a program to mitigate the horrors of war could be used to clarify, in so far as diplomacy is able, the intentions of the opposing sides and it may therefore prevent the catastrophe of an all-out war caused by miscalculation. Even a unilateral declaration of what we understand by limited war would accomplish a great deal, because it would provide a strong incentive to the other side to test its feasibility.

It has been argued that the deliberate ambiguity of our present position, which refuses to define what we understand by limited war or under what circumstances we might fight it, is in itself a deterrent because the enemy can never be certain that military action on his part may not unleash all-out war. But if we wish to pose the maximum deterrent, an explicit declaration of massive retaliation would seem far more advantageous. The purpose of our ambiguity is to combine the advantage of two incompatible courses: to pose the threat of all-out war for purposes of deterrence, but to keep open the possibility of a less catastrophic strategy should deterrence fail. If the ambiguity is to serve any purpose, however, it may have precisely the contrary effect; it may give rise to the notion that we do not intend to resist at all and thus encourage aggression. Or it may cause an aggressor to interpret resistance which we intend to localize as a prelude to all-out war. Instead of strengthening the deterrent and giving scope for a non-catastrophic strategy, the deliberate ambiguity of our position may weaken the deterrent and bring on the most catastrophic kind of war.

Moreover, a diplomatic program designed to convey our understanding of the nature of limited war to the other side may be important because it is not certain that the Soviet leadership has fully analyzed all the options of the nuclear period. In so far as the repeated Soviet denials of the possibility of limited nuclear war represent a real conviction and not simply a form of psychological warfare, an energetic diplomacy addressed to the problem of war limitation can compensate for the lack of imagination on the part of the Soviet General Staff.

Before we can convey our conception of practical limitations to the other side, however, we have to admit their possibility to ourselves and we have to be clear in our own mind about their nature. And at present, as we have seen, no such clarity exists, either among the military or the political leaders. Our services are operating on the basis of partially overlapping, partly inconsistent doctrines, some of which deny the possibility of limited war while others define it so variously that we can hardly be said to possess the capability for limited war, either conceptually or physically.

If wars are to be kept limited, one of our tasks will be to find ways to slow down the tempo of modern war, lest the rapidity with which operations succeed each other prevent the establishment of a relation between political and military objectives. If this relationship is lost, any war is likely to grow by imperceptible stages into an all-out effort. The goal of war can no longer be military victory, strictly speaking, but the attainment of certain specific political conditions which are fully understood by the opponent. A limited war between major powers can remain limited only if at some point one of the protagonists prefers a limited defeat to an additional investment of resources or if both sides are willing to settle for a stalemate in preference to an assumption of increased risk. Since in either case the protagonists retain the *physical* resources to increase their commitment, the ability to conduct a limited war successfully depends on the skill with which we can devise proposals for a settlement that appears to the enemy more favorable than continuation of the war.

For this reason, limited war cannot be conceived as a small, all-out war with a series of uninterrupted blows prepared in secrecy until the opponent's will is broken. On the contrary, it is important to develop a concept of military operations conducted in phases which permit an assessment of the risks and possibilities for settlement at each stage before recourse is had to the next phase of operations. Paradoxical as it may seem in the jet age, strategic doctrine should address itself to the problem of slowing down, if not the pace of military operations, at least the rapidity with which they succeed each other. We must never lose sight of the fact that our purpose is to affect the will of the enemy, not to destroy him, and that war can be limited only by presenting the enemy with an unfavorable calculus of risks. This requires pause for calculation. In so far as possible, every campaign should be conceived as a series of self-contained phases, each of which implies a political objective, and with a sufficient interval between them to permit the application of political and psychological pressures.

Therefore too it will be necessary to give up the notion that direct diplomatic contact ceases when military operations begin. Rather, direct contact will be more than ever necessary to ensure that both sides possess the correct information about the consequences of expanding a war and to be able to present formulas for a political settlement. To the extent that diplomacy can offer alternatives to expanding a conflict, it may deter the enemy from running greater risks. To the extent that military operations can be conducted in stages, so that a sequence of events is approximately concluded before the next commitment is made, it will give an opportunity for evaluation of the circumstances which made a settlement advisable. Not the least of the paradoxes of the nuclear age may be that lack of secrecy may actually assist in the achievement of military objectives and that, in a period of the most advanced technology, battles will approach the stylized contests of the feudal period, which served as much as a test of will as a trial of strength.

If our military staffs could become clear about a doctrine of limited war, we could then use the disarmament negotiations to seek a measure of acceptance of it by the other side. It would not be necessary that such a concept be embodied in an international treaty or even that the Soviet Government formally adhere to it. There should be no illusions, in fact, about the ease with which the Soviets might be induced to forego the advantages of atomic blackmail. The primary purpose of such a program would be to convey our intentions to the Soviet bloc and to encourage it likewise to consider a limitation of war in its own self-interest. Limited war is possible only to the extent that our military policy leaves no doubt that all-out war would mean disaster for the Soviet bloc.

The previous analysis has shown that with a doctrine of limited war many of the long-cherished notions of traditional warfare have to be modified. These include the principle that wars can be won only by dominating the airspace completely. Since an attempt to deprive an enemy of his retaliatory force would inevitably bring on all-out war, the minimum condition of limited war will be the immunity of the opposing strategic striking forces. Another concept which, as we have seen, will have to be modified is the elimination of enemy communication and industrial centers, a goal which was meaningful only so long as the major movement of armies was effected by road or rail. Finally, in a war which will be largely fought by the forces-in-being, the destruction of industrial potential will play a much smaller role than in the past.

Thus it is possible to visualize limitations, at least as to targets and the size of weapons used. We might propose that neither bases of the opposing strategic air forces nor towns above a certain size would be attacked, provided that these bases were not used to support tactical operations and that the towns did not contain military installations useful against armed forces. Such a proposal could be combined with the control schemes of the general disarmament proposals. For example, each side could be required to list its strategic air bases, which would then be immune from attack. It would be helpful, although not essential, that inspectors be admitted to all these bases. No air base within a stated distance of the initial demarcation line, say five hundred miles, could purchase immunity by being declared strategic save by admitting inspectors who would verify that it was not being used for tactical purposes.

Again, all cities within five hundred miles of the battle zone would be immune from nuclear attack if they were declared "open" and if their status was certified by inspectors (although the latter condition is not absolutely essential). An open city would be one which did not contain any installations that could be used against military forces, such as air bases or missile-launching sites. The term "military installation" should be defined literally and not extended to include industrial plants. Cities located at a greater distance than five hundred miles from the battle zone would be immune altogether, whatever installations they contained. The inspectors might consist of a commission of neutrals; it would be preferable if they were experts of the other side, because this would give their reports a much higher credibility. The inspectors would have their own communications system and would operate even during hostilities.

The elimination of area targets will place an upper limit on the size of weapons it will be profitable to use. Since fall-out becomes a serious problem only in the range of explosive power of 500 kilotons and above, it could be proposed that no weapon larger than 500 kilotons will be employed unless the enemy uses it first. Concurrently, the United States could take advantage of a new development which significantly reduces fall-out by eliminating the last stage of the fission-fusion-fission process. We could propose that all weapons above 500-kiloton explosive power should be "clean" bombs.

Such a program would have several advantages over disarmament schemes designed only to prevent surprise attack. It would accomplish most of the goals sought by the general inspection scheme. It would afford warning, in so far as an inspection system is able to do so. In addition it would also serve as an instrument of war limitation. Moreover, it would be self-policing. Within a relatively small combat zone, it will be much more difficult to hide installations against modern means of detection than in the vastness of a continent. And any significant amount of fall-out would indicate a violation of the agreement to limit the size of weapons employed.

Because it is self-policing, such a system would work even without inspection. Nevertheless, it would be desirable to couple it with an inspection scheme. The objection to inspection as a bar to all-out surprise attack is not that inspection is incapable of producing the required information, but that the information it produces does not address itself to the basic security problem. Given the high state of readiness of strategic striking forces, their increasing speed and constantly growing dispersion as the missile age approaches, even a perfect inspection system will not add significantly to the existing warning time. With respect to all-out war, inspection either tells the opposing powers what they already know or it produces information too late to be helpful. In limited war, by contrast, inspection supplies the precise information required to determine whether the opponent is carrying out his side of the bargain. The information will be useful because, at best, the enemy will gain a tactical advantage which can be overcome by re-taliation.

Moreover, in all-out war the aggressor, having already staked his national existence on his decision to launch an all-out surprise attack, will have no incentive to make the inspection system work. In a limited war, on the other hand, the aggressor will be anxious to avoid all-out war; other-wise he would not be fighting a limited war in the first place. He will, therefore, have a strong motive to keep the opponent correctly informed of his adherence to the rules. Given this attitude, both sides will be disposed to overlook occasional violations, or at least to refrain from drawing the most drastic conclusions until the opponent's intentions have been further tested.

Another advantage of a system of inspection is that the inspectors could serve also as points of political contact. Thus the mechanics of arms limitation might also bring about the possibility of a rapid settlement should the con-tenders so desire.

It may be objected that such a program as this would in effect neutralize cities and seriously interfere with mili-tary operations. But the neutralization of cities is inherent in modern technology, quite apart from any arms-limita-tion schemes. It would seem to make little difference whether a city is neutralized by the self-restraint of the protagonists, the presence of inspection teams, or the ex-plosion of megaton weapons. As for impairing military op-erations, the handicap would be the same for both sides, and the military will have to accept the fact that, short of a thermonuclear holocaust, purely military decisions are no longer possible.

Other criticisms assert that a program of war limitation assumes a degree of human rationality for which history offers no warranty. But history offers no example for the extraordinary destructiveness of modern weapons either. A program which sought to establish some principles of war limitation in advance of hostilities would seem to make fewer demands on rationality than one which attempted to improvise the rules of war in the confusion of battle.

Still others argue that an attempt to convey our understanding of limited war to our opponent would tell him the exact price of each piece of real estate and therefore weaken the deterrent. If this is true, however, the deliberate ambiguity of our present position is almost equally dangerous, for it makes sense only if we mean to imply that in certain circumstances we *might* resist locally. Ambiguity has certain advantages in making the calculations of an aggressor more difficult. But it should encompass only the range of alternatives one is willing to carry out. Ambiguity which implies courses of action which are not intended to be adopted approaches a strategy of bluff.

Moreover, the notion that deterrence is achieved only by the threat of maximum destruction deserves close scrutiny. It is an understandable outgrowth of our desire to enjoy our existence without interference from the outside world. As a result, aggression has always had for us the quality of an immoral act undertaken for its own sake, and we have come to think of resistance to it more in terms of punishment than in terms of balancing risks.

But usually aggression is caused by the desire to achieve a specific objective. It is not necessary to threaten destruction of the home base of the enemy to inhibit him; it is sufficient to prevent the aggressor from attaining his goal. An aggressor is not likely to launch an attack if he cannot count on a reasonable chance of success. To be sure, it is unwise to inform an aggressor of the precise price he will have to pay for aggression. But we should make certain that we are prepared to pay whatever price we either express or imply. A wise policy cannot rest on a threat that we are afraid to implement.

The United States should, therefore, shift the emphasis of disarmament negotiations to an effort to mitigate the horror of war. Such a course would have the additional advantage of enabling us to make a distinction between Soviet "ban-the-bomb" propaganda and disarmament, and to appeal to the rest of the world with a display of moderation. We should leave no doubt that any aggression by the Communist bloc may be resisted with nuclear weapons but we should make every effort to limit their effect and to spare the civilian population as much as possible. Without damage to our interest, we could announce that Soviet aggression would be resisted with nuclear weapons if necessary; that in resisting we would use weapons of not more than 500 kilotons explosive power unless the enemy used them first; that we would use "clean" bombs with minimal fall-out effects for any larger explosive equivalent, unless the enemy violated the understanding; that we would not attack the enemy retaliatory force or enemy cities located more than a certain distance behind the battle zone or the initial line of demarcation (say, five hundred miles); that within this zone we would not use nuclear weapons against cities declared open and so verified by inspection, the inspectors to remain in the battle zone even during the course of military operations.

We would lose nothing even if we made such an announcement unilaterally, since our strategy for an all-out war is based in any event on permitting the other side to strike the first blow. In case of a local Soviet attack, limited war could be fought according to rules established well in advance. If the war begins with an all-out surprise attack on us, we would still be free to use every weapon in our arsenal. The same would be true if the Soviet leadership sought to threaten our national existence directly, even if by means short of all-out war.

To be sure, it is not likely that the Soviet Government will formally accept such a proposal, because the belief of the non-Soviet world in the inevitable horror of nuclear war is needed for effective atomic blackmail. In order to undermine the will to resist the Soviet leaders have every interest in painting the consequences of war in the most drastic terms. Nevertheless, the Soviet leaders would face a considerable dilemma if we maintained our position in the face of a Soviet rejection and if we reinforced it by periodically publicizing those aspects of our weapons development which stress the more discriminating uses of our power. The horrors of all-out war would provide a powerful incentive to test our sincerity.

The limitation of war described here is impossible, however, without a strategic doctrine adapted to the new role of nuclear weapons. It presupposes an ability to use force with discrimination and to establish political goals in which the question of national survival is not involved in every issue. It also requires a public opinion which has been educated to the realities of the nuclear age. The possibility of total security has ended with the disappearance of our atomic monopoly. Limited war and the diplomacy appropriate to it provide a means to escape from the sterility of the quest for absolute peace, which paralyzes by the vagueness of its hopes, and of the search for absolute victory, which paralyzes by the vastness of its consequences.

CHAPTER NINE

The Impact of Strategy
on Our Allies and
the Uncommitted

I

Nowhere are the dilemmas of the nuclear age more apparent than in the attempt to construct a system of alliances against Soviet aggression. It reveals once more the problem of establishing a relationship between a policy of deterrence and the strategy we are prepared to implement, between the temptation to pose a maximum threat and the tendency to recoil before it. In our alliance policy these problems are compounded by the vulnerability of our allies and their sense of impotence because they are either junior partners in the atomic race or excluded from it altogether. Moreover, we have never been clear about the strategy behind our alliance policy—whether we mean to defend our allies against invasion or whether we rely on an over-all superiority vis-à-vis the Soviet bloc to defeat aggression. To us this choice may represent a strategic option; to our allies it appears as a matter of life and death.

In the past, coalitions have generally been held together by a combination of three purposes: (1) To discourage aggression by assembling superior power and to leave no doubt about the alignment of forces—this, in effect, is the doctrine of collective security. (2) To provide an obligation for assistance. Were the national interest always clear and constant, each power would know its obligations and the alignment of its potential opponents without any formal pact. But the national interest fluctuates within limits; it must be adapted to changing circumstances. An alliance is a form of insurance against contingencies, an additional weight when considering whether to go to war. (3) To legitimize the assistance of foreign troops or intervention in a foreign country.

An alliance is effective, however, only to the extent that it reflects a common purpose and represents an accretion of strength to its members. The mere assembling of overwhelming power is meaningless if it cannot be brought to bear on the issues actually in dispute. The strongest purpose will prove ineffective if it cannot find expression in an agreed strategic doctrine. Thus the French system of alliances in the interwar period broke down, when put to the test, because its political purpose and the military doctrine on which it was based were inconsistent with each other. The political purpose of the French system of alliances was to assure the integrity of the small states of Central and Eastern Europe. Militarily, this implied an offensive strategy on the part of France, because only by forcing Germany into a two-front war could the latter's pressure on the Central European powers be eased. But with the building of the Maginot line the condition of military co-operation between France and its allies disappeared. In every crisis France was torn between its political and military commitments, and its allies were forced to choose between suicidal resistance or surrender. In the event, whatever course they chose—whether surrender, as Czechoslovakia, or resistance, as Poland—proved equally disastrous. The French system of alliances, so imposing on paper, did not survive any of the tests for which it was designed. It did not discourage aggression because its strategic doctrine made it impossible to assemble superior power, and its calls for assistance went unheeded because a legal obligation by itself will not impel common action if the requirements of national survival seem to counsel a different course. In short, it is not the fact of alliance which deters aggression but the application it can be given in any concrete case.

Since the end of World War II, the United States has

created a vast and complicated system of alliances which includes forty-four sovereign states. We have multilateral pacts in the Western Hemisphere expressed in the Inter-American Treaty of Reciprocal Assistance. We have been instrumental in creating the North Atlantic Treaty for the defense of Western Europe. We were the chief force behind the Southeast Asia Collective Defense Treaty which unites us with Australia, France, New Zealand, Pakistan, the Philippines, Thailand, and the United Kingdom. Then there is the ANZUS Pact signed by us together with New Zealand and Australia. Finally, we have entered into bilateral defense treaties with Japan, Nationalist China, South Korea and the Philippines. Moreover, we are indirectly connected with the Baghdad Pact which unites Iraq with two of our allies in NATO, Britain and Turkey, and one of our partners in SEATO, Pakistan.

The chief purpose of this intricate structure is to surround the Soviet periphery with an alignment of powers, any one of which the U.S.S.R. will hesitate to attack. A world-wide system of collective security hides great complexities, however. For if we examine these alliances in terms of the criteria outlined above, we find that some of them do not share a common purpose, others add little to our effective strength, or both. To us the Soviet threat overshadows all else; but Pakistan is more concerned with India than with the U.S.S.R. and China; the Baghdad Pact is of greater significance for relationships within the Middle East than for defense against Soviet aggression. And in neither SEATO nor the Baghdad Pact are we associated with partners with whom we share the degree of common purpose conferred by the cultural heritage which unites us with our European allies. In such circumstances, a system of collective security runs the danger of leading to a dilution of purpose and to an air of unreality, in which the existence of an alliance, and not the resolution behind it, is considered a guarantee of security.

These problems are magnified, moreover, by the tendency of our strategic doctrine to transform every war into an all-out war. For while it is true that all our security arrangements are regional in nature, they are given a world-wide application because of our reliance on all-out war, both doctrinally and technically. Thus the outbreak of any war anywhere becomes of immediate concern to all our allies and causes them in every crisis to exert pressure for a policy of minimum risk. Nor will these pressures be avoided by declarations that the United States reserves the right of unilateral action, such as Secretary Dulles made to the NATO Council in December 1956. As long as our military doctrine threatens to transform every war into an all-out war, it becomes of inevitable concern to our allies, whether by right or by self-interest, and they will do their best to prevent *any* action on our part which threatens to involve them.

The inconsistency between a reliance on all-out war and the political commitment to regional defense has been the bane of our coalition policy. Our strategic doctrine has never defined how we propose to protect threatened areas: whether to defend them locally or whether to treat an attack on them as *the cause* of war. The former strategy would require resisting aggression where it occurred, at least in areas we wished to deny to the Soviets. The second strategy would treat aggression as a cause of war but it would involve no commitment about the area where we proposed to fight. The latter is, in effect, the doctrine of massive retaliation "at places of our own choosing." In such a strategy, security against Soviet aggression is achieved, if at all, by the over-all strategic balance between us and the Soviet bloc. But whatever the deterrent effect of massive retaliation, it removes the incentive for a military effort by our allies. They realize that in an all-out war they will add to our effective strength only by supplying facilities or by serving as bases; they see little significance in a military contribution of their own. A reliance on all-out war as the chief deterrent saps our system of alliances in two ways: either our allies feel that any military effort on their part is unnecessary or they may be led to the conviction that peace is preferable to war even on terms almost akin to surrender.

Our attempt to take account of this feeling has led to a further strategic distortion. In order to reassure our allies, it has caused us and Great Britain to build up forces in Western Europe too small to resist a concerted attack and too large for police actions. Thus Great Britain has four divisions in Germany, and the United States five of its combat-ready fourteen. Our European allies, in turn, have made just enough of a defense effort to induce us to keep our forces on the Continent but not enough to constitute an effective barrier to Soviet aggression. The result of all these half measures and mutual pretenses has been that we are stationing substantial ground forces in an area where our strategic doctrine explicitly rejects the possibility of local war.[1] On the other hand, in the peripheral areas of Asia and the Middle East, where the possibility of local war is admitted, we have neither forces on the spot nor the mobility to get our strategic reserve into position quickly enough to be effective.

II

The acid test of our system of alliances is the North Atlantic Treaty Organization. It unites us with powers with whom we share both a common history and a similar culture. Of all our alliances it represents the greatest accretion to our strength. Western Europe contains the second largest concentration of industry and skills outside the United States. In a very real sense, the world balance of power depends on our ability to deny the resources and manpower of Western Europe to an aggressor.

Nevertheless, since its inception NATO has been beset by difficulties. It has not found it possible to organize its power effectively or to create a military force which can undertake a meaningful defense. None of the force levels which have been announced periodically with much fanfare has ever been achieved. Almost a decade after its creation NATO is still without a force sufficient to prevent its

[1] See, for example, General Alfred M. Gruenther's final statement on leaving NATO, New York *Times*, November 14, 1956.

members from being overrun by the Soviet Army. Unsure about the implications of nuclear war, uncomfortable with a World War II type of strategy, NATO has attempted to combine elements of both at the price of lessened self-confidence and diminished ability to take decisive action in a time of crisis. It has not resolved the question of the significance of a military contribution by our allies to a strategy which relies on all-out war. It has not clarified to our partners the purpose of conventional forces in a war in which even the local defense of Western Europe will involve the use of nuclear weapons.

A NATO Council decision has declared nuclear weapons an integral part of the defense of Western Europe. But the public opinion of most of our allies and, judging from official statements, many of the leaders as well, tends to identify any explosion of a nuclear weapon with the outbreak of an all-out war. When the outbreak of war has come increasingly to be considered equivalent to national catastrophe, a lagging defense effort is almost inevitable. It is doubly unfortunate that this should have happened at a time when the advent of tactical nuclear weapons in quantity has for the first time brought an adequate ground defense of Western Europe within reach.

There are many causes for the inadequacies of NATO. For one thing, the United States, by its strategic doctrine and its refusal to share atomic information, has inhibited the growth of a sense of common purpose. For another, our European allies have been unwilling to make the economic sacrifices required for a meaningful defense effort and some of them have tended to escape harsh realities by denying their existence.

So long as United States strategic doctrine identifies the defense of Europe with all-out war, a substantial military contribution by our allies is unlikely. They do not have the resources to create a retaliatory force, and their small size and geographic proximity to the U.S.S.R. would make it impossible to protect such a force could it be created. They, therefore, see no sense in making a military contribution of their own except by furnishing facilities or contributing to

a trip wire for our Strategic Air Force. Since the purpose
of a trip wire is not to hold a line but to define a cause of
war, it does not supply an incentive for a major effort.

Moreover, our Strategic Air Command has never been a
part of the NATO structure. Since the alliance has no control over the instrument around which its whole strategy
is built, there has inevitably been an air of unreality about
NATO planning. The force levels of NATO almost necessarily have seemed less important than the determination
of the United States to unleash its retaliatory power if necessary.

Our strongest European ally, instead of striving to com-
plement our forces, has felt obliged to duplicate the armaments in which we are already strongest. At considerable
sacrifice Great Britain has developed a strategic air force
and a nuclear stockpile too small to fight an all-out war
against the Soviet bloc but sufficiently large to drain resources from the British capability for limited war, which,
as events in the Middle East showed in 1956, is a much
greater need for Britain. And our policy of withholding
atomic information has caused the British effort in the field
of strategic striking power to absorb a maximum amount
of resources. Since Great Britain was prevented by our
Atomic Energy Act from profiting from our research and
development, it has had to duplicate much of our own effort and to do so at great expense and with no substantial
benefit to the over-all strategic striking power of the free
world.

Our Continental allies, deprived of access to our information about nuclear matters and without the benefit of the
British wartime experience in nuclear development, have,
in turn, had no choice except to build up the conventional
forces whose utility has constantly been called in question
by the tactical nuclear weapons in the NATO arsenal which
have remained under our exclusive control. Their exclusion
from the nuclear field has made it very difficult for the
Continental powers to assess the meaning of the new technology. It has contributed to the widespread confusion over
the distinction between conventional and nuclear war, over

the significance of tactical nuclear weapons, and over the feasibility of the local defense of Europe, which has beset NATO planning at every step. If the United States retains exclusive control of nuclear weapons our allies will become increasingly vulnerable to Soviet atomic blackmail, which implies that they can escape their dilemmas by refusing to adopt a nuclear strategy.

While the United States has been responsible for many of NATO's inconsistencies, our allies, with the exception of Great Britain, have not helped matters by the eagerness with which they seized upon the ambiguities of our doctrine as a justification for deferring difficult choices. Their self-confidence shaken by two world wars, their economies strained by the recovery effort, they have recoiled before the prospect of fresh conflict. Instead of adopting the austere measures required for a major defense effort, they have tended to deny the reality of the danger or they have asserted that they were already protected by our retaliatory capability. Our Continental allies have been torn between a strategy of minimum risk and the desire for economy, between the wish for protection against Soviet occupation and the reluctance to face harsh realities. But the Atlantic powers must make up their minds: NATO is either a device to defend Europe locally or an instrument to unleash the British and American strategic air forces. It cannot be both and it cannot be the former without a more realistic defense effort by our European allies.

We have insisted for so long that an attack on Europe would be the signal for an all-out war that we may well find ourselves engaged in the most wasteful kind of struggle because other alternatives have never been considered. And even though it may be true that Europe is the chief strategic prize, it does not follow that we will inevitably adhere to a strategy in its defense which is certain to destroy our national substance. It is not reasonable to assume that the United States, and even more the United Kingdom, would be prepared to commit suicide in order to defend a particular area—especially if the Soviet Union shows its customary skill in presenting its challenge ambiguously. What if the Red Army attacks in Europe explicitly to disarm West Germany, offering the United States and the United Kingdom immunity from strategic bombing and promising to withdraw to the Oder after achieving its limited objective? Is it clear that France would fight under such circumstances? Or that the United Kingdom would initiate an all-out war which, however it ended, might mean the end of British civilization? Or that an American President would trade fifty American cities for Western Europe?

It may be argued that the U.S.S.R. faces the same problem, that it too may not be prepared to risk total devastation for a marginal gain. But the psychological bloc against *initiating* all-out war cannot be emphasized often enough. If the Soviets can force us to shoulder the risk of initiating all-out war, there is great danger that soon no areas outside the Western Hemisphere will seem "worth" contending for. It is not simply that there are inherent limitations to the credibility of the threat of suicide; it is above all that the most wasteful and cataclysmic strategy should not be our only possible riposte. There is no logic in conducting a war fought presumably to maintain the historical experience and tradition of a people with a strategy which is almost certain to destroy its national substance.

Thus our alliances should not be considered as a device to strengthen our ability to fight an all-out war but as a means to escape its horrors. In an all-out war few of our allies will add to our striking power, and they will have no incentive to furnish the trip wire to unleash it. But our capacity for all-out war can be used as a shield to organize local defense, and our assistance should be conceived as a means to make local defense possible. In this resides our only chance to avoid the impasse which has been the bane of our coalition policy: the gap between the belief of our allies that they are already protected by our thermonuclear capability, to which they do not feel they have a contribution to make, and their terror of its consequences, which makes them reluctant to invoke it as a strategy for fighting a war. Only by developing a strategy which admits the possibility of local defense can we escape the never-never land where our military contributions to the ground defense of our allies are greater than their own and where current investment in local defense pays no dividends, because we reject any strategy that could make them effective.

The sense of common purpose which has been lacking in our coalition policy can be conferred by the interest we now share with our allies in avoiding all-out thermonuclear war. Instead of merely furnishing a trip wire, our allies should be persuaded that the best means of avoiding thermonuclear war resides in our joint ability to make local aggression too costly. We must convince them that they cannot avoid their dilemmas by neutrality or surrender, for either will bring on what they fear most: confined to the Western Hemisphere, we would have no choice but to fight an all-out war. And all-out war will have almost as fearful consequences for neutrals as for the chief protagonists.

III

A strategic doctrine which poses less absolute sanctions than all-out war would go far toward overcoming another difficulty of our coalition policy: the tendency of our system of alliances to merge into a world-wide system of collective security. For all-out war is of direct concern not only to every ally but also to every neutral. As long as our strategic doctrine threatens to transform every war into an all-out war, our allies will not only be reluctant to make a military effort of their own; they will generally seek to keep us from running major risks ourselves. By the same token, as long as our strategic doctrine relies so heavily on all-out war, our policy makers will be tempted to give our coalition global scope. As a result, in every crisis from Korea to Indochina to the Middle East, we have left the impression that, unless all allies (and sometimes even all powers) resist aggression jointly, no effective action is possible at all. Thus, whatever the specific terms of our commitments, our coalition policy has in practice encountered many of the difficulties found in a system of general collective security.

And a world-wide system of collective security is extremely difficult to implement. The acid test of a military alliance is its ability to achieve agreement on two related problems: whether a given challenge represents aggression and, if so, what form resistance should take. But differences in geographic position, history, power, and domestic structure ensure that a world-wide consensus is difficult to attain except against a threat so overpowering that it obliterates all differences, both about its nature or about the strategy for dealing with it. Against any other danger united action is almost inevitably reduced to the lowest common denominator. Even if there should be agreement that a given act constitutes aggression, the willingness of the powers to run risks to oppose it will differ. A state will not easily risk its survival to defeat an aggression not explicitly directed against its national existence. A North Vietnamese troop movement may be a mortal danger to Laos but it can be of only marginal interest to Italy. A domestic upheaval in Syria may disquiet Turkey; it will seem much less dangerous to Portugal.

Against an aggressor skilled in presenting ambiguous challenges there will occur endless wrangling over whether a specific challenge in fact constitutes aggression and about the measures to deal with it. If the aggression is explicitly less than all-out or if it is justified as the expression of a "legitimate" grievance, at least some of the members of an alliance will be tempted to evade the problem by denying the reality of the threat. They will prefer to "wait and see," until the aggressor has "demonstrated" he is intent on world domination, and he will not have demonstrated it until the balance of power is already overturned.

As long as the challenge is not overwhelming an aggressor may, therefore, actually be aided by a world-wide system of collective security or by a system of alliances which is given world-wide application. For it will be easier to obtain agreement on inaction than on commitment; indeed, inaction may represent the only consensus attainable. Even where there is agreement on the fact of aggression or on what constitutes a just claim, it will still be exceedingly difficult to achieve a common stand as to what action should be taken. The contrast in effectiveness of the United Nations in the Suez and Hungarian crises illustrates this point. In ʰoth cases the United Nations, which exhibits the difficulties of a general system of collective security in their most extreme form, expressed its disapproval. This symbolic act was effective toward Britain and France, primarily because it involved no assumption of substantive risk. It worked because Britain and France recoiled before the mere expression of united world opinion.

By contrast, United Nations resolutions have so far proved ineffective in bringing about the evacuation of Hungary or the unification of Korea. For in these cases a pronouncement as to the merits of the dispute was unavailing against a power prepared to defy the system of collective security. Compliance could be achieved only by a willingness to employ more drastic measures. But the majority which was prepared to go on record condemning Soviet actions was not ready to face perils to have its view prevail. The readiness to pass resolutions always exceeds the willingness to back them up.

To seek to give too generalized an application to a system of alliances may, therefore, have the paradoxical result of paralyzing the power or powers capable of resisting alone. The theoretical gain in strength may be more than outweighed by the dilution of a common purpose. At the same time, in every crisis short of an overriding attack, such a system of collective security gives a veto to the ally with least interest in the matter at issue and with least power to make his views prevail. From Korea to the Chinese offshore islands to Indochina to Suez, some powerful members of our system of coalitions have disagreed with others about the extent of the danger or else they have taken positions which made unity attainable only by foregoing any risks. Our reaction to this was always a heightened determination to "strengthen" the alliance, to seek to compensate for the inability to apply the alliance concretely by escaping into a formal unity. Thus Korea led to the ANZUS Pact, Indochina to SEATO, and the Suez crisis to an effort to "tighten" the bonds of NATO.

The attempt to apply what are, in effect, regional alliances on a world-wide basis has tended to inhibit the action of those powers with most at stake in a given dispute. It has turned our alliances into targets of many national frustrations and therewith confronted many governments with the following dilemma: if they have acted outside the sphere of their primary interest, it has undermined their domestic support and, if they did not, it has strained the alliance. In consequence, formal unity becomes a substitute for common action, or the alliance is blamed for the failure to take measures which the government concerned was most reluctant to undertake in the first place. Thus Secretary Dulles implied that only lack of British support prevented our intervention in Indochina, and the British Cabinet has given the impression that American vacillation was solely responsible for the failure of its policy in the Middle East.

The prerequisite of an effective system of alliances, then, is to harmonize our political and our military commitments by a strategy of local defense and a diplomacy of regional co-operation. Within the region covered by alliances we should concert our efforts militarily and politically. Outside that region we must be free to act alone or with a different grouping of powers if our interest so dictates. Such a course would take account of the fact that the United States alone of the powers of the non-Soviet world is strong enough physically and psychologically to play a global role.

To sustain a regional system of alliances, however, the United States must be willing to exercise its leadership in defining the transformations the alliance is prepared to resist. We cannot rely on the consensus of humanity to define the issues for which to contend. It is not only that our allies, with the possible exception of Great Britain, are too weak to act outside the area of their primary concern; it is also that *within* this area or on the issues most directly affecting it they will be at a serious disadvantage without United States support. Surely one of the lessons of the fiasco of the invasion of Egypt by Britain and France was that none of our allies can fight a limited war and keep it limited by its own effort.

We are required to exercise leadership, moreover, when an understanding of the nature of security has become infinitely complicated. The traditional concept of aggression, as military attack by organized units across a sovereign boundary, presupposed a society of nations in which domination of one power by another was possible only by military victory or by annexation. But in the age of "volunteers" and "arms bases," of guerrilla warfare and economic penetration, the strategic balance may be upset without a clear-cut issue ever being presented. Does Soviet repression of satellite revolts warrant United States intervention? Is a Soviet base in the Middle East aggression when it is stocked with weapons or only when Soviet troops appear against the will of the indigenous government?

It is impossible to answer these questions in the abstract. They demonstrate, however, that we may have as much difficulty identifying the transformations we will resist by force as in assembling the force to resist them. Moreover, while the precise circumstances that might justify recourse to force cannot be laid down in advance, we need to develop some conception of our strategic interest well in advance of crisis situations. Are we opposed only to the forcible expansion of communism, or is the existence of a Communist regime in some areas a threat to our security, however the regime is established? Do we resist Communist domination of an area only when it is "illegal," or because the domination of Eurasia by communism would upset the strategic balance against us? If the former, we would resist only the *manner* of Communist expansion; if the latter, we would resist the *fact* of Communist expansion. It may happen, of course, that in neither case will we be able to arrest developments, as was the case in China, for example. If we are clear about our strategic interest, however, the form of resistance, and indeed the decision whether to resist, will be technical questions. Without such concepts our actions will be haphazard and our alliances uncertain.

While we cannot always refrain from acting simply because we lack a consensus within the coalition, we must refrain from attempting to prescribe to our allies what their interests should be in every situation. This is certain to destroy any alliance. While it is true that our strategic interests transcend those of our allies, our allies may well be more sensitive than we within the region of their primary concern. Because their margin of safety is so much narrower, our allies may well feel threatened by transformations which do not seem to affect our security directly. In such a situation we must be prepared to make concessions to what our allies consider their essential interests.

This is not to say we must support our allies however arbitrary their behavior. Our coalition policy must strike a balance between identifying an alliance with the consensus of its members and the desire for freedom of action in situations where our views and those of our allies diverge. It must be built on an understanding by all partners that our interests and those of our allies cannot be of the same order because the disparity of power and responsibility is too great. We can co-operate on matters of mutual concern, which in almost every case means regional co-operation. But our allies must understand that we have an obligation to maintain, not only a regional equilibrium but the world balance of power as well. Provided our military doctrine does not threaten to transform every war into all-out war, our allies must, therefore, be prepared to let us act alone or with a different grouping of powers outside the area of regional co-operation. We, in turn, should show understanding and compassion for the problems of states whose margin of survival—military, political, and economic—is far smaller than ours. Any other course will make for paralysis: it will cause our allies to hamstring us *outside* the area of mutual concern and it will cause us to frustrate our allies *within* it.

IV

What of the relationship of the uncommitted part of the world to our coalition policy? It is often said that our policy of military alliances is one of the causes of our difficulties with the newly independent nations, and to a certain extent this is correct. We must be careful, however, not to confuse the symptom with the cause of our difficulties nor to judge our policy in terms of its popularity with the newly independent states.

The importance of the newly independent nations cannot be doubted. It is equally beyond question that it is to the American interest that we identify ourselves with their hopes and aspirations and that we seek to prevent an alignment of the colored races of the world against the whites. How this should be accomplished is much less obvious, however.

The revolution that is taking place in the newly independent and the still dependent states can only be narrowly understood as a revolution against colonialism. In a real sense it is a continuation of a revolution *started* by the colonial powers and carried on under their aegis. Moreover, not all the protest movements of formerly subjugated people are of the same order, nor do they all represent the same phenomenon: there is a basic difference between areas in which colonialism ruled directly and those in which it governed indirectly.

The remarkable aspect of colonialism from its beginning was the imposition of rule by a very small group of Europeans over vast populations. This was due not so much to the military superiority of the West—in many respects it is greater today than it was in the nineteenth century—as to the fact that the European powers displaced an existing ruling group in a society where the vast majority of the population neither enjoyed nor expected direct participation in government. The structure of government in what is now the uncommitted third of the world had been feudal for centuries, and in their first appearance the Europeans appeared as a new governing group substituting itself for the existing one, according to a pattern which had characterized these areas for many generations. The domination of vast territories by small groups of Europeans was possible precisely because they were not considered as "foreign"; the notion of their foreignness was introduced in the first instance not by the governed but by their rulers.

For the Europeans were not content with displacing a feudal upper class. They brought with them the twin doctrines of rational administration and popular participation in government, which in time had inevitably to prove inconsistent with their continued domination. The rationalizing of administration led to the consolidation of many areas into viable units for the first time in their history; Indonesia, for example, was nothing but a geographic expression until the Dutch found it more efficient to unite the islands of the Indies under a single administration. At the same time the colonial powers trained a group of indigenous leaders in European universities, where they absorbed the doctrines of the right to self-government, human dignity, and economic advancement which had been the rallying points for European revolutionary and progressive movements throughout the nineteenth century.

The result was two sets of paradoxes. In its revolutionary aspect, colonialism represents one of the greatest conversions in history. Almost without exception the leaders of the newly independent states, as well as the heads of anticolonial uprisings in still dependent countries, are opposing their present or former masters in terms of values they have learned from them. Their challenge to the West is not in terms of a different set of beliefs; on the contrary, they are demanding that the West live up to its own principles. The leaders in the uncommitted third of the world are playing a role drawn from a Western script. As the ideals of the British, French, and American revolutions became diffused, partly through the very spread of colonialism, the seeds were sown for the destruction of colonialism itself. The more successful the teachings of the colonial powers, the more untenable their positions became. Thus the greater the participation of the indigenous population in their own government, the more insistent grew their demands for independence, as is demonstrated by the difference between the British and the Portuguese colonies. What is taking place in the areas once under direct colonial rule is the second stage of the revolution started by the colonial powers. It is an attempt by the leaders of the newly independent states to spread among the masses of their people the values which they themselves acquired from the colonial power and which furnished the original impetus of the revolution.

This leads to the second paradox of the uncommitted third of the world: that conditions are more stable and promising in areas which have been under direct colonial rule than in those where the colonial powers exercised their influence only indirectly. The territories governed directly, such as India, benefited through administrative consolidation and the overthrow of the old feudal order by an outside force. The countries controlled indirectly, such as most of those in the Middle East, suffered the demoralizing influence of foreign control without a corresponding gain in the training of leadership groups or of administrative cohesion. On the contrary, while in areas governed directly boundaries were drawn with an eye to what constituted a viable unit, in other territories they were often drawn to ensure that the countries would *not* be viable. For the most part, boundaries in the Middle East reflected neither a common history nor an economic or administrative necessity. They were drawn to guarantee weakness and rivalry.

In the areas once ruled indirectly, several revolutions are, therefore, going on concurrently. There is, to begin with, the revolt by a small, Western-educated elite against feudal rule; there is the quest for administrative, political, and economic cohesiveness; there is, finally, the attempt to raise the level of economic welfare and of education of the masses. The revolutionary urgency is much greater and the problems more nearly insoluble in these areas than in countries formerly under direct rule, where many of these upheavals were accomplished by the fiat of the colonial power and over a long period of time. Therefore, while a legalistic concept of sovereignty and aggression may be a stabilizing element in Southeast Asia, it invites explosions in areas like the Middle East because it works against the necessary consolidation of inherently volatile and economically unviable units.

These paradoxes make the quest for popularity among the newly independent states a highly treacherous course. For while the leadership groups have been trained in Western universities and have on the whole accepted Western thinking, this very fact may limit the degree to which they can identify themselves with the Western powers politically. It is not so much that these leaders would be suspected by their countrymen of collaboration with the former colonial rulers; the motivation is more complex and more subtle. To sustain the dedication and the suffering of the rebellion against the colonial powers, the leaders of independence movements had to elaborate a distinction between themselves and their rulers which they derived from a claim to superior morality, or at least superior spirituality. But when the battle was won and independence finally achieved, many leaders of newly independent countries have had to realize, at least subconsciously, that they were inwardly a good deal closer to their former rulers than to their own countrymen. It may be too much to say that they resent the West for having taught them patterns of thinking which make them strangers to their own people; it is clear that they require anti-colonialism as a means of achieving a sense of personal identity. Precisely because they are inwardly so close to the West, many of the leaders of the newly independent states cannot afford to align themselves with it politically.

In these terms, neutralism and anti-colonialism are not so much a policy as a spiritual necessity. The constant reiteration of nonalignment may be the means by which the leaders of newly independent nations reassure themselves; they can be certain of their independence only by acting it out every day and on every issue. This explains why the most strident advocates of neutrality are often the very people who in dress, bearing, and manner of thinking are closest to the West—indeed, who often have spent very little of their lives in their own countries. Individuals with firm roots in their own tradition, on the other hand, seem to feel less compulsive about proclaiming their independence daily and seem more prepared to act jointly with the Western powers when their interests coincide.

Therefore too anti-colonialism reflects not so much the extent of past suffering as the difficulty of achieving a national consciousness. For contrary to the nations of Western Europe, from which they drew their ideal of nationhood, many of the newly independent states are based neither on a common language nor on a common culture. Their only common experience is the former colonial rule. Their leaders require anti-colonialism to achieve not only a sense of personal but also of national identity. The collection of islands called Indonesia is meaningful only in terms of the history of Dutch rule; its frontiers follow the frontiers of empire, and so does its national consciousness. Because West New Guinea was part of the Dutch East Indies, Indonesia has laid claim to it, although it is inhabited by people as different from the Polynesian stock of Indonesia as the Dutch themselves. Indonesia does not covet Malaya, although racially and linguistically it is much closer, because no common experience connects it to Malaya. Conversely, Malaya has no desire to join its cultural brethren in Indonesia but will become a state within the boundaries of former British colonial rule.

The close identification of nationalism with the memory of colonial rule also accounts for the seeming blind spot of so many newly independent states with respect to Soviet colonialism. The leaders of the uncommitted nations may condemn such Soviet actions as the repression of the Hungarian revolt. They may dislike Soviet control of the satellite orbit. But they will not be prepared to consider it as the same phenomenon which causes their own frustrations. Until they develop a stronger sense of personal identity and until their nations can develop purposes not drawn from the struggle for independence, anti-colonialism with an anti-Western bias will be an essential psychological need.

In the uncommitted areas, popularity is an unattainable goal. To seek to gear our policy to an inquiry into what people desire may merely force the newly independent states to dissociate themselves from us in order to demonstrate their independence. Indeed, we may drive the newly independent states toward the Soviet bloc by a too ardent embrace. On the other hand, our spiritual kinship with the uncommitted peoples and their policy of political nonalignment can serve our interests. For whatever their protestations, the leaders of almost every newly independent state, particularly in areas which had been under direct colonial rule, are spiritual heirs of the West to a significant degree. The very fact that India considered it a great achievement to obtain Soviet acquiescence to its five principles of coexistence indicates that its assessment of the real threat to peace is not so very different from ours. And no attempt was made to ask for similar agreements from the former colonial powers or from the United States, so often depicted in Asian folklore as imperialist and eager to restore colonial rule. Obviously it was self-evident to India that relations between it and the United States were so firmly based on the principle of peaceful coexistence that no explicit reiteration was necessary.

If, then, we are prepared to exercise leadership, we may be able to induce many of the newly independent nations to travel in a direction to which they already incline, if always a few steps behind us. They will not surrender their nonalignment but they may be willing to act in the pursuance of common interests, provided we are prepared to chart the road and provided we do not insist on intimate association. In the uncommitted nations popularity may be less important than respect.

V

The importance of United States leadership is all the greater because many of the leaders of the newly independent nations have so little understanding of international relations and of the nature of power. Although they distinguished themselves in the struggle with the former colonial powers, the independence movements, almost without exception, provided a poor preparation for an understanding of the element of power in international relations. Based on the dogmas of late nineteenth-century liberalism, especially its pacifism, the independence movements relied more on ideological agreement than on an evaluation of power factors, and to this day the claim to superior spirituality remains the battle cry of Asian nationalism. Moreover, the bad conscience of the colonial powers and their preoccupation with European problems gave the struggle for independence more the character of a domestic debate than of a power dispute. To be sure, many of the leaders of the newly independent powers spent years in jail and suffered heroically for their cause. It is no reflection on their dedication to assert that the results achieved were out of proportion to their suffering. Empires which had held vast dominions for hundreds of years disappeared without a battle being fought.

And if it is difficult for the leaders to retain a sense of proportion, it is next to impossible for the mass of the population. On the whole they were involved in the struggle for independence only with their sympathies; to them the disappearance of the colonial powers must seem nothing short of miraculous. Moreover, most of the people of the newly independent states live in pre-industrial societies. It would be difficult enough for them to grasp the significance of industrialism; it is too much to expect them to comprehend nuclear technology. It is therefore understandable that in most former colonial areas there is an overestimation of what can be accomplished by words alone. Nor is this tendency diminished by the rewards that fall to the uncommitted in the struggle for allegiance by the two big power centers.

But however understandable, it is a dangerous trend. In the present revolutionary situation, the dogmatism of the newly independent states makes them susceptible to Soviet "peace offensives," and their lack of appreciation of power relationships causes them to overestimate the protection afforded by moral precepts. Indeed, their very insistence on principle contributes to the demoralization of international politics, for it tempts them to accept at face value the protestations of peaceful intentions with which the Soviets inevitably accompany their aggressive moves. It reinforces the quest for a "pure" case of aggression, and this almost insures that actual aggression will not be dealt with; indeed, it may not even be recognized. Moreover, to the extent that the independent states are aware of power, they are likely to be more impressed by two hundred Chinese divisions—an element of power that is familiar, concrete, and near—than by the more remote and esoteric power of the United States.

Thus considerations of both power and principle combine to inspire the newly independent nations with caution. In every crisis they exercise a pressure for solutions which combine abstractness with minimum risk and in many situations they may provoke a crisis by their attempt to inject domestic standards of conduct into the international field.

It is imperative that the uncommitted powers understand not only the benefits but also the duties of independence. Many of the leaders of the newly independent states have found the temptation to play a major role in international affairs almost overwhelming. Domestically, their problems are intractable; even a major economic advance would fall short of the aspirations of their people, and many countries will have a serious problem to maintain their standard of living in the face of rising birth rates. In domestic policy every course of action has a price and sometimes a high one. Even so well-established a leader as Jawaharlal Nehru found that reshaping the boundaries of the Indian states could provoke major communal riots. But in the international field, the division of the world into two contending camps exalts the role of the uncommitted, and the collapse of the old international system creates a fertile field of manipulation for ambitious men. These conditions produce an almost irresistible temptation to defer the solution of difficult domestic problems by entering the international arena, to solidify a complicated domestic position by triumphs in the international field. Unless the newly independent nations learn that every action has a price in the international field as well, they will increasingly seek to play a global role that is beyond either their strength or the risks they are willing to assume.

Condescending as it may seem to say so, the United States has an important educational task to perform in the uncommitted third of the world. By word and deed we must demonstrate that the inexorable element of international relations resides in the necessity to combine principle with power, that an exclusive reliance on moral pronouncements may be as irresponsible as the attempt to conduct policy on the basis of considerations of power alone. To be sure we should, wherever possible, seek to identify ourselves with the aspirations of the newly independent states. But we must also be prepared to preserve the conditions in which these aspirations can be fulfilled. We should never give up our principles nor ask other nations to surrender theirs. But we must also realize that neither we nor our allies nor the uncommitted can realize any principles unless we survive. We cannot permit the balance of power to be overturned for the sake of allied unity or the approbation of the uncommitted.

The challenge to our leadership is all the greater if we consider the inevitable spread of nuclear technology. Within a generation, and probably in less time than that, most countries will possess installations for the peaceful uses of nuclear energy and, therefore, the wherewithal to manufacture nuclear weapons. And even if this should not prove to be the case, the Soviets may find it advantageous to increase international tensions by making nuclear weapons available to other powers, on the model of their arms sale to Egypt and Syria. But nuclear weapons in the hands of weak, irresponsible, or merely ignorant governments present grave dangers. Unless the United States has demonstrated a military capability that is meaningful for the newly independent states, many parts of the world will play the role of the Balkans in European politics: the fuse which will set off a holocaust. The United States, therefore, requires a twentieth-century equivalent of "showing the flag," an ability and a readiness to make our power felt quickly and decisively, not only to deter Soviet aggression but also to impress the uncommitted with our capacity for decisive action.

It is thus misleading to assert that strategic considerations play no role in our relations with the uncommitted powers. On the contrary, much as in our policy of alliances, the capability for local action is the prerequisite for an effective policy in the uncommitted areas of the world. But while strategy can help to establish a framework within which to build relations with the newly independent states, here the main thrust of our policy must be in fields other than military. In fact, our insistence that security is achieved primarily by a military grouping of powers has been one of the chief difficulties in our relations with many of the newly independent states.

The military contribution of SEATO and the Baghdad Pact (to which we belong in all but in name) does not compensate for the decision of India and Egypt to stand apart and for the domestic pressures these instruments generated in some of the signatory countries. The primary function of these pacts is to draw a line across which the U.S.S.R. cannot move without the risk of war and to legitimize intervention by the United States should war break out. But the line could have been better drawn by a unilateral declaration, as in the Truman doctrine for Greece and Turkey, and the Middle East doctrine of President Eisenhower. Behind this shield we could then have concentrated on the primary problem of creating a sense of common purpose by emphasizing shared objectives—for example, by striving for a grouping of powers to assist in economic development. Had we emphasized these nonmilitary functions of SEATO, it would have been much more difficult for India or Indonesia to stay aloof. As these political groupings gained in economic strength, their own interest would dictate a more active concern for common defense; at the least it would provide the economic base for a meaningful defense. A powerful grouping of states on the Russian borders would tend to restrain the Soviet Union, whether or not the purpose was primarily military. And by the same token, such groupings are desirable from the American point of view, even if they do not go along with our every policy.

The problem of the uncommitted states cannot be solved, however, merely by an economic grouping of powers. It is related to the whole United States posture. Anti-Americanism is fashionable today in many parts of the globe. As the richest and most powerful nation we are the natural target for all frustrations. As the power which bears the primary responsibility for the defense of the free world, we are unpopular with all who are so preoccupied with their own national development that they are unwilling to pay sufficient attention to foreign threats. We should, of course, seek to allay legitimate grievances but we would be wrong to take every criticism at face value. A great deal of anti-Americanism hides a feeling of insecurity, both material and spiritual. Many of our most voluble critics in Southeast Asia would be terrified were our military protection suddenly withdrawn. The neutrality of the uncommitted is possible, after all, only so long as the United States remains strong, spiritually and physically.

In its relations with the uncommitted, the United States must, therefore, develop not only a greater compassion but also a greater majesty. The picture of high American officials scurrying to all quarters of the globe to inform themselves on each crisis as it develops cannot but give an impression of uncertainty. The nervousness exhibited in our reactions to Soviet moves must contrast unfavorably with what appears to be the deliberate, even ruthless, purposefulness of the Soviets. Our attempt after every crisis to restore the situation as closely as possible to the *status quo ante* may well convey the lack of a sense of direction. To gear our policy to what the uncommitted powers will accept may merely increase their feeling of insecurity or force them to move away from us to demonstrate their independence. Firmness might induce the uncommitted powers to develop formulas which meet us at least part way. The bargaining position of such countries as India depends, after all, on their skill in finding a position *between* the two major powers.

A firm United States posture is made all the more necessary by the desire of many of the uncommitted nations for peace at almost any price. Because they consider us the more malleable of the two superpowers, they choose in every crisis to direct their pressures against us as a means to preserve the peace or to resolve an issue. To the degree that we can project a greater sense of purpose, some of these pressures may be diverted against the Soviet bloc. A revolution like Egypt's or even India's cannot be managed by understanding alone; it also requires a readiness on our part to bear the psychological and military burden of difficult decisions.

The problem of American relations both with our allies and the uncommitted, therefore, depends on a close relationship of power and policy. Without a military policy which poses less fearful risks than all-out war, our alliances will be in jeopardy, and the uncommitted areas will vacillate between protestations of principle and a consciousness of their impotence. But even the wisest military policy will prove sterile if our diplomacy cannot elaborate a concept of aggression which is directed to the most likely dangers. In our relation to both our allies and the uncommitted, we must realize that common action depends on a combination of common purpose and effective power. It is the task of our diplomacy to bring about common purpose but it can do so only if our military policy is able to develop a strategy equally meaningful to all partners.

Nevertheless, we must beware not to subordinate the requirements of the over-all strategic balance to our policy of alliances or to our effort to win over the uncommitted. In some situations, the best means of bringing about a common purpose is by an act of leadership which overcomes fears and permits no further equivocation. The price of our power is leadership. For what else is leadership except the willingness to stand alone if the situation requires? The failure to assume these responsibilities will not result in a consensus of humanity; it will lead to the creation of a vacuum.

CHAPTER TEN

The Need for
Doctrine

I

Whatever the problem, then, whether it concerns questions of military strategy, of coalition policy, or of relations with the Soviet bloc, the nuclear age demands above all a clarification of doctrine. At a time when technology has put in our grasp a command over nature never before imagined, power must be related to the purpose for which it is to be used. Research and development will soon overwhelm the military services with a vast number of complex weapons. And the usual answer that a service can never possess a too varied capability will no longer do, for it is prohibitively expensive. In the 1930's each service had to select among perhaps two weapons systems; during World War II this had risen to eight or ten. In the 1950's the number is over a hundred, and in the 1960's it will be in the thousands. Only a doctrine which defines the purpose of these weapons and the kind of war in which they are to be employed permits a rational choice.

Strategic doctrine transcends the problem of selecting weapons systems. It is the mode of survival of a society, relating seemingly disparate experiences into a meaningful pattern. By explaining the significance of events *in advance* of their occurrence it enables society to deal with most problems as a matter of routine and reserves creative thought for unusual or unexpected situations. The test of a strategic doctrine is whether it can establish a pattern of response—a routine—for the most likely challenges. If a society faces too many unexpected contingencies, the machinery for making decisions will become overloaded. "Nothing is easier to effect," said Machiavelli, "than what the enemy thinks you will never attempt to do." An unexpected situation forces improvisation and takes away the advantage of sober calculation. While improvisation may only inhibit the best performance of an individual, it can have far more serious consequences for a society. In extreme cases, members of the group may take independent action and thereby complicate an effective over-all response. Or it may lead to panic, the inability to make any response to a challenge except by fleeing from it.

The Romans stampeded the first time they confronted Hannibal's elephants, not because the elephants were particularly effective but because the Romans had never considered a mode for dealing with such a contingency. Within a few years they had developed a "doctrine"; the charges of the beasts became an "expected" tactic to be confronted through discipline instead of through flight. In 1940 the rapid German tank thrusts demoralized the French Army above all because maneuvers of this kind had been explicitly rejected by French doctrine. A German tank force actually inferior in numbers was able to rout its opponent because French commanders possessed no concept for dealing with it. Before the end of the war the strategic doctrine of the allies had caught up with German tactics and, indeed, improved on them. Armored warfare was transformed from a tactic of surprise into a matter of routine. Surprise can take two forms, then: an unexpected timing and an unexpected mode of action. The secret of Napoleon's victories was that he confused his enemies by the speed of his maneuvers. Conversely, it is possible to be aware that an attack is imminent and yet be unprepared for the form it takes. In 1941 we knew that Japan was planning a military move, but our strategic doctrine did not foresee an attack on Hawaii.

The basic requirement for American security is a doctrine which will enable us to act purposefully in the face of the challenges which will inevitably confront us. Its task will be to prevent us from being continually surprised. Our doctrine must be clear about the nature of our strategic interest in the world. It must understand the mode of Soviet behavior and not make the mistake of ascribing to the Soviet leaders a pattern of behavior based on our own standards of rationality. Since our policy is so explicitly based on deterrence, our doctrine must pay particular attention to determining how the other side calculates its risks. Deterrence is achieved when the opponent cannot calculate any gain from the action we seek to prevent; and what is considered a gain is, for purposes of deterrence, determined by his criteria, not ours. Strategic doctrine, finally, must be able to assess the forces which move contemporary events and find the means for shaping them in the desired direction.

In the absence of a generally understood doctrine, we will of necessity act haphazardly; conflicting proposals will compete with each other without an effective basis for their resolution. Each problem as it arises will seem novel, and energies will be absorbed in analyzing its nature rather than in seeking solutions. Policies will grow out of countermeasures taken to thwart the initiatives of other powers; our course will become increasingly defensive.

Many of our problems in the postwar period have been produced by our failure to accept the doctrinal challenge. We have tended to ascribe our standards of reasonable behavior to the Soviet leaders. We have had difficulty in defining our purposes in relation to the revolutionary forces at large in the world. Above all we have had a penchant for treating our problems as primarily technical and for confusing strategy with the maximum development of power. Yet at the moment when we have at our disposal an unparalleled degree of power, we are driven to realize that the problems of survival can be solved only in the minds of men. The fate of the mammoth and the dinosaur serves as a warning that brute strength does not always supply the mechanism in the struggle for survival.

II

Of course we do possess a strategic doctrine expressed in the decisions of the Joint Chiefs of Staff and of the National Security Council. But the decisions of the Joint Chiefs and of the National Security Council give a misleading impression of unity of purpose. The officials comprising these bodies are either heads of military services, in the case of the Joint Chiefs, or heads of executive departments, in the case of the National Security Council. As administrators of complex organizations they must give most of their attention to reducing the frictions of the administrative machine, both within their departments and in the relation of their departments to other agencies. Their thoughts run more naturally to administrative efficiency than to the elaboration of national objectives. In the committees where national policies are developed they become negotiators rather than planners, and the positions they seek to reconcile inevitably reflect a departmental point of view in which administrative or budgetary considerations play a major role. The heads of departments do not stand above the battle of the bureaucracy; they are spokesmen for it. In fact, the departmental viewpoint is sometimes purposely exaggerated in order to facilitate compromise.

As a result, the conclusions of both the Joint Chiefs of Staff and the National Security Council reflect the attainable consensus among sovereign departments rather than a sense of direction. Because agreement is frequently unattainable except by framing conclusions in very generalized language, decisions by the Joint Chiefs of Staff or the National Security Council do not end serious interdepartmental disputes. Instead they shift them to an interpretation of the meaning of directives. And departments or services whose disagreements prevented the development of doctrine in the first place will choose the exegesis closest to their original point of view. Seeming unanimity merely defers the doctrinal dilemma until either some crisis or the requirements of the budgetary process force a reconsideration under the pressure of events.

The disputes among the services have grown so bitter because force levels, which determine appropriations, are set on the basis of each service's primary mission. Since, in purely military terms, the primary mission cannot be achieved without defeating the enemy completely, each service will always consider its force levels inadequate and will insist that one reason for this inadequacy is a transgression by a sister service on its field of jurisdiction.

The dispute between the Army and the Air Force regarding the importance of airlift provides an illustration. The significance of their dispute resides not in the arguments advanced on either side, but in the fact that in terms of the primary mission of each service it is insoluble. The Air Force, charged with defeating the enemy air arm, must look on an investment in planes of no tactical or strategic combat effectiveness as a diversion of resources. The Army, on the other hand, charged with destroying its enemy counterpart, cannot carry out its primary mission if it cannot get rapidly to the theater of combat. For it, airlift is the condition of all effective action.

The rigid division of functions among the services, therefore, prevents the consideration of airlift in terms of overall strategy. The Army, to which the airlift is essential, is precluded by the Key West agreement from developing one, while the Air Force is impelled by its primary mission to consider airlift a marginal requirement. Nor can such problems be avoided by administrative fiat, as has been demonstrated repeatedly. Interservice rivalries are inherent in the definition of missions. They result inevitably from a division of roles based on means of locomotion, at a time when technology makes a mockery of such distinctions.

The intimate connection between primary mission and budgetary rewards impels our Joint Chiefs, with the best intentions in the world, to become essentially advocates of a service point of view. The Joint Chiefs have risen to their position through a lifetime of dedication to one service. They are a product of its problems, its training schools, its environment. Maintaining the morale of their service can never be far from their minds. And mastering the primary mission of each service is becoming so difficult that the effort almost inevitably inhibits a consideration of its relationship to an over-all mission; or, more accurately, it leads to a psychological distortion in which over-all strategy tends to be equated with a service's primary mission.

Another factor inhibiting the development of strategic doctrine is the predominance of fiscal considerations in our defense planning. This is not even always a question of deliberate choice. One of the reasons for the emphasis on fiscal policy and technology has been that the position of the advocates of economy has usually been explicit and that the pressures of technology have brooked no delay. In the process of co-ordinating diverse policies, which is the primary function of the National Security Council, there always exists a clear fiscal policy, largely because governmental economy is the *raison d'être* of the Bureau of the Budget and because only one agency—the Treasury Department—is responsible for setting objectives in the fiscal field. But there is rarely, if ever, an equally clear National Security policy to oppose it. On the contrary, each contending service is tempted to enlist the backing of the Treasury Department and the Bureau of the Budget by claiming that its particular strategy will help to promote governmental economy. The fiscal viewpoint, therefore, often comes to predominate by default. In a conceptual vacuum, the side with the clearest and most consistent position will hold the field.

Whatever the reason, every Administration since World War II has at some time held the view that this country could not afford more than a certain sum for military appropriations. Now the imposition of a budgetary ceiling is not inevitably pernicious. Removing all budgetary restrictions would inhibit doctrine even more, because it would lead each service to hoard weapons for every eventuality—as occurred to some extent during the Korean War. And the proliferation of weapons systems unrelated to doctrine will cause strategic decisions—which always involve choices

—to be made in the confusion of battle. The difficulty with our present budgetary process is, that by giving priority to cost over requirement, it subordinates doctrine to technology. Budgetary requests are not formulated in the light of strategic doctrine. Rather doctrine is tailored and, if necessary, invented to fit budgetary requests.

The predominance of fiscal considerations makes for doctrinal rigidity, because it causes each service to be afraid that a change in doctrine will lead to a cut in appropriations. Thus in 1950 a violent controversy broke out between advocates of strategic air power and a group of scientists at the Lincoln Laboratory of the Massachusetts Institute of Technology, who were accused of advocating a cut in our retaliatory force. The remarkable thing about this dispute was that the M.I.T. group explicitly denied underrating the importance of strategic air power. They insisted that their recommendations had been solely concerned with building up our air defense. Yet the partisans of strategic air power were probably correct in assuming that a new capability could in practice be developed only at the expense of an existing one.

As a result, budgetary pressures compound the inherent conservatism of the military and encourage a subtle form of waste. Each service pushes weapons development in every category without much regard for the program of other services and each service seeks to obtain control over as many different weapons as possible as a form of insurance against drastic budgetary cuts in the future. Because to relinquish a weapons system may mean to relinquish the appropriations that go with it, each service has a powerful incentive to hold on to every weapon even after it has outlived its usefulness. A weapons system, no matter how obsolescent, represents a budgetary category. There is no guarantee that a replacement will find acceptance among the budgetary authorities, and in any case justifying a new item involves a long process fraught with serious danger of budgetary reduction.

While there is undoubtedly an upper limit of defense spending beyond which injury to the economy would outweigh the gain in military strength, it is also the case that this theoretical ceiling has consistently been underestimated. In 1949, during the B-36 hearings, it was generally agreed that our economy could not support indefinitely a military budget of $14.6 billion, and yet within a year military expenditures had reached four times that amount. From 1953 to 1957 the military budget was stabilized at around $35 billion on the same argument used for a much smaller budget in 1949—that higher expenditures would have a deleterious effect on the economy. With the steady rise since 1953 in the gross national product, the percentage devoted to defense expenditures has actually been declining, at least until fiscal 1959. To be sure, there is no requirement that defense expenditures should rise with the gross national product. Such an approach is as mechanical as that which led to the imposition of a budgetary ceiling. It does indicate, however, that even according to the strictest canons of fiscal orthodoxy, the ceiling need not be as rigid as its advocates maintain. It also means that if the current defense budget is too low even to maintain our retaliatory force, as was argued by the chiefs of each service before the Symington Committee, an increase in expenditures is essential, both to improve our readiness for all-out war and to bring about the capability for limited war.

The limitations imposed by the predominance of fiscal considerations is not compensated for by an increase in civilian control either within the Executive Branch or by Congress. Effective control over military programs is made very difficult by the fiction of the annual review of programs and by their technical complexity. The yearly review has become increasingly out of phase with the substantive realities of defense planning. The hiatus between development, procurement, and operation is several years in the case of most weapons. The introduction of a new weapon into a unit implies that all units will be so equipped over a period of time. Thus the first order for B-52's logically carried with it the obligation to continue procurement until all heavy bomber wings of the Strategic Air Command were composed of jet planes. Similarly, starting the construction on an aircraft carrier makes almost inescapable future appropriations to complete it.

In these circumstances, a yearly review does not bring about effective control; it does ensure that no dispute is ever finally resolved. Each year the same arguments about the efficacy of limited war, airlift, and the relative merits of carrier and land-based aviation are repeated. They are not settled until some technical development outstrips the dispute or an administrative decision allocates roles and missions which the losing service accepts only because it has every prospect of reopening the issue in the following year. In the absence of doctrinal agreement, interservice disputes can be resolved only by compromises which may define only the least unacceptable strategy or by a proliferation of missions and weapons systems.

The technical complexity of most disputes complicates civilian control and, particularly, Congressional control even further. Within the Department of Defense the multiplication of civilian officials, often in office for only a year or two, causes the Secretaries and Assistant Secretaries to become less agents of control than a device for legitimizing interservice disputes. Their short term in office makes it difficult, if not impossible, for them as civilians to become familiar with the subtleties of strategic problems. Instead of being able to establish a unified concept, they are largely dependent on the advice of their professional staff, whose spokesmen they almost inevitably become.

As for Congressional control, the only forum where the over-all defense program can be considered is in the Appropriations Committee. A meaningful judgment by Congress on the defense budget would require it to assess the military strength achieved by a given expenditure and to correlate this strength to an agreed set of national security objectives. Neither condition is met by current practice. To be sure, the budget is introduced by testimony of the service chiefs and their civilian superiors regarding the gravity of the international situation. But no attempt is made to show the relationship of strategy to events abroad beyond the general implication that the proposed program will ensure the security of the United States. In turn, the Congressional committees can make their judgments only in terms of a vague assessment of the international situation. They will hesitate to reduce the budget if they feel the situation to be grave and they will be disposed to pare requests drastically when they think the situation is less serious than has been represented.

In order to create a favorable climate for their budgetary requests, the services tend to emphasize the most ominous aspects of the United States security problem. Aware that there is greater receptivity to programs which seem to offer total solutions, each service is tempted to stress the part of its mission which poses the most absolute sanctions. Thus in 1951 the Army produced the "atomic cannon," a cumbersome, hybrid, and already obsolescent weapon, partly to gain access to the nuclear stockpile. Similarly, after the B-36 hearings the Navy abandoned its opposition to identifying deterrence with maximum retaliatory power. In fact it adopted the theory as its own and in its budgetary presentations has emphasized its contribution to the strategic striking force more than its less dramatic task of antisubmarine warfare. And Congressional hearings leave little doubt that within the Air Force the Strategic Air Command has the highest prestige value.

Thus the budgetary process places a premium on the weapons systems which fit in best with the traditional preconceptions of American strategic thought. It is not that the belief in the importance of strategic striking forces is wrong; indeed, the Strategic Air Command must continue to have the first claim on our defense budget. It is simply that the overemphasis on total solutions reinforces the already powerful tendency against supplementing our retaliatory force with subtler military capabilities which address themselves to the likelier dangers and involve a less destructive strategy.

III

The test of an organization is how naturally and spontaneously it enables its leadership to address itself to its most severe challenges. There is little in the organization of our national defense establishment that impels the service chiefs in a spontaneous fashion to consider over-all strategic doctrine. The proper attitude of mind cannot be demanded by fiat after our military leaders have achieved eminence; it must be cultivated throughout their careers. Therefore unification is as important at the lower and intermediary echelons, where attitudes are formed, as at the top, where often little can be done except to provide a forum for well-established views.

It may well be that the separation of the Army and the Air Force in 1948 occurred two decades too late and at the precise moment when the distinction between ground and air strategy was becoming obsolescent. Instead of making the Army Air Corps independent, it would probably have been wiser to mix the two organizations more thoroughly and to develop a single service focused neither on exclusive ground nor on exclusive air strategy. Instead the separation of the two services was achieved to the detriment of both. Different service academies, training schools, and war colleges inevitably emphasize a particular aspect of our strategic problem instead of an over-all doctrine in which traditional distinctions should be disappearing, in which the Army would begin to approach the mobility of the Air Force and the Air Force to develop the relative discrimination of ground warfare.

It would still be the wisest course to move in the direction of a single service initially by amalgamating the Army and the Air Force. The Navy's strategic problems may remain sufficiently distinct not to require integration, and in any case resistance in the Navy to complete unification would be so bitter as to obviate its advantages. A unified service with a single system of service schools would force officers at a formative stage of their careers into a framework less narrowly addressed to the concerns of a particular service. Loyalty to a service, which is one of the most attractive traits of the military and which now necessarily produces a rigid adherence to a service point of view, could in this manner be utilized to help produce an over-all strategic doctrine.

To be sure, the officers of all services attend each other's war colleges even now. But it is one thing to attend a service school as an outsider to learn the point of view of another service; it is quite another to provide incentives, from the earliest stages of an officer's career, to consider strategic problems apart from the interests of a service. In a single service, a staff officer would be judged less by his skill in defending his service's point of view in the co-ordinating procedure of the Pentagon than by his contribution to an over-all doctrine or, at least, by his ability to operate within it. Doctrine would no longer be a tool of interservice rivalry but a subject to be considered on its own merits.

Complete unification among the services is probably out of the question. The traditions from which each service derives its strength would bring about overwhelming resistance to the concept of a single uniform and a single system of service schools. It may even be that a single service would be too unwieldy and would still require a subdivision according to the strategic tasks which have to be performed. It may, therefore, be best to begin reorganization by creating two basic commands, each representing a clearly distinguishable strategic mission. The Army, Navy, and Air Force could continue as administrative and training units, much as the training commands *within* the various services operate today. But for all other purposes, two basic organizations would be created: the Strategic Force and the Tactical Force. The Strategic Force would be the units required for all-out war. It would include the Strategic Air Command, the Air Defense Command, the units of the Army required to protect overseas bases, and the units of the Navy which are to participate in the retaliatory attack. The Tactical Force would be composed of the Army, Air Force, and Navy units required for limited war. The

Strategic Force would probably be under Air Force command, the Tactical Force under Army command. The training and doctrine of each Force should be uniform, and its officers should attend the same technical and service schools. The schools would continue to be administered by a parent service but the curriculum and student body should be determined by the Force commander.

Such a division would reflect the realities of the strategic situation. While the Tactical Force might be required in an all-out war and for such a purpose would come under the command of the Strategic Force, the Strategic Force should not be utilized for limited war and should be as self-contained as possible even for all-out war. The Strategic Force should not be utilized for limited war, because by training and doctrine it is not suited for it and because its unimpaired power represents the only guarantee for the war remaining limited. If an enemy could bring about a significant attrition of the Strategic Force by means of a limited war, he would tilt the strategic balance in his favor however the limited war ended. Moreover, any utilization of the Strategic Force in a limited war might create doubts about our intentions to keep the war limited and thereby unleash a retaliatory blow.

Both the Strategic and the Tactical Forces should be self-contained, because if the Tactical Force is considered an auxiliary to an all-out strategy, we will always be tempted to conserve it for a final showdown. And as we have seen, the training, weapons systems, and doctrine for limited war differ basically from that appropriate for all-out war. Moreover, the Tactical, just as the Strategic, Force should be able to accomplish its mission with the forces-in-being. It cannot afford to rely on substantial mobilization because this might be taken by the enemy as a prelude to an all-out showdown. In any case, half-trained reserves would probably not be adequate for the speed and complexity of modern war.

The division of our military establishment into a Strategic and a Tactical Force would reflect the real nature of the strategic problem we confront: the necessity for being

THE NEED FOR DOCTRINE

protected against all-out war as the prerequisite of all other measures, and the capability to fight limited war as the form of conflict where the cost is commensurate with the issues actually under dispute.

In such an organization too the Joint Chiefs of Staff would change their character. They would then consist of a Chairman, the Chief of the Tactical Force, the Chief of the Strategic Force, and the Chief of Naval Operations (to represent operations such as antisubmarine warfare which do not fit into any of the above categories). Such a group would in its very nature be more oriented toward doctrine than the present Joint Chiefs of Staff. The Chief of each Force would represent an integrated strategic mission and not a means of locomotion. Since service chiefs would continue to administer the traditional services, the Chief of each Force would be freed of many of the routine problems of administration which, as Admiral Radford pointed out before the Symington Committee, make the Chairman the only member of the present group who can give his full attention to problems of over-all strategy.

The advantage of the proposed organization for the conduct of military operations is demonstrated by the fact that in every recent war we have set up joint commands reflecting the same basic concept. The new organization would create in peacetime the structure which the requirements of combat would impose on us in any case. To be sure, the same contest over appropriations as is now going on might take place between the Chiefs of the Strategic and the Tactical Forces. And there would be the same temptation to invent doctrine in support of budgetary requests. But with each Force representing a distinguishable strategic mission, self-interest and the requirements of strategic doctrine would be identical.

The change in the organization of the services should be supplemented by similar action on the civilian side of the Department of Defense. At present the Secretary of Defense is at best an arbiter of doctrinal disputes. He possesses neither the staff nor the organization to shape them. Implicit in the present organization is the notion that strategic doctrine reflects "purely" military considerations. Thus the Chairman of the Joint Chiefs reports directly to the President and attends meetings of the National Security Council. Although the special relationship between the President and the Chairman of the Joint Chiefs is implicit in the fact that the President is also commander in chief, it has contributed to the practical autonomy of the military in matters of doctrine.

Such a separation of strategy and policy can be achieved only to the detriment of both. It causes military policy to become identified with the most absolute applications of power and it tempts diplomacy into an overconcern with finesse. Since the difficult problems of national policy are in the area where political, economic, psychological, and military factors overlap, we should give up the fiction that there is such a thing as "purely" military advice. The Secretary of Defense would gain greatly from instituting some form of Strategic Advisory Council, whose work should be closely related to the deliberations of the Joint Chiefs of Staff. The two groups might, for example, meet jointly on all issues save purely technical matters of procurement or weapons development. Both the civilian officials and the Joint Chiefs would profit from an amalgamation of their functions. At every stage of formulation of strategy, doctrine would be considered as a combination of political, economic, and military factors instead of a compromise between "purely" military and "purely" political considerations.

The services should also be given some relief from the almost incessant effort of either preparing, negotiating, or justifying budgets. The yearly budget review encourages irresponsibility. Almost inevitably it diverts energies from problems of over-all strategy and causes the budget to be justified in terms which flatter prevailing predilections. A great deal would be gained by an extension of the budget cycle for defense appropriations. Some constitutions which provided for a yearly review of the budget have made exceptions in the case of military appropriations. It would be a great advance if our military budget could be extended over a two-year period. Thus the military budget would coincide with the term of the House of Representatives. And, as we have seen, many of the essential commitments for major procurement in any case extend over several years.

To be sure, in its initial stages the proposed procedure might sharpen interservice rivalries because commitments would now be more fundamental. But bringing the interservice dispute into the open would produce healthy consequences in the long run. The failure to resolve doctrinal disagreements and the pretense of harmony at each budgetary hearing cause the conflict to rage by subterfuge, by planned leaks to newspapers or to sympathetic Congressmen. A two-year budgetary cycle would free the service chiefs from the constant pressure of short-term considerations; it might encourage planning to turn from the essentially defensive task of justifying force levels to a consideration of the purpose of those forces.

With the emergence of an agreed strategic doctrine within the Department of Defense, the whole process of formulating security objectives within the Executive Branch would gain in balance. The clear fiscal point of view could then be confronted by an explicit Department of Defense position. With a better structure for producing discussions and a longer interval between the need for preparing budgetary requests (and even in its absence), the interservice disputes would lose a great deal of their tenseness. Doctrine would then be directed not merely to the acquisition of the tools of war but to a more imaginative conception of their varied uses.

IV

It would be a mistake, however, to expect too much from organizational remedies. For many of the difficulties described in this chapter and in this book have been caused by national traits which are deeply ingrained in the American experience. As in all tragedies, many of our problems have been produced in spite of our good intentions and have been caused not by our worst qualities but by our best.

Foremc_t among the attitudes which affect the making of our policy is American empiricism and its quest for certainty: nothing is "true" unless it is "objective," and it is not "objective" unless it is part of experience. This makes for the absence of dogmatism and for the ease of social relations. But it has pernicious consequences in the conduct of policy. Policy is the art of weighing probabilities; mastery of it lies in grasping the nuances of possibilities. To attempt to conduct it as a science must lead to rigidity. For only the risks are certain; the opportunities are conjectural. One cannot be "sure" about the implications of events until they have happened, and when they have occurred it is too late to do anything about them. Empiricism in foreign policy leads to a penchant for *ad hoc* solutions. The rejection of dogmatism inclines our policy makers to postpone committing themselves until all facts are in; but by the time the facts are in, a crisis has usually developed or an opportunity has passed. Our policy is, therefore, geared to dealing with emergencies; it finds difficulty in developing the long-range program that might forestall them.

A symptom of our search for certainty is the vast number of committees charged with examining and developing policy. The very multiplicity of committees makes it difficult to arrive at decisions in time. It tends to give a disproportionate influence to subordinate officials who prepare the initial memoranda and it overwhelms our higher officials with trivia. Because of our cult of specialization, sovereign departments negotiate national policy among themselves with no single authority, except an overburdened President, able to take an over-all view or to apply decisions over a period of time. This results in the gap previously noted between grand strategy and particular tactics, between the definition of general objectives so vague as to be truistic and the concern with immediate problems. The gap is bridged only when a crisis forces the bureaucratic machinery into accelerated action, and then the top leadership has little choice but to concur in the administrative proposals. In short, we are trying to cope with political problems by administrative means.

Our inward doubt makes for vulnerability to Soviet maneuvers in two ways: on the one hand, every Soviet change of line is taken to some extent at face value. We cannot be certain that the Soviets may not "mean" it this time until they have proved they do not; and they will try their best not to prove it until the new tactic has served its purpose. On the other hand, we have found it difficult to adjust our tactics to new situations, so that we always tend to speak in the categories of the most recent threat but one. Moreover, we hesitate not only in the face of Soviet blandishments but also before Soviet intransigence. Every Soviet aggressive move finds us debating its implications and creates pressures for deferring a showdown for the "clear" case of aggression the Soviet leaders are trying very hard not to present. The paradoxical result is that we, the empiricists, often appear to the world as rigid, unimaginative, and even somewhat cynical, while the dogmatic Bolsheviks exhibit flexibility, daring, and subtlety. This is because our empiricism dooms us to an essentially reactive policy that improvises a counter to every Soviet move while the Soviet emphasis on theory gives them the certainty to act, to maneuver, and to run risks. The very fact of Soviet action forces us to assume the risks of countermoves and absorbs our energies in essentially defensive measures.

The willingness to act need not derive from theory, of course. Indeed, an overemphasis on theory can lead to a loss of touch with reality. In many societies—in Great Britain, for example—policy developed from a firmly held tradition of a national strategy. For more than two centuries, it was a tenet of British policy that Antwerp should not fall into the hands of a major power. This was not backed by an elaborate metaphysics but simply by a tradition of British sea power whose requirements were so generally understood that they were never debated. The absence of a tradition of foreign policy exaggerates the biases of our empiricism. As a result we find it difficult to conduct our policy with a proper regard for the timing of measures. To be sure, our cumbersome administrative mechanism adds immeasurably to the problem. But in addition our deliberations are conducted as if a course of action were eternally valid, as if a measure which might meet exactly the needs of a given moment could not backfire if adopted a year later.

For this reason our policy lacks a feeling for nuance, the ability to come up with variations on the same theme, as the Soviet leaders have done so effectively. We consider policy making concluded when the National Security Council has come to a decision. And, in fact, the process of arriving at a decision is so arduous, and a reappraisal is necessarily so "agonizing," that we are reluctant to reexamine policies after they have outlived their usefulness. But a written statement of policy is likely to amount to a truism; the real difficulty arises in applying it to concrete situations. And while we have often come up with proper measures, we have not found it easy to adapt our approach to changing conditions over a period of time.

Another factor shaping our attitude toward foreign affairs is our lack of tragic experience. Though we have known severe hardships, our history has been notably free of disaster. Indeed, the American domestic experience exhibits an unparalleled success—great daring rewarded and great obstacles overcome. It is no wonder, therefore, that to many of our most responsible men, particularly in the business community, the warnings of impending peril or of imminent disaster sound like the Cassandra cries of abstracted "eggheads." For is not the attribute of the "egghead" his lack of touch with reality, and does not American reality show an unparalleled wealth coupled with an unparalleled growth?

There has been much criticism of former Secretaries George M. Humphrey and Charles E. Wilson for their emphasis on holding down the defense budget. But, in fairness, the psychological background of their decisions should be understood. Despite all the information at their disposal, they simply could not believe that in the nuclear age the penalty for miscalculation may be national catastrophe. They might know in their heads but they could not accept in their hearts that the society they helped to build could disappear as did Rome or Carthage or Byzantium, which probably seemed as eternal to their citizens. These characteristics make for an absence of a sense of urgency, a tendency to believe that everything can be tried once and that the worst consequence mistakes can have is that we may be forced to redouble our efforts later on. The irrevocable error is not yet part of the American experience.

Related to this is our reluctance to think in terms of power. To be sure, American expansion, both economic and geographic, was not accomplished without a judicious application of power. But our Calvinist heritage has required success to display the attribute of justice. Even our great fortunes, however accumulated, were almost invariably held to impose a social obligation; the great foundation is after all a peculiarly American phenomenon. As a nation we have used power almost shamefacedly, as if it were inherently wicked. We have wanted to be liked for our own sakes and we have wished to succeed because of the persuasiveness of our principles rather than through our strength. Our feeling of guilt with respect to power has caused us to transform all wars into crusades and then to apply our power in the most absolute terms. We have rarely found intermediary ways to use our power and in those cases we have done so reluctantly.

But foreign policy cannot be conducted without an awareness of power relationships. To be sure, force alone will not overcome the contemporary revolution. An imaginative diplomacy and bold programs are required if we are to identify ourselves with the aspirations of humanity. But unless we maintain at least an equilibrium of power between us and the Soviet bloc, we will have no chance to undertake any positive measures. And maintaining this equilibrium may require some very difficult choices. We are certain to be confronted with situations of extraordinary ambiguity, such as civil wars or domestic coups. Certainly we should seek to forestall such occurrences. But once they have occurred, we must find the will to act and to run risks in a situation which permits only a choice among evils. While we should never give up our principles, we must also realize that we cannot maintain our principles unless we survive.

The obverse of our reluctance to think in terms of power has been our notion of the nature of peace. We assume that peace is the "normal" pattern of relations among states, that it is equivalent to a consciousness of harmony, that it can be aimed at directly as a goal of policy. These are truisms rarely challenged in our political debate. Both major political parties maintain that they work for a lasting peace, even if they differ about the best means of attaining it. Both make statements which imply that on a certain magic day, perhaps after a four-power conference, "peace will break out."

No idea could be more dangerous. To begin with, the polarization of power in the world would give international relations a degree of instability even if there were no ideological disagreement, and the present volatile state of technology is likely to compound this sense of insecurity. Whenever peace—conceived as the avoidance of war—has become the primary objective of a power or group of powers, international relations have been at the mercy of the state willing to forego peace. To entrust the fate of a country entirely to the continued good will of another sovereign state is an abdication of statesmanship; it means that survival is completely dependent on factors outside of one's own control. Peace, therefore, cannot be aimed at directly; it is the expression of certain conditions and power relationships. It is to these relationships—not to peace as such —that diplomacy must address itself.

A power can survive only if it is willing to fight for its interpretations of justice and its conception of vital interests. The test comes in its awareness of where to draw the line and for what issues to contend. That is why it is so crucial for the United States to become clear about the nature of our strategic interests in the world. It would be comforting if we could confine our actions to situations in which our moral, legal, and military positions are completely in harmony and where legitimacy is most in accord with the requirements of survival. But as the strongest power in the world, we will probably never again be afforded the simple moral choices on which we could insist in our more secure past. The thrust of Soviet aggression will always be directed at the weak points in our armor and to issues in which our psychological inhibitions are at a maximum. To deal with problems of such ambiguity presupposes above all a moral act: a willingness to run risks on partial knowledge and for a less than perfect application of one's principles. The insistence on absolutes, either in assessing the provocation or in evaluating possible remedies, is a prescription for inaction.

In the process of defining our strategic interest we cannot avoid facing another fact of the nuclear age little in accord with our predilections: the difficulty, if not impossibility, of holding a perimeter of twenty thousand miles while always remaining on the defensive politically, militarily, and spiritually. A major part of the perimeter encompasses countries which are in rapid flux. Even if we were omniscient, it would seem inevitable that in some countries forces hostile to our interests will gain ascendancy. To be sure, communism has never come to national power by peaceful means. But the boundary between peace and war has been steadily eroded; and communism may well have a different meaning for the newly independent nations of Asia and the Middle East than for the countries of Western Europe. If, then, every addition to the Soviet orbit becomes immunized against United States influence while the Soviet bloc remains free to exacerbate all tensions within the non-Soviet world, our eventual expulsion from Asia and the Middle East and perhaps even from Europe will be almost inevitable.

To overcome this danger requires a more dynamic conception of world affairs. A great historical movement which is represented by the coming together of communism and the anti-colonial revolution cannot be mastered by negative motives. A policy impelled primarily by a desire to prevent an expansion of the Soviet sphere ensures that militarily we will be forced always to fight at the point of our greatest weakness; that diplomatically we will always contest issues of maximum embarrassment to us; that spiritually we will convey an impression of uncertainty. In any conflict the side which is animated by faith in victory has a decided advantage over an opponent who wishes above all to preserve the *status quo*. It will be prepared to run greater risks because its purpose will be stronger. The advantage of initiative is that each move opens the possibility of several further steps. If carried far enough, it will force the opponent to protect itself against an ever growing number of contingencies and, therefore, to concentrate on purely defensive measures.

This does not mean preventive war. Considerations of principle would prohibit such a course apart from the enormous destructiveness of modern weapons. However, we should be as ready to profit from opportunities in the Soviet orbit as the Soviet bloc feels free to exploit all the difficulties of the non-Soviet world. In foreign policy courage and success stand in a causal relationship.

V

We thus reach our final problem: the adequacy of our leadership groups for dealing with the challenges we are likely to confront. This is an aspect of a more general problem faced by any society: where to strike a balance between the requirements of organization and the need for inspiration. Organization expresses the importance of continuity; the routine by which it operates represents a recognition that a society must be able to assimilate and utilize mediocrity. Inspiration, on the other hand, is the mechanism of growth; it is the ability to transcend a framework which has come to be taken for granted. The stability of a society depends on its skill in organization, which enables it to react mechanically to "ordinary" problems and to utilize its resources to best effect. The greatness of a society derives from its willingness to chart new ground beyond the confines of routine. Without organization every problem becomes a special case. Without inspiration a society will stagnate; it will lose the ability to adapt to new circumstances or to generate new goals. The experience of a people tends to be confined to the level of its average performance. But leadership is the refusal to confine action to average performance; it is the willingness to define purposes perhaps only vaguely apprehended by the multitude. A society learns only from experience: it "knows" only when it is too late to act. But a statesman must act as if his inspirations were already experience, as if his aspiration were "truth." He must bridge the gap between a society's experience and his vision, between its tradition and its future.

In this task his possibilities are limited because there is an inherent tension between the mode of action of a bureaucracy and the pattern of statesmanship. A smoothly working bureaucracy creates the illusion of running by itself; it seeks to reduce all problems to administrative terms. The basic motivation of a bureaucracy is its quest for safety; its preference is in favor of a policy of minimum risk. A bureaucracy, therefore, tends to exaggerate the technical complexities of its problems and to seek to reduce questions of judgment to a minimum. Technical problems are susceptible to "objective" analysis, whereas questions of judgment contain too many uncertain elements. An administrative mechanism has a bias in favor of the *status quo*, however arrived at. Short of an unambiguous catastrophe, the *status quo* has the advantage of familiarity. No "objective" criteria can prove that a change of course will yield superior results. The inclination of a bureaucracy is to deny the possibility of great conception by classifying it as "unsound," "risky," or other terms which testify to a preference for equilibrium over exceptional performance. It is no accident that most great statesmen were opposed by the "experts" in their foreign offices, for the very greatness of the statesman's conception tends to make it inaccessible to those whose primary concern is with safety and minimum risk.

A society owes its vitality to its ability to strike a balance between the requirement of organization and the need for inspiration. Too much stress on organization leads to bureaucratization and the withering of imagination. Excessive emphasis on inspiration produces a tour de force without continuity or organizational stability. The best solution is a bureaucracy which runs sufficiently smoothly to take care of ordinary problems as a matter of routine, but which is not so pervasive as to inhibit the creative thought which is inseparable from statesmanship.

The complexities of contemporary life inhibit the establishment of this balance, however. For the mastery of any one field, whether it be politics, science, or industry, is so difficult that it discourages reflection about its relationship to other activities. The structure of most organizations is growing so intricate that learning to manipulate it tends to leave little energy for reflecting on its purpose. The ultimate in bureaucratization comes about when the internal problems of an administrative mechanism approach the complexity of the external problems with which it was designed to deal, a condition rapidly being reached in many aspects of modern life.

Thus at a moment when the capacity to think conceptually was never more important, technical problems have become so complicated that they tend to pre-empt all attention. A strong leadership group is developed when the qualities which are encouraged in reaching the top approximate the qualities required for providing effective over-all guidance. But the structure of a modern society tends to run counter to this need. The skill required in attaining eminence within a large administrative mechanism is essentially manipulative: the ability to adapt to prevailing standards and to improve efficiency within a framework which is given. But the qualities required for leadership are primarily creative: to set the framework within which administration will then operate. The patterns of thinking developed in the rise to eminence may, therefore, inhibit effectiveness once eminence has been reached. The rewards in a bureaucracy are for skill in adjusting to an equilibrium. The requirement of leadership is the ability to galvanize an organization and to prevent the equilibrium from becoming an end in itself.

Many of the difficulties of our governmental apparatus are common to our entire society and arise primarily from our sudden emergence as the major power in the free world. The character of our leadership groups was formed during a century or more of preoccupation with domestic development. Politics was considered a necessary evil, and the primary function of the state was the exercise of police powers. Neither training nor incentives impelled our leadership groups to think in political or strategic terms. This emphasis was compounded by our empiricism, with its cult of the expert and its premium on specialization.

The two professions which are most dominant in the higher levels of government—industry and the law—can serve as an illustration. The rewards in industry, particularly large-scale industry, are for administrative competence; they, therefore, produce a tendency to deal with conceptual problems by administrative means, by turning them over to committees of experts. And the legal profession, trained to deal with a succession of discrete individual cases, produces a penchant for *ad hoc* decisions and a resistance to the "hypothetical cases" inherent in long-range planning. Our leadership groups are, therefore, better prepared to deal with technical than with conceptual problems, with economic than with political issues. Each problem is dealt with "on its merits," a procedure which emphasizes the particular at the expense of the general and bogs down planning in a mass of detail. The absence of a conceptual framework makes it difficult for them even to identify our problems or to choose effectively among the plethora of proposals and interpretations produced by our governmental machinery.

This explains many postwar Soviet successes. Whatever the qualities of Soviet leadership, its training is eminently political and conceptual. Reading Lenin or Mao or Stalin, one is struck by the emphasis on the relationship between political, military, psychological, and economic factors, the insistence on finding a conceptual basis for political action and on the need for dominating a situation by flexible tactics and inflexible purpose. And the internal struggles in the Kremlin ensure that only the most iron-nerved reach the top. Against the Politburo, trained to think in general terms and freed of problems of day-to-day administration, we have pitted leaders overwhelmed with departmental duties and trained to think that the cardinal sin is to transgress on another's field of specialization. To our leaders, policy is a series of discrete problems; to the Soviet leaders it is an aspect of a continuing political process. As a result, the contest between us and the Soviet system has had many of the attributes of any contest between a professional and an amateur. Even a mediocre professional will usually defeat an excellent amateur, not because the amateur does not know what to do but because he cannot react with sufficient speed and consistency. Our leaders have not lacked ability but they have had to learn while doing, and this has imposed too great a handicap.

To be sure, many of the shortcomings of our leadership groups reflect the very qualities which make for the ease of relationships within American society. The condition for our limited government has been the absence of basic social schisms, the regulation of many concerns not by government fiat but by "what is taken for granted." A society can operate in this fashion only if disputes are not pushed to their logical conclusions and if disagreements are blunted by avoiding dogmatism. And, in fact, the fear of seeming dogmatic permeates our social scene. Opinions are usually introduced with a disclaimer which indicates that the proponent is aware of their contingency and claims no superior validity for them. This produces a preference for decisions by committee, because the process of conversation permits disagreements to be discovered and adjustments made before positions have hardened. Our decision-making process is, therefore, geared to the pace of conversation; even departmental memoranda on which policy decisions are ultimately based are written with an eye to eventual compromise and not with the expectation that any of them will be accepted in their entirety.

It would be a mistake to be pessimistic. When World War II ended no one would have supposed that the United States would assume commitments on such a world-wide scale. Our shortcomings are imposing only because of the magnitude of the threat confronting us. Moreover, the performance of the United States, for all its failings, compares favorably with that of the other nations of the non-Soviet world. Our difficulties are, therefore, only a symptom, and by no means the most obvious one, of an inward uncertainty in the free world. To be sure, by the nature of their institutions democracies cannot conduct policy as deviously, change course as rapidly, or prepare their moves as secretly as dictatorships. But the crisis of the free world lies deeper. The tragic element in foreign policy is the impossibility of escaping conjecture; after the "objective" analysis of fact there remains a residue of uncertainty about the meaning of events or the opportunities they offer. A statesman can often escape his dilemmas by lowering his sights; he always has the option to ignore the adversary's capabilities by attributing peaceful intentions to him. Many of the difficulties of the non-Soviet world have been the result of an attempt to use the element of uncertainty as an excuse for inaction. But in foreign policy certainty is conferred at least as much by philosophy as by fact. It derives from the imposition of purpose on events.

This is not to say that we should imitate Soviet dogmatism. A society can survive only by the genius that made it great. But we should be able to leaven our empiricism with a sense of urgency. And while our history may leave us not well enough prepared to deal with tragedy, it does teach us that great achievement does not result from a quest for safety. Even so, our task will remain psychologically more complex than that of the Kremlin. As the strongest and perhaps the most vital power of the free world we face the challenge of demonstrating that democracy is able to find the moral certainty to act without the support of fanaticism and without a guarantee of success.

INDEX